Selected Readings in Classic British and American Poetry

英美经典诗歌选读

张跃军◎主编

厦门大学出版社 XIAMEN UNIVERSITY PRESS
国家一级出版社
全国百佳图书出版单位

图书在版编目(CIP)数据

英美经典诗歌选读/张跃军主编.—厦门:厦门大学出版社,2018.7
ISBN 978-7-5615-6803-3

Ⅰ.①英… Ⅱ.①张… Ⅲ.①英语-阅读教学-高等学校-教材②诗集-英国③诗集-美国
Ⅳ.①H319.4:I

中国版本图书馆 CIP 数据核字(2017)第 304908 号

出 版 人 郑文礼
责任编辑 王扬帆 高奕欢
封面设计 夏 林
技术编辑 朱 楷

出版发行 厦门大学出版社
社 址 厦门市软件园二期望海路 39 号
邮政编码 361008
总 编 办 0592-2182177 0592-2181406(传真)
营销中心 0592-2184458 0592-2181365
网 址 http://www.xmupress.com
邮 箱 xmupress@126.com
印 刷 厦门市金凯龙印刷有限公司

开本 787 mm×1 092 mm 1/16
印张 18.5
字数 379 千字
印数 1～1 500 册
版次 2018 年 7 月第 1 版
印次 2018 年 7 月第 1 次印刷
定价 45.00 元

厦门大学出版社
微信二维码

厦门大学出版社
微博二维码

编 委 会

序 言

“英语诗歌选读”是《全国高等学校英语专业英语教学大纲》要求开设的“专业知识”课程。“英美诗歌”可独立开设，或作为“英美文学”这门主干课程的重要组成部分。诗歌因其形式美和便于操作（短诗自不待言，长诗常以片断出现）而广受欢迎，不仅成为英语专业的授课内容，而且常常成为非英语专业文化素质课程的热门之选。本教材便是因应目前国内高校英美诗歌教学的需要，组织力量编选的。

本教材参照《全国高等学校英语专业英语教学大纲》和《大学英语课程教学要求》，旨在夯实学生的英语语言和文化基础，强化其对于英美文学，尤其是英美诗歌名篇的鉴赏能力，增强对其文学和文化修养以及综合素质的培养，使之全面发展。内容安排上，本教材将英国诗歌和美国诗歌分开，分别以上篇和下篇的形式出现，并粗略地划出诗人诗作所处的时代，如英国诗歌分为中世纪、16—18世纪、浪漫主义时代，等等。这样，师生在教学中便有了宏观的时代背景，便于理解作品。诗人的选择方面，入选者皆为英美诗坛重要诗人，所选作品无论是表现主题还是形式方面均具有经典性与代表性。考虑到教材的使用中不可避免的课时等因素，入选篇目以短篇为主，同时也不乏《丁登寺旁》《墓园挽歌》《杰·阿尔弗瑞德·普鲁弗洛克的情歌》这样篇幅较长的名篇，以及长篇（如《失乐园》）的节选。所选篇目对于一门课程的教学来说，可能数量较多，但我们有意为之，旨在较全面展示英美诗歌的丰富性和多元性，教师在教学中则可根据实际情况加以选用，有些作品可布置学生课下自学。上下篇分别包含18节和14节，每节包括如下几项内容：诗人介绍、诗歌文本、文本注释、作品分析、思考题、中译文。注释包括作品题解和语言点的解释，前者有时包含对诗歌形式即文类（genre）的介绍；作品赏析立足不同视角，从主题表现、形式特征、叙事方式、对诗歌传统的继承与发展，以及与其他作品的比较等方面着手。如此编排既有利于教师授课，又有助于学生自学，可作为英语专业和其他专业本科生、研究生学习英美诗歌和英美文学的教材。

已出同类教材的内容和篇幅差别甚大，内容编排上也各有特色。《英美经典诗歌选读》具有如下特色：

（1）质量高：编者多具有博士学位和高级职称，学术水平较高，保证了教材的学术性和高质量；（2）适用性强：编者皆来自高校教学科研第一线，熟悉学生的需要，保证了教材的适用性，不会产生教与学的脱节；（3）注重操作性和实践性：注释、作品分析与思考题着眼于启发功能，鼓励学生进一步思考有关问题；（4）具有全面性和引领性：注释和文本分析等环节，有时突出重点，有时则着眼全局。如华兹华斯一节，从形式（包括遣词造句、音韵效果、词法与句法、篇章结构）和内容等方面综合考察，着眼于行文的字面意义以及字里行间的意蕴，从诗学、美学和哲学层面深入剖析。另外，与美国哲学家和散文大师爱默生《论自然》的论断相比较，引导读者理解英美浪漫主义文学传统之发展流变，而这同时也是思想传统的比较。莎士比亚部分，则考察了莎士比亚在中国的流布，同时把十四行诗的结构与八股文的“起承转合”加以类比，使中国读者对这位英国文艺复兴时期的伟大诗人有更加切身的感受。

本教材的分工如下：张跃军（博士，广西民族大学、厦门理工学院教授，博士生导师）负责诗人及诗歌篇目的确定与分工，确立编写体例，审阅全书并定稿，并执笔上篇的第 8 单元以及下篇的第 19、22、25、29 单元；周丹（博士，武汉理工大学副教授）撰写上篇的第 11、12、16、17 单元，并协助审阅上篇的英国诗歌部分；邹雯虹（博士，江西财经大学讲师）执笔下篇的第 20、23、30、31、32 单元，并协助审阅下篇的美国诗歌部分；陈尚真（博士，岭南师范学院副教授）执笔上篇的第 1、4、6、7 单元；廖永清（硕士，广西民族大学副教授）执笔上篇的第 2、3、5 单元；吕爱晶（博士，湖南科技大学教授）撰写上篇的第 13 单元，以及第 10 单元中的文本二（《咏锡雍》）部分；李成坚（博士，西南交通大学教授、博士生导师）执笔上篇的第 14、15、18 单元；肖小军（博士，深圳职业技术学院教授）撰写下篇的第 21、26、27、28 单元；刘朝晖（博士，深圳职业技术学院教授）撰写上篇的第 9 单元，第 10 单元中的诗人介绍和文本一（《她走在美的光影中》）部分，以及下篇的第 24 单元。编选的过程中，在注释等技术性环节，我们参阅了国内外相关著述，如 *Norton Anthology of English Literature*（《诺顿英国文学选集》）、*Norton Anthology of American Literature*（《诺顿美国文学选集》）、《英国文学名篇选著》、《英美诗歌名篇详注》等，在此特表谢忱。同时感谢厦门理工学院教材建设项目的支持。限于水平和时间，本书定有诸多不足之处，请读者不吝赐教，以利编者改正。

编　者

2018 年 5 月

CONTENTS

上篇　英国诗歌

The Middle Ages

Unit 1　Geoffrey Chaucer 3

Text: The Canterbury Tales: The General Prologue (Excerpt) 4

The 16th to the 18th Century

Unit 2　William Shakespeare 10

Text1: Sonnet 18 11

Text2: Sonnet 105 14

Unit 3　John Donne 18

Text: A Valediction: Forbidding Mourning 19

Unit 4　John Milton 26

Text1: Paradise Lost (Excerpt of Book Four) 27

Text:2 When I Consider How My Light Is Spent 32

Unit 5　Thomas Gray 34

Text: Elegy Written in a Country Churchyard 35

The Romantic Period

Unit 6　Robert Burns 53

Text1: A Red Red Rose 54

Text2: Auld Lang Syne 56

Unit 7　William Blake 61

Text1: The Sick Rose 62

Text2: The Tyger 64

Unit 8　William Wordsworth 68

Text: Lines Composed a Few Miles above Tintern Abbey on Revisiting the Banks of the Wye During a Tour, July 13, 1798 69

Unit 9 Samuel Taylor Coleridge 86
Text: Kubla Khan Or a Vision in a Dream. A Fragment. 87
Unit 10 George Gordon Byron 94
Text1: She Walks in Beauty 95
Text2: On the Castle of Chillon 98
Unit 11 Percy Bysshe Shelley 101
Text1: Ode to the West Wind 102
Text2: Ozymandias 111
Unit 12 John Keats 115
Text: Ode on a Grecian Urn 116

The Victorian Age

Unit 13 Elizabeth Barrett Browning 123
Text: Sonnets from the Portuguese (21) 124
Unit 14 Alfred Tennyson 127
Text: Ulysses 128
Unit 15 Robert Browning 135
Text1: My Last Duchess 136
Text2: Meeting at Night 141

The 20th Century

Unit 16 William Butler Yeats 145
Text1: The Lake Isle of Innisfree 146
Text2: Sailing to Byzantium 149
Unit 17 W. H. Auden 156
Text: Musée des Beaux Arts 157
Unit 18 Seamus Heaney 161
Text1: Clearances In Memoriam M. K. H., 1911-1984 162
Text2: Punishment 164

下篇　美国诗歌

Transcendentalism and American Poetry of the 19th Century

Unit 19 Ralph Waldo Emerson 171
Text: Days 172
Unit 20 Edgar Allan Poe 175
Text1: To Helen 176

Text2: Annabel Lee 179
Unit 21 Walt Whitman 184
Text1: Song of Myself (Excerpt) 185
Text2: O Captain! My Captain! 188
Unit 22 Emily Dickinson 192
Text1: 712 (Because I could not stop for Death) 193
Text2: 258 (There's a certain Slant of light) 196

Modern American Poetry

Unit 23 Robert Frost 201
Text1: The Road Not Taken 202
Text2: Nothing Gold Can Stay 205
Unit 24 Wallace Stevens 208
Text1: Anecdote of the Jar 209
Text2: The Snow Man 212
Unit 25 William Carlos Williams 216
Text: Spring and All 217
Unit 26 Ezra Pound 222
Text1: In a Station of the Metro 223
Text2: The River-Merchant's Wife: A Letter 225
Unit 27 T. S. Eliot 231
Text: The Love Song of J. Alfred Prufrock 232
Unit 28 Langston Hughes 247
Text1: The Negro Speaks of Rivers 248
Text2: A Dream Deferred 251

Postmodern and Contemporary American Poetry

Unit 29 Elizabeth Bishop 255
Text: The Fish 256
Unit 30 Allen Ginsberg 262
Text: Howl (Excerpt) 263
Unit 31 Gary Snyder 270
Text: I Went into the Maverick Bar 271
Unit 32 Sylvia Plath 275
Text: Lady Lazarus 276

英国诗歌

THE MIDDLE AGES

Unit 1　Geoffrey Chaucer

Introduction to the Author

Geoffrey Chaucer (1343-1400), poet, courtier and diplomat, is known as the Father of English literature. Chaucer was born into a wine merchant family of the new wealthy middle class in London. He probably spent his childhood in the business atmosphere of the kingdom's capital, met people of all sorts, and practiced several languages. After schooling of Latin, Chaucer was sent as a page in his teenage to the countess of Ulster, a prominent aristocrat in England who was married to the second son of Edward Ⅲ. During the Hundred Years' War, Chaucer was captured by the French in one of Edward's campaigns and released after the king of England contributed 16 pounds to his ransom. Being a member from the king's household, Chaucer had the chance to visit Spain, France and Italy as a diplomat when he was young. Chaucer served as a high official on several posts at court during his prime of life. In his later years, he was the clerk of the royal palace and was granted a sum of pension when he retired from the office. Chaucer was buried as the first poet in the Poets' Corner of Westminster Abbey.

Chaucer was a professional courtier. His writing was probably his spare time's recreation, a sideline rather than a vocation. His diplomatic travel into Italy brought him in contact with Italian literature. *Troilus and Criseyde*, one of his important works and one of the outstanding poems in European medieval literature, takes Boccaccio as its source. The poetical features of the poem also reflect the influence of Dante and Petrarch. Chaucer's representative work is his unfinished *The Canterbury Tales*, one of the great poems in world literature, which profoundly influences English literature and the English language. His other works include *The Book of the Duchess*, *The House of Fame* and *The Legend of Good Women*, etc.

Chaucer's contribution to the English language and literature lies in three aspects. Firstly, he improved and enriched the Middle English, the vernacular of the British people, with his prolific and versatile writing to enable it to compete with the dominant literary languages of Latin and French. Secondly, he set up one example for the following generations of literary people in his writing by combining the influence of foreign literature and the influence of English tradition with his own sense of nativeness. Thirdly, he left the modern English poets a rich legacy in versification, e.g. the introduction of the European continental accentual-syllabic meter into the English prosody, the invention of the rhyme royal, and the arrangement of the rhymed couplets with the iambic pentameter.

The Canterbury Tales: The General Prologue (Excerpt)[1]

When April's gentle rains have pierced the drought
Of March right to the root, and bathed each sprout
Through every vein with liquid of such power
It brings forth the engendering of the flower;
When Zephyrus[2] too with his sweet breath has blown
Through every field and forest, urging on
The tender shoots, and there's a youthful sun,
His second half course through the Ram[3] now run,
And little birds are making melody
And sleep all night, eyes open as can be
(So Nature pricks them in each little heart),
On pilgrimage then folks desire to start.
The palmers[4] long to travel foreign strands
To distant shrines[5] renowned in sundry lands[6];
And specially, from every shire's end[7]
In England, folks to Canterbury wend[8]:
To seek the blissful martyr[9] is their will,
The one who gave such help when they were ill.
Now in that season it befell one day
In Southwark[10] at the Tabard[11] where I lay,
As I was all prepared for setting out
To Canterbury with a heart devout[12],
That there had come into that hostelry

At night some twenty-nine, a company
Of sundry folk whom chance had brought to fall
In fellowship[13], for pilgrims were they all
And onward to Canterbury would ride.
The chambers and the stables there were wide,
We had it easy, served with all the best;

And by the time the sun had gone to rest
I'd spoken with each one about the trip
And was a member of the fellowship.
We made agreement, early to arise
To take our way, of which I shall advise.
But nonetheless, while I have time and space,
Before proceeding further here's the place
Where I believe it reasonable to state
Something about these pilgrims—to relate
Their circumstances[14] as they seemed to me,
Just who they were and each of what degree
And also what array they all were in[15].
And with a Knight[16] I therefore will begin.

1. 乔叟的《坎特伯雷故事集》是用中古英语写成的，例如《序诗》开头的四行：

   Whan that April with his[0] showres soote[0]　　its / fresh
   The droughte of March hath perced to the roote,
   And bathed every veine in swich[0] licour[0]　　such / liquid
   Of which vertu engendred is the flowr;

   为方便读者阅读，选文采用罗纳德·艾科（Ronald L. Ecker）和尤金·克鲁克（Eugene J. Crook）的现代英语译文。
2. Zephyrus：西风，古希腊神话里的西风神（Greek god of the west wind）。
3. Ram：[天文学]白羊（星）座。…there's a youthful sun / His second half course through the Ram now run；朝气蓬勃的太阳/正运行在白羊座的后半程。依西方古代天文学和占星术说法，太阳沿着黄道带运行到白羊座的时候是春分时节，大地万物复苏，生机勃勃。而白羊座的后半程是指春夏之交的时节，在英国是一年之中气候宜人的季节。
4. palmers：旧时带着象征荣耀的棕榈叶从圣地回来的朝圣者。
5. shrines：圣地，圣殿，神龛。

6. sundry lands：各式各样的国度。第 13～14 行的大意是：曾经满载荣耀的朝圣者在这个时候渴望旅行到陌生海岸，寻访不同国度那遥远的圣迹。
7. from every shire's end：从每个郡的角落。
8. folks to Canterbury wend：人们去往坎特伯雷。wend：去（direct one's way；go）
   Canterbury：坎特伯雷，英国英格兰东南部城市，距伦敦市中心约 98 公里。大主教圣托马斯·贝克特（Saint Thomas à Becket）在坎特伯雷大教堂被国王的卫士杀害，后被罗马教廷封圣。这一事件使得坎特伯雷成为宗教圣地，英国人朝圣的热门地。乔叟的《坎特伯雷故事集》也是以此朝圣习俗为其故事背景。
9. blissful martyr：蒙主赐福的殉道者，这里指的是圣托马斯·贝克特，被谋杀的坎特伯雷大主教。
10. Southwark：伦敦的一个区。
11. Tabard：旅店名。
12. with a heart devout：带着一颗虔诚的心。
13. a company / Of sundry folk whom chance had brought to fall / In fellowship：一群各色民众凑巧结成伙伴。
14. circumstances：情况，状况。
15. what array they all were in：他们处在什么样的阶层。
16. Knight：骑士，在中世纪时英国贵族中层级较低的一种，在公爵 Duke（Duchess 公爵夫人）、侯爵 Marquis（Marchioness 侯爵夫人）、伯爵 Earl（Countess 伯爵夫人）、子爵 Viscount（Viscountess 子爵夫人）和男爵 Baron（Baroness 男爵夫人）等五级爵位（peerages）之下（中国人通常以周朝以前可世袭罔替的五等爵位名称对应翻译英国的贵族封号）。现代英国也把"骑士"称号授予有杰出贡献的人。

Text Analysis

Chaucer's writing plan is shown in "The General Prologue" of *The Canterbury Tales*. He had intended to write one hundred and twenty stories, making each pilgrim telling four stories, two on the way to Canterbury and two more on the way back. However, he actually wrote only twenty-two complete stories and two fragments.

Yet this incomplete work is great enough to establish Chaucer's monumental position in the history of world literature, for there are many inventions in his writing. Chaucer adopts the traditional topic during the Middle Ages, the pilgrim's progress, but reconstructs it with new subject and new organization. In *The Canterbury Tales*, the pilgrims are no longer lonely legendary figures with heroic quality; instead, they are only a group of common people from the London middle class. Tales told by the pilgrims are not mainly about the religious deeds or heroic adventures, but stories about the general citizens and their lives. The way of telling the tales is not the mode of single speaker in the traditional pilgrim's progress which is either the pilgrim himself or the narrator in the third person, but rather, a new arrangement of making all the pilgrims join in the story telling: points of view are enriched from the first person to the omniscient, and the dialogues are also introduced in the narration; thus the arrangement presents a panoramic view of a society in the work. Chaucer carefully matches the tale and the teller, making the subject, the theme and even the language of the story united with the narrator's identity.

The tales told by Chaucer's pilgrims reflect vividly the social life of his time, a time when secular performance gradually replaces the spiritual one as the center of common people's life. In the beginning part of "The General Prologue", the figurative language and metaphorical accounts present the vigorous scenes of people's activities in April, a beautiful season fit for excursion in the countryside, making the religious travel a lively and joyous tour. The pilgrim's progress is but a ritually religious activity; the spurring desire for people to the shrine of St. Thomas Becket in Chaucer's *The Canterbury Tales* matches the exuberant spring time when the showers and gentle winds awaken the earth, bringing the spiritual renewal to the world. The setting in "The General Prologue" is suggestive too. The starting point of the travelers' journey is an inn named Tarbard in Southwark of London, and their destination is Canterbury. The former place represents the city, new center of human society; and the latter, a life far from city people. The route of the travelers is from the secular to the spiritual world and then back to the original place. It may suggest that these pilgrims will never be away from their familiar social life. An inn is a common meeting place in the tales of the medieval era, only that the visitors are often the heroic knights or warriors. But in Chaucer's story it becomes a place of new social order, where people from all ranks of the middle class share the duty and pleasure.

Different from other English authors writing tales of pilgrim's progress in verse form, Chaucer successfully invents his own iambic pentameter by learning from the Italian and French syllabic lines and combining them with the English conventional accentual ones. He arranges the iambic pentameter lines into rhymed couplets and rhyme royal stanza (also known as Chaucerian stanza). Chaucer's new poetical form expresses more exactly the musicality of the English language.

Questions

1. Please interpret the first four lines of "The General Prologue" in your own words.
2. What is an iambic pentameter line?

3. Please try to summarize Chaucer's innovative writing features according to the excerpt of "The General Prologue".

Chinese Translation

当四月的甘霖渗透了三月枯竭的根须，沐灌了丝丝茎络，触动了生机，使枝头涌现出花蕾；当东风吹香，使得山林莽原遍吐着嫩条新芽，青春的太阳已转过半边白羊宫座，小鸟唱起曲调，通宵睁开睡眼，是自然拨弄着它们的心弦：这时，人们渴想着朝拜四方名坛，游僧们也立愿跋涉异乡。尤其在英格兰地方，他们从每一州的角落，向着坎特伯雷出发，去朝谢他们的救病恩主、福泽无边的殉难圣徒。

在这时节，有一天，我正停憩在伦敦南岸萨得克的泰巴客店，虔心诚意，准备去坎特伯雷朝圣，到了晚上，客店中来了二十九位形形色色的朝客，凑巧结成了旅伴，他们都不约而同，要赴坎特伯雷的盛会；当时客店的屋舍马厩却很宽敞，我们舒舒服服地安顿下来。简单说来，到了夕阳西沉的时分，我已同每人相识交谈，约定了一齐早起出发。可是，在我开讲这故事之前，我想暂抽一部分时间，先谈一下每人的个别情况，由我的角度看去，他们是何种人物，属于哪一个社会阶层，穿着怎样。现在我将先讲一个武士。

（方重　译）

THE 16TH TO THE 18TH CENTURY

Unit 2 William Shakespeare

Introduction to the Author

William Shakespeare (1564-1616), actor, playwright and poet, was born in Stratford-up-on-Avoninto into a family of some prominence. Little is recorded about Shakespeare's early life; he might have attended the Stratford grammar school, where he received an education in Latin, but he did not go on to Oxford or Cambridge after then. He later went to London and worked there as an actor, working for the theatrical troupe, the Globe; meanwhile he was also a shareholder and eventually became the troupe's most important playwright.

Shakespeare was a prolific writer, with 13 comedies, 13 historical plays, 6 tragedies, 4 tragicomedies, as well as 154 sonnets, which were mostly dedicated to his patron, Henry Wriothsley, the Earl of Southampton. His works include, among others: comedies *Comedy of Errors*, *The Taming of the Shrew*, *Love*'s *Labor*'s *Lost*, *A Midsummer Night*'s *Dream*, *The Merchant of Venice*, *Much Ado About Nothing*, *As You Like It*, *Twelfth Night*, *Merry Wives of Windsor*, *All*'s *Well That Ends Well* and *Measure for Measure*; history plays *Henry* Ⅳ, *Henry* Ⅴ, *Richard* Ⅲ, *Julius Caesar*, *Antony and Cleopatra*; tragicomedies *Romeo and Juliet*, *Timon of Athens*, *Cymbeline*, *The Winter*'s *Tale*, and *Tempest*; he was especially famous for the four great tragedies *Hamlet*, *Othello*, *King Lear* and *Macbeth*.

Shakespeare's plays were based on old literary texts or folk legends but incorporated into them his own thinking, and greatly refreshed the old subjects. In play writing, he inherited the classical Greek and Roman tradition, the medieval English tradition, and the European tradition of the Renaissance period, but moved away from the three unities, broke the boundaries of tragedy and comedy, and greatly expanded the development of drama as a literary genre. His friend, the playwright Ben Jonson, remarked that Shakespeare belonged not only to his age but to all times.

Starting from the 17th century, Shakespeare's plays were spread to Europe, and then to America and other places of the world. Shakespeare was introduced into China in the mid-19th century by the missionaries, though serious interest in him did not begin until the beginning of the 20th century; his plays were known to the Chinese readers by way of Charles Lamb and his sister's *Tales from Shakespeare*. By far, Shakespeare study has been an important part of scholarship in foreign literature and culture studies in China.

Besides the plays, Shakespeare remained a poetic genius throughout the years, publishing a renowned and critically acclaimed sonnet cycle in 1609 (mostly written between 1590-1598). His contributions to this popular poetic genre are all the more amazing in his break with contemporary notions of subject matter. Shakespeare idealized the beauty of man as an object of praise and devotion (rather than the Petrarchan tradition of the idealized, unattainable woman). In the same spirit of breaking with tradition, Shakespeare also treated themes previously considered off limits—the dark, sexual side of a woman as opposed to the Petrarchan ideal of a chaste and remote love object. He also expanded the sonnet's emotional range, including such emotions as delight, pride, shame, disgust, sadness, and fear. Shakespeare is adept at using this genre, and displays rich vocabulary, simple yet expressive wording, unexpected metaphors, refreshing structure and strong musical effect. He is especially good at the last two lines, i.e. the couplet, characteristic for its startling conception while in logic consistent with the central argument of the poem.

Sonnet 18[1]

Shall I compare thee[2] to a summer's day[3]?
Thou art more lovely and more temperate[4]:
Rough winds do shake the darling buds of May[5],
And summer's lease hath all too short a date[6];
Sometime[7] too hot the eye of heaven shines,
And often is his gold complexion dimmed[8];
And every fair from fair sometime declines[9],
By chance or nature's changing course untrimmed[10];
But thy eternal summer shall not fade,
Nor lose possession of that fair thou ow'st[11],
Nor shall Death brag thou wand'rest in his shade[12],
When in eternal lines to Time thou grow'st[13]:
So long as men can breathe, or eyes can see,
So long lives this, and this gives life to thee.[14]

1. 莎士比亚的十四行诗一般以第一行命名，或者以标号称呼。十四行诗（sonnet）始于中世纪民间抒情诗，13 至 14 世纪流行于意大利。常见的十四行诗的诗体有：意大利体或彼特拉克体（Italian or Petrarchan sonnet），由 1 个 8 行诗节（octave）和 1 个 6 行诗节（sestet）组成，尾韵形式为 abba, abba 或 abab，abab 和 cde, cde 或 cd, cd, cd；英国式或莎士比亚式（English or Shakespearean sonnet），由 3 个 4 行诗节（quatrain）和 1 个 2 行诗节（couplet）组成，尾韵为 abab, cdcd, efef, gg；斯宾塞式（Spenserian sonnet），同样由 3 个 4 行诗节和 1 个 2 行诗节组成，尾韵为 abab, bcbc, cdcd, ee。此外，还有一些变体。
2. thee：古英语中，thee 作为第二人称单数代词的宾格形式，thou 为第二人称单数代词的主格形式，第二人称单数的所有格形式为 thy 或 thine。第二人称复数的主格形式是 you 或 ye（ye 也可用作第二人称单数主格 thou 的尊称），宾格为 you，所有格为 your 或 yours。另外，与第二人称单数主格 thou 连用的动词，其后接 -est, -st, -t，如本诗的第 10 行中的 ow'st（owest），第 12 行中的 grow'st（growest）；动词 be 的第二人称单数现在时为 art，如本诗第 2 行中的 Thou art（You are）。
3. 该句可能是从谚语“As good as one shall see in a summer's day”（夏天时间漫长，可以看到很多的东西）而来。day 的意思是 period，term（时段），如 Henry Ⅵ，Ⅱ. 1.2 中有“I saw not better sport these seven years' day”之说。在这句诗中，day 可以表示一天的 24 小时，或者按照通常的理解，表示 period（时段），如在本诗的第 4 和第 9 行中，夏天都指一个季节。
4. temperate: even-tempered，moderate，equable.
5. 16 世纪 90 年代，英国日历的日期（历法）比欧洲晚几天（直到 18 世纪后期才纠正过来）。因此该诗中的五月实际上是六月，是夏天的时令了。
6. lease：allotted time，本意是土地或房屋的租赁期限，这里是指夏天租赁给人们的期限，该行的意思是说夏天过于短暂。该行最后的 date 和第 2 行末尾的 temperate 押长元音“a”，例如在英国的南方，bat 和 bad 中的“a”同样是发长音。
7. sometime：第 5 行和第 7 行中的 sometime 连用，即 sometimes… sometimes…，表示 from time to time，意思是“有时……有时……”；另外，sometime 可以理解为双关词，除了上述意思外，表示 eventually (at some time)，即“终归，终究”。
8. 第 5 至 6 行用了隐喻，the eye of heaven 指 the sun（太阳），第 7 行延续了这个隐喻。
9. 正常的语序应该是 And every fair sometime declines from fair, 意思是 every beautiful thing or person loses its beauty at some point。该句中，第一个 fair 可以指美丽的事物或人，第二个 fair 指人或物之美。
10. changing course：through altering seasons, in unpredictable weather，指四季的更迭；untrimmed: stripped of ornament, robbed of trimming.
11. that fair thou ow'st：that beauty you own，你所拥有的美。

12. Echoing Psalms 23:3, "Yea though I walk through the valley of the shadow of death, I will fear no evil: for thou art with me, thy rod and thy staff be the things that do comfort me".
13. to time thou grow'st: thou growest to time，你与时间同在。时间有两种：暂时的、终有尽时的时间，以及无始无终、臻于永恒的时间，后一种时间克服了时间的暂时性从而得以永恒，因此有"你与时间同在"之说。
14. this: this poem, this sonnet, written in "eternal lines".

This is a love poem. The speaker compares his beloved to the summer, yet he goes on to say that the beloved surpasses summer since summer is too short and it is subject to the changes of the sun, which is casted into shadow at times. Every ordinary beauty will lose her beauty as time goes on, however, the beauty of the speaker's beloved will remain what it is, since she will live forever in his eternal poetic lines. This poem provides us with two popular themes in Renaissance：greatness of man and immortality of literature and art. The beloved is immortal because she lives in the immortal poetry, and hence her greatness because of the immortality ; her immortality matches that of literature. The beloved can be immortal because she is imbued with man's quality of being immortal：man is immortal and hence her immortality as an individual man.

The structural development of the sonnet matches well its thematic treatment. Structurally speaking, the Shakespearean sonnet is similar to the Chinese "eight-part essay"：the first quatrain begins an argument, and the second follows it, the third "turns" by arguing the other way round, and the couplet concludes the argument by offering a conclusion to the argument of the poem. The pattern is obvious in this sonnet.

The sonnet follows the traditional belief that man is a small cosmos echoing the big cosmos of the world. The different time periods of the man are identical to the four seasons：the speaker compares his lover to summer, implying the best time of her life. The metaphor of the sun goes throughout the poem, sustained and developed with the writing moving forward.

1. Why is the beloved of the speaker compared to summer instead of any other seasons of the year? How do you understand the metaphor of the sun in the poem?

2. From the Text Analysis, we understand the beloved in the poem to be a female. Is it possible for it to be a male?

3. Can you give some examples, in English and American literature or in Chinese literature, that have similar thematic concerns?

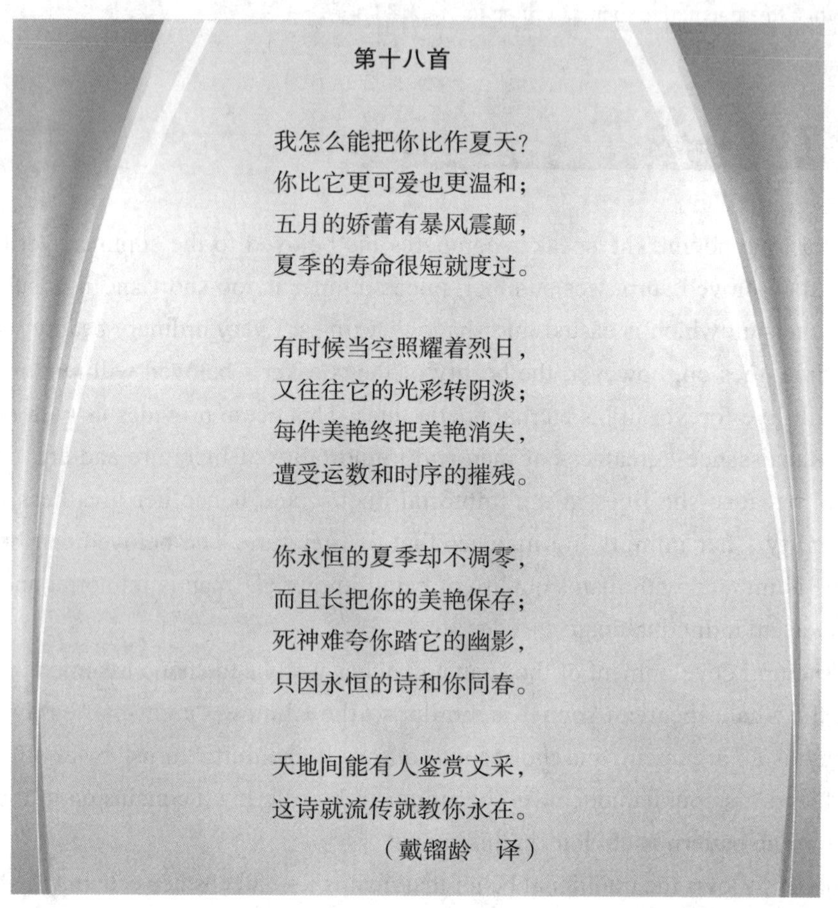

第十八首

我怎么能把你比作夏天?
你比它更可爱也更温和;
五月的娇蕾有暴风震颠,
夏季的寿命很短就度过。

有时候当空照耀着烈日,
又往往它的光彩转阴淡;
每件美艳终把美艳消失,
遭受运数和时序的摧残。

你永恒的夏季却不凋零,
而且长把你的美艳保存;
死神难夸你踏它的幽影,
只因永恒的诗和你同春。

天地间能有人鉴赏文采,
这诗就流传就教你永在。

（戴镏龄　译）

Sonnet 105

Let not[1] my love be called idolatry[2],
Nor my beloved as an idol show[3],

Since all alike my songs and praises be
To one, of one, still such, and ever so[4].
Kind[5] is my love to-day, to-morrow kind,
Still constant[6] in a wondrous excellence;
Therefore my verse, to constancy confined[7],
One thing expressing, leaves out difference[8].
　"Fair, kind and true" is all my argument[9],
　"Fair, kind, and true," varying to other words[10];
And in this change is my invention spent[11],
Three themes in one[12], which wondrous scope affords[13].
Fair, kind, and true, have often lived alone[14],
Which three till now never kept seat in one[15].

1. Let not: on no account.
2. idolatry: excessive devotion, worship of many gods，偶像崇拜。
3. show: appear, display.
4. 第 3 至 4 行：since 指 in fact。对于有的批评家来说，这两行是指责该诗中的诗人偶像崇拜的根据，而对另外的批评者而言，这恰好是对该指责的辩护的开始。两种解释都是成立的，因为诗人在第 1 行中指出别人对自己的指责，而后他对此的反驳又非常坚决。第 4 行中的语义模糊增加了另一种含义：如果 still such, and ever so 指第 3 行中诗人的 songs and praises，则第 3 至 4 行更多地指向偶像崇拜，而不是对此的辩护；反之，如果 still such, and ever so 用来说明第 4 行中出现的 one（第 6 行说他 constant，即忠诚不二），则另一种可能性成立。对于这两种可能性，诗的后 6 行提出了解释，但并不能解决这种混乱：后 6 行指出，诗人只是描述了诗中提到的这位青年。
5. Kind：参看对第 9 行的解释。
6. Still: always，总是；constant: the same, faithful，忠实的。
7. to constancy confined: restricted in the subject-matter to the theme of sameness and fidelity，在写作主题上限于忠实。对此可做如下解释：诗歌受限于诗人的情绪，而诗人忠诚于那位忠实的青年。
8. leaves out difference: ignores other literary subjects，即不考虑其他的文学题材，因为其爱人是如此的忠贞不变。
9. Fair: beautiful, just; kind: loving, generous; true: genuine, faithful. 三者即美、善、真。all: much 或 everything；前面的三个形容词扩大了彼此的内涵，使它们不仅相互包括（参见第 12 行的 Three themes in one），还包括了所有的美德。argument: theme.
10. varying to other words: expressed in different terms, expressed in various.
11. change : change of words ; invention: inventiveness, creative ingenuity ; spent : employed ;

used up, exhausted, squandered.

12. in one: (1) united in one theme, encompassed in a single virtue; (2) contained in a single person (the "one" of line 4). Three themes in one：这里隐含着基督教的三位一体的概念，即圣父、圣子、圣灵是一体的。
13. wondrous scope affords: provides an amazing range of literary opportunities，提供了广阔的文学表现主题。
14. lived alone: lodged separately (in different people)，在不同的人身上分别存在。
15. kept seat: resided, lived; were enthralled.

Text Analysis

This is also supposed to be a love poem. The usual understanding goes that among Shakespeare's 154 sonnets, the first 126 are devoted to a handsome young man while the rest to a dark lady. (For a long time, much controversy exists, such as regarding Shakespeare's sex orientation.) In this regard, the sonnet is to the poet's male friend.

In the beginning of the poem, the poet refutes the charge of idolatry by demonstrating that his love is just and his beloved is worthy of all this—for his unique blend of being fair, kind and true. Therefore, in subject-matter the poet excludes any other issues and works merely on this: love towards his beloved. One might blame the poet for his "blind" love, yet he tries to appear rational by showing a sound argument, despite of our inclination probably not to follow this argument. Besides, though polytheism was idolatrous for most Elizabethan readers, yet idolatry is not necessarily polytheistic, and the tone of the sestet—in the poet's effort to offer a sound defence for his love—implies a suggestion that he thinks his friend is a worldly god, an idol.

The poet not only praises his faithful love, by doing this, he but also eulogizes all men with the virtues of beauty, generosity and truth. Here lies William Shakespeare's aesthetic and world outlook. This position of him is not merely seen in this poem, but also in some other poems, such as in sonnets 54, 69 and 98. Shakespeare's aesthetic views remind us of similar ones held by the English poet John Keats in "Ode on a Grecian Urn."

Questions

1. Do you think the poet's self-defence in the poem is persuasive? Why or why not? If you are to offer a self-refutation of the same sort, what will you do?

2. How do you think of Shakespeare's aesthetic viewpoints as shown in this sonnet? A hint: his aesthetic and artistic views could be found in other places as well, such as in *Hamlet*, in the scene of play within the play.

3. The blending of truth, kindness and beauty is not coincidental in this sonnet, and not even in Shakespeare. Can you give as examples other writings (poems) that have similar concerns in writing?

4. What writing features do you see in this sonnet? Better take into consideration of Shakespeare's writing features as displayed in other of his writings as well.

Chinese Translation

第一百零五首

别把我的爱唤作偶像崇拜，
也别把我爱人看成是一尊偶像，
尽管我所有的歌和赞美都用来
献给一个人，讲一件事情，不改样。
我爱人今天温柔，明天也仁慈，
拥有卓绝的美德，永远不变心；
所以，我的只颂扬忠贞的诗词，
就排除驳杂，单表达一件事情。
真，善，美，就是我全部的主题，
真，善，美，变化成不同的辞章；
我的创造力就用在这种变化里，
三题合一，产生瑰丽的景象。
　　真，善，美，过去是各不相关，
　　现在呢，三位同座，真是空前。

（屠岸　译）

Unit 3 John Donne

Introduction to the Author

John Donne (1572-1631) was born in London. His father was a prosperous merchant; his mother was a devout Catholic whose family had suffered religious persecution and exile. Donne attended Oxford and Cambridge, but he was unable to obtain a degree from either institution because of his Catholicism. In his youth, Donne spent much of his considerable inheritance on women, literature, pastimes and travel. Inheritance from his father was insufficient for his economic independence, so he had to use his wide interests and talents to make a living. In 1621, he was elected dean of St. Paul's. After then he preached widely, both at court and abroad, and his sermons were received with both acclaim and punishment.

Few of Donne's poems were published in his lifetime; the first collected edition of his poetry appeared in 1633. Donne's earliest poems showed a developed knowledge of English society coupled with sharp criticism of its problems, such as corruption in the legal system, mediocre poets, pompous courtiers, and false belief in religion. His early career was also notable for his bawdy and cynical verses, especially his elegies, in which he employed unconventional metaphors, such as a flea biting two lovers being compared to sex. Having converted to the Anglican Church, Donne quickly became noted for his sermons and religious poems. Towards the end of his life, Donne wrote works that challenged death, and the fear that it inspired in many men, on the grounds of his belief that those who die are sent to Heaven to live eternally. One example of this challenge is "Death, Be Not Proud".

Donne's poetry differed much from his predecessors. Poetry in the Elizabethan time was flown in imagery, while Donne and some other 17th century English poets like George Herbert and Andrew Marvell were greatly influenced by the Baroque style of the Continent; they employed Christian mysticism and erotic subjects, and tried to produce surprising effect with "unpoetical" objects like encompass and mosquito. The fear and anxiety displayed in their poetry reflected results of modern cosmological and geographical discoveries, and their challenge to traditional thoughts. Donne is considered a master of the metaphysical conceit, an extended metaphor that combines two vastly different ideas into a single idea, and often uses imagery. The blending of sensation and ration, together with direct and violent metaphors often met with ambivalence from his immediate successors. Critics like John Dryden and Dr. Samuel Johnson disliked the "metaphysical" writing, and the Neoclassical poets regarded his conceits as abuse of metaphor. However, when readers of late 19th and early 20th century had too much of the late Romantic and late Symbolist poetry, they were attracted to Donne and other "metaphysical" poets. T. S. Eliot highly praised metaphysical poetry for its "association of sensibility", and the New Critics further popularized this way of writing by their close reading of the metaphysical poems.

John Donne's poetry represents a shift from classical forms to more personal ones. His works are witty, often employing paradoxes, puns, and subtle yet remarkable analogies. He often experiments with ideas and concepts, and with rhythm and stanza forms at the same time. Donne is noted for his poetic meter, which was structured with changing and jagged rhythms that closely resemble casual speech. His poetry is forceful in rhythm, vivid in language, bold and particular in imagination.

John Donne wrote sonnet, love poetry, religious poetry, proverb, song, elegy, etc. His major writings, among others, include *Songs and Sonnets*, *The Elegies*, *The First and Second Anniversaries*, *Holy Sonnets*, *Devotions upon Emergent Occasions*, etc.

A Valediction: Forbidding Mourning[1]

As virtuous men pass mildly away[2],
　　And whisper to their souls to go,
Whilst[3] some of their sad friends do say
　　The breath goes now, and some say, no;

So let us melt[4], and make no noise,
　　No tear-floods, nor sigh-tempests move[5],
'Twere profanation of our joys
　　To tell the laity[6] our love.

Moving of th' earth[7] brings harms and fears,
　　Men reckon what it did[8] and meant;
But trepidation of the spheres[9],
　　Though greater far, is innocent[10].

Dull sublunary[11] lovers' love
(Whose soul is sense[12]) cannot admit[13]
Absence, because it doth remove
Those things which elemented[14] it.

But we, by a love so much refined[15]
That our selves know not what it is[16],
Inter-assurèd of the mind[17],
Care less, eyes, lips, and hands to miss[18].

Our two souls therefore, which are one,
Though I must go, endure not yet[19]
A breach, but an expansion[20],
Like gold to airy thinness beat[21].

If they be two[22], they are two so[23]
As stiff[24] twin compasses are two;
Thy soul, the fixed foot[25], makes no show[26]
To move, but doth, if th' other do[27].

And though it in the centre sit,
Yet when the other far doth roam,
It leans and hearkens after it,
And grows erect, as that comes home[28].

Such wilt thou be to me, who must
Like th' other foot, obliquely run[29].
Thy firmness makes my circle just[30],
And makes me end where I begun[31].

1. 据沃尔顿（Izaak Walton）著《多恩传》（*Life of Donne*）记载，约翰·多恩于1611年的冬季出使巴黎，他在出发之前创作该诗，献给妻子。Valediction：告别辞。
2. As：该词在这里可以有两种解释：like（正如），或 when（当……的时候）。pass away：die，辞世。第1个诗节是"As"引导的状语从句，而主句则在第2节，由"So"引导。无论从内容还是从表现形式来看，该诗起首即不落俗套，大胆而具有戏剧性。

3. Whilst: while.
4. melt：指二人的肉体熔化，从而合二为一。这一描写回应了第一节中的死亡意象。
5. move：stir up，搅起；其宾语是 No tear-floods nor sigh-tempests。这里的语序变化是为了照顾尾韵的工整。本行体现了玄学派诗歌典型的“玄思”（conceit）意象，此处沿用意大利诗人彼特拉克（Petrarch）的比喻，把眼泪比作洪水，把叹息比作风暴。按照人体和宇宙对应说，作为小宇宙的人的眼泪与叹息，对应着大宇宙中的洪水与风暴；这种用法也为第 3 节中的譬喻打下了基础。诗人在这一行中使用 tear-floods 和 sigh-tempests，把简单的词并用，简洁蕴藉，极大地增强了表现力。
6. the laity：俗人，教会神职人员以外的普通人。诗人把自己与妻子之间的爱情比喻为宗教，是精神和灵魂的活动，而凡俗之人的爱情则是感官的交流，是流俗之举，因此把“我们”（诗人和妻子）的圣洁的精神和心灵之爱告诉凡俗之人，是对爱情的亵渎和不洁。“我们”的分别应该是寂静祥和的，不能像世俗之人那样弄出很大的动静。
7. Moving of th’ earth：earthquake，地震。相传地震的原因在于上帝的震怒，是一种天谴行为，是人类的灾难。
8. what it did：what harms it (the earthquake) did，地震将带来何等伤害。
9. trepidation of the spheres：天体的震动。托勒密（Ptolemy）的天文体系认为，宇宙是一个以地球为中心的圆形，外围有九重天，最外围一重的运动牵引着内部各重天，这样便导致天体的震动，导致春分秋分发生差错。这种运动时宇宙的自然规律是正常的和谐的运动，不会对人产生不好的影响。在诗中，诗人表示精神之侣的分离就像天体的震动，虽然动静不小，却不会形成任何伤害；反之，世俗之人的离别则会引发地震，因为他们无法像精神之侣那样保持精神的平静从容。
10. innocent：harmless，这里指不会对人类产生伤害。
11. sublunary：月下的。月亮之下是世俗世界，是俗人生活的地方。sublunary love（月下的爱）即俗人之爱，是可变的，因此不是恒久的。相反，和“月亮之下”对应的便是“天国”，那里的一切都是神圣的、宗教的爱，是不变的、恒久的，那里的爱情当然也不例外。这是中世纪宇宙论的观点。诗人在第 4 节和第 6 节中，把两种爱情做了反衬。
12. Whose soul is sense：soul 指实质；sense 意思是 the sense(s)，感官，或 sensual，追求感官刺激，与精神之爱（Platonic love）相对而言。
13. admit：tolerate，stand 承受，忍受。
14. elemented：构成，组成。以上 4 节，诗人极力渲染他和妻子的神圣之爱与凡俗者的爱情的区别：俗世之爱不能忍受彼此的分离，因为这种分离必然是身体的分离，而他们的爱就是建立在身体的基础上的，因此身体的分离是他们不能接受的。对于下文将要讨论的精神之侣的分离，这里已然做了铺垫。
15. refined：提炼，该意象来自中世纪的炼金术，暗示一种精神化的过程，正如芜杂之物中可以提炼出纯金，神圣的精神伴侣也可以从低贱的肉欲中升华出纯洁的爱情。“提炼”的意象引导出接下来的锻造黄金的比喻。

16. ourselves know not what it is：我们不知道爱情是何物，it 指爱情。
17. Inter-assurèd of the mind：彼此知晓对方的心思，即心心相印，相互盟誓（有法律的庄严保证之意）。
18. Care less，eyes，lips and hands to miss：Care less to miss eyes，lips and hands。care less 可以理解为 care less than…，也可以理解为 careless。诗人并没有完全排除肉体和感官享受在爱情生活中的作用，但更强调精神的作用，认为这是超越世俗之爱，因而是更高级的爱的形式。第 17 至 20 行的正常语序是：But we，inter-assured of the mind by a love which is so refined that ourselves know not what it is，care less to miss eyes，lips and hands。
19. endure not yet：yet not endure，nevertheless do not suffer（忍受）。
20. breach：parting，leaving each other 分离，分裂。expansion：扩展，扩充，这里指诗人及其妻子之间的爱情并没有因为双方身体的离开而分裂，反而得以扩大，覆盖了英吉利海峡，连接处于英法两国的二人。
21. Like gold to airy thinness beat：like gold，which is beaten into thin gold leaf，锻造成稀薄如空气的金箔。据称，一两黄金可以打造成一片 250 平方英尺的叶片。airy thinness：指神圣的精神之爱是空灵的，和浊重的世俗之爱（sublunary love）形成反差。
22. If they be two：if they should be two，虚拟语气，表假设。以下引入一个新的譬喻，这是另一个"玄思"意象：圆规画圆，意味着变化中（圆周脚）的坚定（圆心脚），而作为其过程的圆则象征着圆满和完美。诗人在此以圆规的两只脚比喻相爱中的两个人，即诗人自己和妻子。圆规历来是坚贞的象征，同时圆又象征着圆满。据考证，圆规的意象最早源于 11 世纪末波斯诗人哈亚姆（Omar Khayyam）的《鲁拜集》（*The Rubaiyat*），后传入欧洲。相关诗行是："你同我都是一个圆规的形骸——/ 虽有两只脚却只有一个脑袋；/ 当圆弧的中心我们一旦确定，/ 两只脚尖我们就并它在一块。"（黄皋炘译）然而，圆规的意象还可以上溯到《圣经》中的《旧约 · 箴言》（8: 27）："When he prepared the heavens，I was there；when he set a compass upon the face of the depth."（他立高天，我在那里；在渊面的周围放上圆规）这是引自 The Holy Bible，King James Version，即钦定本《圣经》，其他各版本有时行文有所不同，如 when he drew a circle on the face of the deep 或 when he inscribed a circle on the face of the deep 或 when he stretched the horizon across the ocean，等等。另外，弥尔顿的《失乐园》也有相关描写，参见第 7 卷第 224～232 行。
23. so: in such a way.
24. stiff: firm, stable.
25. fixed foot：圆心脚，圆规作为支撑的那只脚，在此指诗人的妻子。这一节和下一节中的 the other 指另外一只脚，即圆周脚，圆心脚会随着圆周脚而动。这里的圆周脚指诗人自己。
26. show：sign，迹象。

27. if th' other do：这是条件句，动词 do 前省略了 should。下一行是让步句，单数第三人称 it 后面的动词 sit 也用了原形。
28. 这两节描述了圆规运动的过程：圆心脚开始时静止不动，但当圆周脚开始运动，它也随之而动，并在整个过程中一直倾斜着朝向圆周脚；当圆周脚完成了一周的运动，连点成线，画出一个圆，回到起点，倾斜的圆心脚便直立起来，于是二者并拢，合二为一。诗人以圆规的运动比喻他旅欧期间和妻子的关系：妻子是中心，像圆心脚，他则像圆周脚在外奔波，一旦完成使命，便回归到妻子的身边。
29. Like th' other foot，obliquely run：就像另一只脚（指圆周脚），倾斜地转圈。
30. Thy firmness makes my circle just：你的坚定使我的圆画得好。just: full.
31. And makes me end where I begun：使我在出发的地方止步，指圆周脚在画了一个圆后，在开始的地方结束，这是一解；第二解，圆周脚在完成画圆后，回到圆心脚身边；此外，第 1 节以死亡比喻离别，而离别在西方宗教的意义上也意味着告别今生，进入来世。这个"离别—死亡—离别"的模式似乎也是在画圆，从起点出发，转了一圈后又回到了起点；这个模式呼应了圆规运动的轨迹。全诗以生死循环的圆开始，以圆规所画的圆结束，暗含了"止步在起点"，这在写法上也是一个圆满，强化了全诗的主题。

Text Analysis

Unlike some of John Donne's other works that are more bawdy and cynical in nature, such as the poem "The Flea" or the song "Go, and Catch a Falling Star", "A Valediction：Forbidding Mourning" is centered on a spiritual love that transcends the physical. As a metaphysical poem, this work is unusual in numerous ways, for example the beginning, which is serious and calm in tone but unexpected and dramatic in the idea it employs: the parting of the lovers is compared to death. Of course, the most famous writing in the poem, and probably one of the most famous, if not the most famous, metaphors of the metaphysical poetry is the compass that is compared to the two lovers. It is a typical metaphysical conceit, a type of analogy that compares something physical to something spiritual or beyond physical. The compass is metallic, and will get rusty sometimes: in the common understanding, compass is hardly compared to the lovers. However, Donne takes full advantage of the image, by elaborating on the movement of its two feet. Besides, Donne compares his wife to the fixed foot, while comparing himself to the running foot: this breaks away from usual understanding of the relationship between husband and wife at that time, since wife is usually attached to the husband and could hardly be the center of the family. This sonnet also displays Donne's interests and knowledge in science, religion, love and other fields.

Donne's writings are often ironic and cynical, especially when regarding love and human motives. Common subjects of his poems are love (especially in his early life), death (especially after his wife's death), and religion. These elements find themselves in this poem as well. One difference between this poem (which is from his later career) and his early pieces is that his early poems like "Song" ("Go, and Catch a Falling Star"), which comes from his early playboy years, are cynical and show his androgyny. With time passing, especially when he was devoted to religion, he was serious to woman, and his writings show genuine love and respect to woman, such as this love song to his wife.

This poem is a perfect combination of sense and sensibility, to quote Jane Austen, or association of sensibility, in T. S. Eliot's words. It is intense in imagination and artistic creativity, and is a fine piece of literary work. It is written with an "abab" end rhyme scheme in iambic tetrameter.

Questions

1. John Donne is usually considered as the foremost poet of metaphysical poetry. What features of this school of poetry can be seen from this poem?

2. What evidence of the development in science and technology can be detected in the poem?

3. Why earthquake is employed to set off the difference between ordinary and extraordinary ("our") love?

Chinese Translation

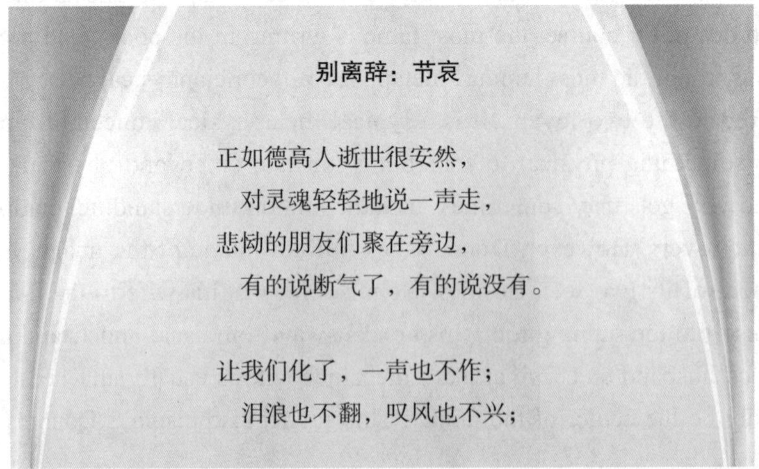

别离辞：节哀

正如德高人逝世很安然，
　对灵魂轻轻地说一声走，
悲恸的朋友们聚在旁边，
　有的说断气了，有的说没有。

让我们化了，一声也不作；
　泪浪也不翻，叹风也不兴；

那是亵渎我们的欢乐——
　要是对俗人讲我们的爱情。

地动会带来灾害和惊恐，
　人们估计它干什么，要怎样，
可是那些天体的震动，
　虽然大得多，什么也不伤。

世俗的男女彼此的相好
　（他们的灵魂是官能）就最忌
别离，因为那就会取消
　组成爱恋的那一套东西。

我们被爱情提炼得纯净，
　自己都不知道存什么念头
互相在心灵上得到了保证，
　再不愁碰不到眼睛、嘴和手。

两个灵魂打成了一片，
　虽说我得走，却并不变成
破裂，而只是向外伸延，
　像金子打到薄薄的一层。

就还算两个吧，两个却这样
　和一副两脚规情况相同；
你的灵魂是定脚，并不像
　移动，另一脚一移，它也动。

虽然它一直是坐在中心，
　可是另一个去天涯海角，
它就侧了身．倾听八垠；
　那一个一回家，它马上挺腰。

你对我就会这样子，我一生
　像另外那一脚，得侧身打转；
你坚定，我的圆圈才会准，
　我才会终结在开始的地点。

（卞之琳　译）

Unit 4 John Milton

Introduction to the Author

John Milton (1608-1674), poet, statesman, is the last great liberal intelligence of the English Renaissance. He was born in London into a middle-class family, educated at St. Paul's School, then at Christ's College, Cambridge. He began his apprentice writing of poetry when he was a college student. After graduation, he went to his father's country house at Horton in Buckinghamshire, leading almost seclusively a life of extensive reading in English, Latin, Greek and Italian of important works under his own direction for six years. In 1638, Milton went abroad on his grand tour to complete his education. A year later, just as he avidly visited famous scholarly figures and historical sites, Milton learned the impending of English Civil War. This event cut short his tour of Europe. Milton returned home and settled down in London, and began his complex and troubling career during this turbulent age. In the time of English Civil War, Milton served as a civil servant for the Commonwealth of England under Oliver Cromwell. He wrote pamphlets to advocate radical political topics which include the freedom of the press. Hard work damaged his eyesight; Milton was completely blind by 1651. After the Restoration, Milton was persecuted and was forced to live in seclusion in the countryside for the rest of his life.

Milton's writing, according to the three stages of his life, can be divided as the time of apprenticeship during which he composed *Lycidas* (1637) and some of his early sonnets, the time of prose writing of which the topics are mainly political and social, and the time of his returning to literary writing and during which he published his three major poems, *Paradise Lost* (1667), *Paradise Regained* (1671), and *Samson Agonistes* (1671).

Milton's works express the values of humanism, such as tolerance, freedom and self-determination, and at the same time reflect the influence of new scientific knowledge. He is a great lyrical poet; his sonnets expand the thematic quest in this exquisite literary genre: *On His Blindness* and *Methought I Saw My Late Espousèd Saint* are such examples among the best English sonnets which touch the readers with profound meditation and deep feelings. Milton is a great prose writer; his celebrated *Areopagitica* (written in condemnation of pre-publication censorship), for instance, is one influential essay in defending the free speech and the freedom of the press. Milton is a great master of epic; his three epic poems, *Paradise Lost*, *Paradise Regained*, and *Samson Agonistes*, display a grand and graceful style which combines the sublimity of Greek tragedy and the stately eloquence of Latin prose, and into which he infuses sharply Miltonic controversy of human beings' loss and gain that other writers may not be able to reach.

Milton has got his international fame in his lifetime for his scholarly prolific writings in English, Latin and Italian. His fame is strengthened especially after the publication of *Paradise Lost*. Milton casts a formidable shadow over English literature for centuries, becoming a monumental model for generations of poets and prose writers.

Paradise Lost (Excerpt of Book Four)

Two of far nobler shape, erect[1] and tall,
God-like erect, with native honour clad
In naked majesty, seemed lords of all,
And worthy seemed; for in their looks divine
The image of their glorious Maker shone[2],
Truth, wisdom, sanctitude[3] severe and pure—
Severe, but in true filial freedom[4] placed,
Whence true authority in men: though both
Not equal[5], as their sex not equal seemed[6];
For contemplation[7] he and valour[8] formed,
For softness she and sweet attractive grace;
He for God only, she for God in him[9].
His fair large front[10] and eye sublime[11] declared
Absolute rule; and Hyacinthine[12] locks
Round from his parted forelock manly hung
Clustering, but not beneath his shoulders broad:
She, as a veil[13] down to the slender waist,
Her unadornèd[14] golden tresses[15] wore
Dishevelled[16], but in wanton[17] ringlets waved
As the vine curls hertendrils[18]—which implied
Subjection, but required with gentle sway,

And by her yielded, by him best received—
Yielded, with coy[19] submission, modest pride[20],
And sweet, reluctant, amorous delay.
Nor those mysterious parts[21] were then concealed:
Then was not guilty shame. Dishonest[22] shame
Of Nature's works, honour dishonourable,
Sin-bred[23], how have ye troubled all mankind
With shews instead, mere shews[24] of seeming pure
And banished from man's life his happiest life,
Simplicity and spotless innocence!
So passed they naked on, nor shunned[25] the sight
Of God or Angel; for they thought no ill[26]:
So hand in hand they passed, the loveliest pair
That ever since in love's embraces met—
Adam the goodliest man of men since born
His sons; the fairest of her daughters Eve[27].

1. erect：直立。弥尔顿用这个词暗示人比用四足行走的动物更高贵，也更具有神的品性。
2. image of their glorious Maker shone：他们荣耀创造者（上帝）的形象熠熠生辉。此处是指亚当和夏娃是上帝按照自己的样子所塑造的，因而他们身上泛着神圣光辉。
3. sanctitude：圣洁（holiness; saintliness）。
4. filial freedom：亚当和夏娃在上帝呵护下享受着儿女们才有的自由。
5. Not equal：不一样，指亚当和夏娃在性别上的差异。
6. as their sex not equal seemed：似乎因为性别表现出（他们个性的）不同。（这些都是作为旁观者魔王的所见所想。）
7. contemplation：沉思（thought, meditation）。
8. valour：健壮而勇敢（strong, courageous）。"For contemplation he and valour formed, / For softness she and sweet attractive grace"这两行的意思是：亚当既健壮勇敢又善于思考，夏娃温柔甜美，有着迷人的优雅。
9. she for God in him：亚当由上帝创造，夏娃是上帝从亚当创造；弥尔顿的意思是亚当比夏娃更接近上帝。
10. front：前额（forehead, as if a large forehead indicates intelligence）。
11. sublime：庄严、崇高（oriented heavenward）。
12. Hyacinthine：风信子。Hyacinthine locks：弥尔顿用典把亚当的发式与希腊神话中受太阳神钟爱的海辛瑟斯相比，让读者联想属于古典时期智慧男子的英俊形象——

《荷马史诗》里描述雅典娜专注于奥迪修斯时所看到他的发式也是这样。诗中描绘夏娃时的用词也是用典，clustring（成束的）使人遐想维纳斯的 fair clustering tresses（一绺绺美丽的长发），同样也具有古典的典雅美。

13. veil：长发垂到腰间像是遮盖的东西。
14. unadornèd：不装饰的（not decorated）。
15. tresses：一绺一绺的长发（a long lock of a woman's hair）。
16. Dishevelld：不整齐（untidy），自然不修整。
17. wanton：浓密（growing profusely; luxuriant）。
18. tendrils：卷发（slender ringlets of hair）。
19. coy：羞涩（shy or reserved）。
20. modest pride：谦逊的自豪。弥尔顿描述亚当的时候集中在他的头部，暗示亚当的重要品性是其智慧。而提到夏娃的时候，弥尔顿的描述则从头扩展到整个形体，意指夏娃的天性是其美丽和典雅。
21. mysterious parts：私处（genitals）。
22. Dishonest：不诚实（impure or unchaste）。
23. bred：导致（led to, produced）
24. mere shews：只是炫耀。
25. shunned：shun（avoid and stay away from deliberately）的过去式。
26. they thought no ill：他们不觉得邪恶；ill：邪恶（morally evil）。
27. Adam the goodliest man of men since born / His sons; the fairest of her daughters Eve：诗人这种不合逻辑的写法意在强调亚当和夏娃是世界上最纯美的一对，特别是他们尚在伊甸园，没有堕落到尘世生儿育女的时候。因此相比较他们尘世间的儿女们，在乐园里的亚当最英俊，夏娃最美丽。goodly：好看（of good appearance）。

Text Analysis

Paradise Lost tells the story of the fall of man, a story Milton borrows from the Holy Bible. However, the fall of man is reinterpreted in the long poem: human beings fall from a state of perfection into a state of human reality. During the process of falling, it seems that the man also gains some worthy things. The state of perfection suggests naiveté. When Adam and Eve fall from the paradise, they have got the wisdom of gods. They are full of hope as they start a new life on the earth. The cause of the fall of man is the fall of Satan, the original archangel in the heaven. Satan drops from heaven to the bottom of hell; yet his thought and will never fall. This devil of heroic quality escapes (or rather rises) from the hell, coming up to the paradise, a perfect place of God's creation between heaven and hell. With his energy, resolution, wit, and power of the born leadership, Satan subtly tempts Eve to eat the fruit of wisdom; and she in turn persuades Adam to taste it, too. The temptation of Satan is like inspiration and enlightenment. The tone of Milton's story is very different from the original religious tale. And the theme expressed in *Paradise Lost* is different from that of epics in history. Milton vaguely suggests that the age of heroes has passed, but human beings today may still yearn for the glorious era, and that we who live in the real secular world, admiring the vanished heroic age, do not need to be pessimistic.

In the text, the perfect state of Adam and Eve is presented in a sublimely lyrical style to Satan who steals into the paradise, and to the readers who seem to stand by the devil. Adam is handsome and Eve is beautiful. They are in nakedness, both their body and their mind, like two purest babies. They are an independent unity; they love and cherish each other.

To achieve the style of stately eloquence, Milton composes his lines with blank verse, displaying in an easy grace the harmonious relation of Adam and Eve.

Questions

1. How are the figures of Adam and Eve described?
2. What relationship between Adam and Eve is explained in the text?
3. What do you think are the possible symbolic implications of the passage?

Chinese Translation

失乐园（节选）

其中屹立两个高大挺拔的华贵形象，
他们的高大挺拔俨然神的挺立。
即使以本身原有的光彩，
披在庄重的裸体上，
看成万物灵长也很名副其实。
因为造物主的光辉影子，
即真理、智慧和严肃、清纯的圣洁，
在那神样的容颜，映照出来，他们严肃，
却有真正子女的自由意志为基地，

人间真正的权威从此而来；
虽然二人各异，似乎是两性的差异：
他机智而勇敢，她却柔和而妩媚，
富有魅力；他为神而造，
而她为他里面的神而造。
绝对的治权在他那俊美的广额
和高尚的眼神显露无余，
青紫色的鬈发从前额分开，
一绺绺地下垂，但没有垂到两个广阔的肩膀。
她那没有装饰的金发，
像头巾披垂到她的纤纤细腰，乱蓬蓬的，
好像葡萄的卷须，曲成波轮，
这意味着她的服从，要她使用委婉的主权，
她的服从，含着羞怯，带着骄矜，
温情脉脉，欲顺故忤，欲爱还嗔，
这样的态度，受他的极度欢迎。
那时人体的神秘部分袒露着；
但还没有不纯洁的羞耻。
对天造之物的不纯洁的羞耻，
不荣誉的荣誉心，罪恶的根源啊，
你的外表，貌似纯洁，
却是多么的使全人类烦恼呀！
你从人的生活中驱除最幸福的生活，
以及单纯和无瑕的天真！
他们这样赤身裸体地行走，
也不躲避上帝和天使的视线；
因为他们心中坦坦荡荡。
他们这样手牵手地行走，
自从他们邂逅作爱的拥抱以后，
便是最可爱的一对：那亚当，
他的子孙中没有比他更善良的，
那夏娃，后代的一切女人没有比她更美的。

（朱维之　译）

When I Consider How My Light Is Spent

When I consider how my light is spent[1]
Ere half my days[2], in this dark world and wide,
And that one talent[3] which is death to hide
Lodged with me useless[4], though my soul more bent
To serve therewith[5] my Maker, and present
My true account[6], lest he returning chide;
"Doth God exact[7] day-labour, light denied?"
I fondly[8] ask; but Patience[9] to prevent
That murmur, soon replies: "God doth not need
Either man's work or his own gifts[10]; who best
Bear his mild yoke[11], they serve him best. His state
Is kingly. Thousands at his bidding speed
And post[12] o'er land and ocean without rest:
They also serve who only stand and wait."

1. light is spent：这个从句表达了两层意思：我如何度日；我如何用尽我的视力。
2. Ere half my days：在我半辈子的时候（Before half my life is over）。
3. talent：天分。弥尔顿提及"that one talent which is death to hide"，似是隐喻《马太福音》中有关天分的寓言。
4. useless：没有用过的（unused）。
5. therewith：于是，因此（by that means，by that talent；with it）。
6. account：价值（record of accomplishment；worth）。
7. exact：要求（demand，require）。
8. fondly：不明智地（foolishly, unwisely）。
9. Patience：此处是拟人化用法。
10. God doth not need / Either man's work or his own gifts：上帝不需要人为他工作或者给他供奉自己的天分。
11. yoke：负担（burden, workload）。
12. post：旅行（travel）。

Text Analysis

"When I Consider How My Light Is Spent" is one of the best known sonnets of John Milton. The poem was possibly written when Milton's blindness was essentially complete. The theme of the poem is that God judges man on whether he works for Him to the best of their ability. No matter how disabled he is, the man remains worthy in the eyes of God.

The poem is written in Petrarchan (or Italian) sonnet with iambic pentameter, rhyming abba, abba, cde, cde. The literary devices adopted in the poem are metaphor in the first line, alliteration in the second line, pun in the third line, and personification in the line eight.

Questions

1. Please explain "but Patience to prevent / That murmur, soon replies: 'God doth not need / Either man's work or his own gifts ; who best / Bear his mild yoke, they serve him best.' "

2. Please point out the allusion "talent" used in the poem and discuss it.

Chinese Translation

一想到我视力如何竟耗竭用尽

一想到我视力如何竟耗竭用尽，
没活半辈子，这世界黑暗迷茫，
这一天赋理该要死亡才埋葬，
我却已虚有其表，越发我心灵
想借以竭诚侍奉我的主，奉呈
我真诚的业绩，唯恐他怒而见谤；
难道让白日劳动，上帝不给光，
我愚蠢地质问，但是耐心不容忍
怨艾，马上回敬，上帝不需要
人效劳，或报答他自己的恩赐，最忍受
他轻微羁轭的，也最尽职守，他威仪
若君王，令一下，万千天使忙奔跑，
遍世界海陆穿梭，拔蹄难收，
只侍立左右的也一样是执役。

（金发燊　译）

Unit 5 Thomas Gray

Introduction to the Author

Thomas Gray (1716-1771) was born in 1716 into a family of a London exchange broker and a milliner. Gray was educated at Eton College, where he and his three close friends, Horace Walpole (son of the Prime Minister Robert Walpole), Thomas Ashton, and Richard West prided themselves on their sense of style, sense of humour, and appreciation of beauty. In 1734, Gray went up to Cambridge but he found the curriculum dull. Although intended by his family for the law, he spent most of his time as an undergraduate reading classical and modern literature, and playing classical music for relaxation. After four years at Cambridge he left without a degree, to tour France and Italy with Walpole. He returned to Cambridge after 1742, pursuing his studies and indulging his tastes. He was knowledgeable in the classical and modern literatures as well as history, though he claimed to be lazy by inclination. Gray was a brilliant bookworm, a quiet, abstracted, dreaming scholar, often afraid of the shadows of his own fame; he refused the post of Poet Laureate offered to him in 1757. This poet best loved by "the common reader" (in Dr. Johnson's remarks) lived a quiet life as a university professor (in 1768 he held the Regius chair of Modern History at Cambridge) in the stagnant atmosphere of the mid-18th century Cambridge. He spent most of his life as a scholar in Cambridge, and only later in his life did he begin travelling again.

Gray published only thirteen poems and his collected works published during his lifetime amounted to fewer than 1,000 lines, yet he is regarded as the foremost English-language poet of the mid-18th century. Gray is known as one of the "Graveyard poets" of the late 18th century, along with Oliver Goldsmith, William Cowper, and Christopher Smart. They write about their observations on death, mortality, and the finality and sublimity of death. Gray's "Elegy Written in a Country Churchyard" is a representative poem of the Graveyard School of poetry, and the label actually comes after the poem.

Gray highly praised his two Pindaric odes "The Progress of Poesy" and "The Bard". He also wrote light verse, including "Ode on the Death of a Favourite Cat, Drowned in a Tub of Gold Fishes", a mock elegy concerning Horace Walpole's cat. Besides poetry, Gray's learning and interests display themselves also in his letters which show his sharp observation and playful sense of humour. He is well known for his phrase, "where ignorance is bliss, 'tis folly to be wise" from his "Ode on a Distant Prospect of Eton College". This is one of the most often misunderstood statements: Gray is not promoting ignorance, but reflecting nostalgically on a time when he was allowed to be ignorant, i.e. his youth.

Gray traveled widely, if his duties allowed, throughout Britain in search of picturesque landscapes and ancient monuments. These elements were not generally valued in the early 18th century, when the popular taste ran to classical styles in architecture and literature. Gray combined traditional forms and poetic diction with new topics and modes of expression, and may be considered as a classically focused precursor of the romantic revival.

Gray died on 30 July 1771 in Cambridge, and was buried beside his mother in the churchyard of Stoke Poges, the setting for "Elegy Written in a Country Churchyard". His grave can still be seen there.

Elegy Written in a Country Churchyard[1]

The curfew tolls the knell of parting day[2],
　　The lowing herd winds slowly o' er the lea[3],
The plowman homeward plods his weary way,
　　And leaves the world to darkness and to me[4].

Now fades the glimmering landscape on the sight[5],
　　And all the air a solemn stillness holds[6],
Save[7] where the beetle wheels his droning flight[8],
　　And drowsy tinklings lull the distant folds[9];

Save that from yonder ivy-mantled tower
　　The moping[10] owl does to the moon complain
Of such[11], as wandering near her secret bower[12],
　　Molest her ancient solitary reign[13].

Beneath those rugged elms, that yew-tree' s shade,

Where heaves the turf[14] in many a mouldering heap,
Each in his narrow cell for ever laid[15],
The rude[16] forefathers of the hamlet sleep.

The breezy call of incense-breathing[17] morn,
The swallow twittering from the straw-built shed[18],
The cock' s shrill clarion, or the echoing horn[19],
No more shall rouse them from their lowly bed[20].

For them[21] no more the blazing hearth shall burn,
Or busy housewife ply her evening care[22];
No children run to lisp[23] their sire' s return,
Or climb his knees the envied[24] kiss to share.

Oft did the harvest to their sickle yield,
Their furrow oft the stubborn glebe has broke[25];
How jocund did they drive their team[26] afield!
How bowed the woods beneath their sturdy stroke[27]!

Let not[28] Ambition[29] mock their useful toil,
Their homely joys, and destiny obscure;
Nor Grandeur hear with a disdainful smile
The short and simple annals[30] of the Poor.

The boast of heraldry, the pomp of power[31],
And all that beauty, all that wealth e' er gave[32],
Awaits[33] alike the inevitable hour.
The paths of glory lead but[34] to the grave.

Nor you, ye proud[35], impute to these the fault[36],
If Memory[37] o' er their tomb no trophies raise,
Where through the long-drawn aisle[38] and fretted vault
The pealing anthem[39] swells the note of praise.

Can storied urn or animated bust[40]
Back to its mansion call the fleeting breath[41]?
Can Honour' s voice provoke the silent dust[42],
Or Flattery soothe[43] the dull cold ear of Death?

Perhaps[44] in this neglected spot is laid
Some heart once pregnant with celestial fire[45];
Hands[46] that the rod of empire[47] might have swayed,
Or waked to ecstasy the living lyre[48].

But Knowledge to their eyes her ample page[49]
Rich with the spoils of time[50], did ne' er unroll;
Chill Penury repressed their noble rage[51],
And froze the genial current[52] of the soul.

Full many a gem[53] of purest ray serene,
The dark unfathomed caves of ocean bear:
Full many a flower is born to blush unseen,
And waste its sweetness on the desert air[54].

Some village-Hampden[55], that with dauntless breast
The little tyrant of his fields withstood;
Some mute inglorious Milton[56] here may rest,
Some Cromwell, guiltless[57] of his country' s blood.

The applause of listening senates[58] to command[59],
The threats of pain and ruin to despise,
To scatter plenty o' er a smiling land[60],
And read their history in a nation' s eyes[61],

Their lot forbade: nor circumscribed[62] alone
Their growing virtues, but their crimes confined[63];
Forbade[64] to wade through slaughter to a throne,
And shut the gates of mercy on mankind,

The struggling pangs of conscious truth to hide[65],
To quench the blushes of ingenuous shame[66],
Or heap the shrine of Luxury and Pride
With incense kindled at the Muse' s flame[67].

Far[68] from the madding crowd' s ignoble strife[69],
Their sober wishes never learned to stray[70];

Along the cool sequestered[71] vale of life
They kept the noiseless tenour[72] of their way.

Yet even these bones from insult to protect[73]
Some frail memorial still erected nigh[74],
With uncouth rhymes and shapeless sculpture decked[75],
Implores the passing tribute of a sigh[76].

Their name, their years, spelt by the unlettered Muse[77],
The place of[78] fame and elegy supply:
And many a holy text[79] around she[80] strews,
That teach the rustic moralist to die[81].

For[82] who to dumb Forgetfulness a prey,
This pleasing anxious being e' er resigned[83],
Left[84] the warm precincts of the cheerful day,
Nor cast[85] one longing lingering look behind?

On some fond breast[86] the parting soul relies,
Some pious drops the closing eye requires[87];
Even from the tomb the voice of Nature[88] cries,
Even in our ashes live their wonted fires[89].

For[90] thee[91], who mindful of the unhonour' d dead
Dost in these lines their artless[92] tale relate;
If chance[93], by lonely contemplation led,
Some kindred spirit[94] shall inquire thy fate.

Haply some hoary-headed swain may say[95],
"Oft have we seen him at the peep of dawn
Brushing with hasty steps the dews away
To meet the sun upon the upland lawn.

"There at the foot of yonder nodding beech
That wreathes its old fantastic roots so high[96],
His listless length[97] at noontide would he stretch,
And pore upon the brook that babbles by[98].

"Hard by yon wood, now[99] smiling as in scorn,
Muttering his wayward fancies[100] he would rove,
Now drooping, woeful wan[101], like one forlorn,
Or crazed with care, or crossed in hopeless love[102].

"One morn I missed him on the customed hill[103],
Along the heath, and near his favourite tree;
Another came; nor yet beside the rill[104],
Nor up the lawn, nor at the wood was he[105];

"The next with dirges due in sad array[106]
Slow through the church-way path we saw him borne[107].
Approach and read (for thou canst read) the lay[108]
Graved on the stone beneath yon aged thorn[109]."

The Epitaph[110]

Here rests his head upon the lap of Earth
A youth to Fortune and to Fame unknown[111].
Fair Science frowned not[112] on his humble birth,
And Melancholy marked[113] him for her own.

Large was his bounty[114], and his soul sincere,
Heaven did a recompense as largely[115] send:
He gave to Misery all he had, a tear[116],
He gained from Heaven ('twas all he wished) a friend[117].

No farther seek[118] his merits to disclose,
Or draw his frailties from their dread abode[119]
(There they[120] alike in trembling hope repose),
The bosom of his Father and his God.

Notes

1. It is believed that Gray began writing this poem in the graveyard of the church in Stoke Poges, Buckinghamshire, in 1742. Some of its stanzas (together with the "Eaton Ode") are associated with the memories of the poet's close friend Richard West. After several years of leaving it unfinished, he completed it in 1750. The poem was rather widely circulated before its publication in 1751 upon which it became a literary sensation. Technically, it contains altogether 32 quatrains of iambic pentameter, with a rhyme scheme of abab for each stanza.
2. curfew：evening bell，宵禁钟声。按中世纪习俗，晚 8 点敲钟，通知市民已到熄灯就寝时间。knell：丧钟；白天已尽，夜晚钟声仿佛在向白天告别。该行的 5 个重音中，4 个是长音，而 knell 构成的短音居中，似乎是为了平衡；从意义上看，它暗示着一天即将过去，永不再来；短音 knell 似乎还提醒人们钟声短促却悠远，消失缓慢。
3. The lowing herd winds slowly o'er the lea：lowing，牛的哞哞鸣叫声；该词切不可和第 20 行 lowly 中的 low 混淆。请注意这一行的 l 声，以及第 3 行中的 pl 和 w，第 10 行中的 m，第 14 行中的 h 等；双声词和头韵的巧妙使用，显示出该诗在音调方面的考究。
4. leaves：其主语为 plowman。这行诗的内容和意境，在诗人威廉 · 柯林斯（William Collins）的《黄昏颂》（"Ode to Evening"，1746）中已经出现，在其他诗人作品中也出现过，并非作者独创。这种孤独情绪是 18 世纪英国文学中的感伤主义（sentimentalism）的一种表现。在表达方式方面，古典主义诗人遵循罗马理论家贺拉斯的论调，认为内容虽然重要，表达形式同等重要，但只有真正的诗人才能表达得好，即亚历山大 · 蒲柏（Alexander Pope）所谓 "What oft was thought，but ne'er so well expressed"，因此他们刻意在表达上争奇斗胜。
5. sight：eyesight，眼睛，视线，指眼睛已看不清昏暗中的景色。
6. holds：governs，统辖，统治；其主语为 stillness，宾语为 air。诗中往往因音节排列的关系，动词放在最后，同时动词主语、宾语位置往往前后不一致，或主语在先，或宾语在先，读者应能辨别下列各行中的主语和宾语：第 26，34～35，38，47，49～50，53～54，57～58，61～65，81～82，90，93～94，103，122 行。
7. Save：除了。
8. the beetle wheels his droning flight：beetle，甲虫；wheels，旋转飞翔；droning flight，飞翔时嗡嗡作响。以下 6 行写寂静的夜晚中，少有的声响来自甲虫和猫头鹰（猫头鹰很少发出声音）。柯林斯在《黄昏颂》中也描写过甲虫嗡嗡叫着盘旋的景象，而柯林斯又脱胎于弥尔顿的《利西达斯》（*Lycidas*）。格雷和 18 世纪许多英国诗人服膺弥尔顿、莎士比亚等作家，常套用他们的诗句，"寻章摘句"。本诗中这种例子甚多，以下不一一列举。
9. tinklings：羊颈上的铃声；这是移就（transferred epithet）的用法。folds：羊圈。
10. moping：烦躁不安。
11. such：可以指人，但更可能指其他动物，如飞禽、昆虫之类。
12. secret bower：女孩的闺房、绣房，外人不可随意闯入。

13. Molest：损害。该词暗示猫头鹰对擅入者（牛群和牧牛人）的不悦，用得极佳，显示出诗人高超的炼字功夫。以上 3 节是诗的“开篇”，意在设景。以下 4 节点出墓中埋葬的人物（当地农民），表示惋惜，并追忆其生前生活。
14. turf：墓园的地上长着一层乱草，这片草地上拱起了（heaves）一堆堆（heap）的坟墓，这些坟墓已坍塌败坏（mouldering）。
15. 这一行的施事者为下行中的 forefathers。cell：指墓穴。
16. rude：朴质的，没有文化的。
17. incense-breathing：突出芬芳。incense 不作焚香解。
18. straw-built shed：茅棚，用于储藏农具，饲养牲畜等。
19. clarion：鸡鸣在英诗中常用来比作司晨号角。horn：打猎人在清晨的号角声。
20. lowly bed：以死亡比睡眠，以坟墓比床榻，以上 3 句写清晨的声音，这些声音已不能把死者从长眠中唤醒；lowly 为双关语（pun）。
21. For them：参看诗人詹姆斯·汤姆逊（James Thomson）《四季诗》（“The Seasons”）中的《冬季》（“Winter”，1726）第一章第 276 行以下，写一走投无路的农民在暴风雪中倒下，临终时想到妻子为他生火烤衣，孩子们在窗前张望父亲归来的情景。此处的写法极为类似。这些都是当时流行的“感伤”情绪的流露。
22. ply her evening care：忙于晚上的家务事，如把火添旺，烧晚饭，陪孩子等。
23. lisp：指咿呀学语的孩子含含糊糊地喊着父亲回来了。
24. envied：争抢着分享的。
25. furrow：此处应该指犁子；glebe：土地，天地；broke：松土。
26. team：指三两头套在一起的耕畜（组成一个“团队”），这里是指下田耕田。
27. stroke：指伐木运斧。
28. Let not：第 29～32 行对“大人物”发出警告，在死亡面前人人平等。这 4 行诗曾被苏格兰诗人彭斯（Robert Burns）作为他的《佃农的星期六之夜》（“*The Cotter's Saturday Night*”）的序诗。
29. Ambition：“野心”，寓言式的人物。这些抽象名词代表了 18 世纪人性的普遍特征，本诗中其他的例子还有：Grandeur（第 31 行），Memory（第 38 行），Honour（第 43 行），Flattery and Death（第 44 行），Knowledge（第 49 行），Penury（第 51 行），Luxury and Pride（第 71 行），Forgetfulness（第 85 行），Nature（第 91 行），以及 Misery（第 123 行）。
30. annals：编年史，此处指农民一生的历史。
31. heraldry：指世袭贵族；pomp：显赫的声势。
32. gave：yielded，所能获致的。
33. Awaits：主语为 the inevitable hour（死亡）。初稿为 await，义亦通。修改后，说法与第 36 行相反，而内容相同。
34. but：only，只是。

Notes

35. you，ye proud：you 用于独立的呼格（vocative）；与名词或形容词合用时，常用 ye，如 Ye blessed creatures (Wordsworth)。
36. these：指埋葬在这里的农民；impute the fault：把过错（第 38～40 行）归于……
37. Memory：指人们为了纪念死者，把能代表他生前荣光的物品（trophies）如军旗、雕像之类，悬挂或安放在教堂内他的墓上。这是英国许多大教堂内常见的景象。
38. aisle：从教堂大门通向神坛的主要甬路称 nave，其左右两侧平行甬路称 aisle。此处泛指教堂内的甬路。
39. The pealing anthem：大风琴奏出的洪亮的赞美歌。参看弥尔顿，《沉思者》（Il *Penseroso*），161～163 行。
40. storied urn：指“大人物”墓上的一种装饰，一个石雕或浮雕的瓮，上面刻着他生平某些事迹；animated bust：指墓上（或其他地方）设置的死者半身石像；animated 意为栩栩如生。
41. its mansion：宅邸，此处指已死的躯体；its 指 breath。fleeting breath：短促的生命。
42. provoke：召唤，此处指重新赋予生机。dust：按照基督教《圣经》的说法，人是上帝用泥土造成的，死后复归泥土的；此处指死者。
43. soothe：以甜言蜜语打动死神，使他闭而不闻的耳朵听从人们的请求。
44. Perhaps：接下来 7 节，诗人惋惜这些淳朴农民的遭遇使他们的潜力与天才未能发挥，但又对他们的地位使他们不致犯大错这一点表示庆幸。对于诗人的观点，我们可以保留自己的看法。
45. Pregnant：filled；celestial fire：天国之火，指宗教热忱。农民中可以产生宗教家，也有解作诗才者，则与第 48 行重复。
46. Hands：虽是复数，但与之搭配的动词仍借用第 45 行中的 is laid。
47. rod of empire：掌握统治大权。从罗马人开始，作为刑具的棒或一束棒（fasces）成为权力的象征。农民中可能产生治国之材。
48. lyre：古希腊的一种弦乐器，琴身为 U 形，这里引申为音乐、诗歌的象征。农民中可产生大诗人、大音乐家。
49. her ample page：her 指 Knowledge，page 指书本。
50. spoils of time：人类历来积累下来的经验、智慧。
51. Penury：贫困；rage：渴望，理想。
52. genial current：诗人把农民的创造力比作川流，故用 froze。genial 原意为“适宜生物滋衍的”，引申为赋予创造力的。贫困导致农民不能发挥其创造力。
53. Full many a gem：full 在古英语中作副词，以加重语气。many a：形式是单数，实际内容为复数；参看第 14 行。gem：诗人把农民比作埋藏在海底的明珠。
54. 这两行中，诗人把农民比作在荒漠中自生自灭、无人赏识的香花（flower），即李贺所谓“无人柳自春”。这一意象在 17、18 世纪诗人中颇普遍。sweetness：芬芳。
55. 这一节中出现的 Hampden（汉普登），Milton（弥尔顿）和 Cromwell（克伦威尔）

都是17世纪英国资产阶级革命时期的革命领袖。汉普登以反对查理一世的横征暴敛受到迫害而闻名，故第57—58行称有些农民反抗地主，表现了大无畏的精神，不愧为农民中的汉普登。

56. mute inglorious Milton：不是说弥尔顿不光荣，而是说农民中可能产生过弥尔顿这样的革命诗人，但没有机会发表自己的思想（mute），没有获得弥尔顿那样的荣耀。

57. guiltless：可以有两种相反的理解：(1) 农民中可以产生克伦威尔这样的革命英雄，但手上没有像他那样沾着同胞的血；(2) 克伦威尔本人就不是沾上同胞血的罪人。二说以前者为是，我们不能指望诗人正确理解17世纪历史事件的意义。“Hampden，Milton，Cromwell”均以“may rest here”为谓语。在初稿中，诗人用了三个罗马历史人物“Cato，Tully，Caesar”，后来的修改说明引用古代神话、历史典故的古典主义方法已不能适应时代的需要。

58. senates：Senate为罗马元老院（立法机关），此处指议会。

59. to command：赢得，to command，to despise，to scatter，(to) read均为第65行forbade的谓语。

60. To scatter plenty：造福，施舍。smiling是造福、施舍的结果；由于得到恩惠，国人（land）笑逐颜开。

61. And read their history in a nation's eyes：read意为declare, relate；history即life-history, career，可以引申为great deeds。in a nation's eyes：举国上下，有目共睹。

62. nor circumscribed：主语仍是their lot。他们的命运不仅限制了他们的优秀品德的发展。nor…alone相当于not…only。

63. confined：主语为lot，宾语为crimes。

64. Forbade：主语仍是lot，宾语为to wade，(to) shut，to hide，to quench，(to) heap。每一宾语代表一种罪恶行为。

65. to hide：真理挣扎着要出示（pangs），自己也明知其为真理（conscious），但因种种原因不甘吐露真情（hide），极言虚伪、谎言之徒的矛盾痛苦。联系全句主语，意为穷人纯朴老实。

66. ingenuous shame：natural sense of shame，天生的羞耻之心。

67. 第71～72行的大意是：以诗歌奉承权贵。诗人以古代祭礼为比喻：“把在诗神的火焰上燃着的香（实物，与第17行芬芳的气息不同）堆到富贵人的神坛上（奉献给他们）。”

68. 以下5节的大意是：虽然这些农民一生平淡无奇，似乎也不应该被人遗忘。

69. Far from the madding crowd's ignoble strife：他们的愿望（wishes）不是去（far from）干疯狂的人群所干的不光彩的、你争我夺的勾当。小说家哈代（Thomas Hardy）曾以该句诗的前五个词作为一部小说的标题。如把strife后的逗号删掉，第73、74两行将自相矛盾，不合逻辑。又，Far from固然可以说是形容wishes，但按意义说，应该是They being far…。

Notes

70. stray：脱离正道。
71. sequestered：isolated，与世隔绝，平静。
72. tenour：continuous course，持续的进程。主语为 memorial（第 78 行），谓语为 implores（第 80 行）；erected（第 78 行）和 decked（第 79 行）是形容词，形容主语。
73. insult：指被人铲平或践踏之类；protect：指 erected 之目的。
74. frail memorial：一块薄碑，或朴素的墓碑；still：古义 always。
75. uncouth rhymes：not fine verses，鄙陋的诗句；decked with：decorated with，装饰着。
76. Implores the passing tribute of a sigh：恳求过路人馈赠（tribute）一声叹息。
77. unlettered Muse：乡村里没有什么学问的诗人。
78. The place of：代替了。
79. holy text：《圣经》中的词句。
80. she：指第 81 行中的诗神。
81. That：指 holy texts，动词用复数；rustic moralist：指读墓碑的乡人；to die：how to die，以何种态度对待死亡。
82. 以下两节一问一答，皆从 to die 衍生而来。
83. 第 85～86 两行，有两种解释：（1）who，being a prey to dumb forgetfulness，任何人死后都要被人遗忘；（2）who ever resigned this pleasing anxious being so as to become a prey to dumb forgetfulness？有谁愿意舍弃这可爱而又令人不安的生命，被人遗忘，再不被人提起（dumb）呢？以第 2 种解释为佳。
84. Left：动词，主语仍是 who。
85. Nor cast：and did not cast，without casting.
86. on 接动词 relies；fond breast：fond 意为 affectionate，具有慈爱心肠的人。
87. requires：主语是 eye，宾语是 drops。
88. voice of Nature：天性的呼声。
89. our ashes：在我们身后；their：指先我们而故去的墓中人；fires：精神、天性、激情等。
90. 以下至本诗末均为诗人假设自己死后的情景。“墓园派”（Graveyard School）诗歌的特点之一是对贫困人的同情，具有一定程度的民主性；另一特点是沉浸于对死亡、孤独的玄想 t 之中。
91. For thee：as for thee，至于你自己。此处为诗人对自己说话。
92. artless：朴素的。
93. chance：by chance.
94. kindred spirit：person like you.
95. Haply：古英语用法，意思是 perhaps；hoary-headed：白发的；swain：乡下人。
96. beech：山毛榉，一种英国常见的大树；wreathes：盘成环状。
97. listless length：百无聊赖的身躯，躺卧。此处为双声。
98. pore upon：专心注视；babbles：小儿学语状，此处指流水潺潺，“b”音有拟音的效果。

99. now…now：时而……时而。
100. wayward fancies：飘忽而不可捉摸的遐想。
101. woeful wan：sad and pale，这是头韵的用法。
102. crazed with care：忧愁得近于疯癫；crossed：受挫折。
103. missed him：发现他不见了；customed：accustomed，他常去的。
104. Another：another day；nor：neither；rill：小溪。
105. 以上 8 行（105～112 行），后人刻在诗人墓碑上，作为墓志铭。
106. The next：the day after the next，第三天；dirges：葬歌；due：死者应得的，恰当的；in sad array：穿着丧服，或作悲哀的行列，此处指送葬人，但送葬人一词未在句中出现。
107. borne：in his coffin.
108. for thou canst read：询问者（第 96 行）必然是个读过书的人；当时并非人人识字。lay：短歌，此处指诗，也就是最后三节的墓志铭。
109. aged：请注意，该词发双节音；thorn：hawthorn tree。
110. 这仍是诗人想象中（参见注 90）乡人指点给访客看的诗人墓志铭。
111. A youth：全句主语。作者作此诗时年仅 28 岁。unknown 形容 a youth。长期以来，关于这位叙述者为何对自己称"你"（第 93 行），批评界一直众说纷纭。有观点称，诗人可能出现了笔误，以"你"代替了"我"（第 96 行）。有学者则认为，故去的叙述者就是那位写"鄙陋诗句"的乡野诗人（第 79～81 行），但是这位故去青年的科学知识（第 119 行）明显地排除了这种可能性。还有人认为，诗人自己是那位叙述者，但格雷完成这首诗时已 35 岁，已不那么年轻。因此，这首"挽歌"应不是出自格雷，而是出自一位"剧中人"（dramatic persona），该诗是逝者与生者关于死亡的对话。
112. science：指一般知识；frowned not：不因他出身卑微而歧视他，因他有一定的学问。
113. marked：忧郁女神在他（青年）身上打上标志表明他是属于她的。青年天性忧郁。
114. bounty：恩泽，此处指这青年有博爱的性格。
115. recompense：send 的宾语，指第 124 行的 friend。as largely：as liberally，as generously，与前一行 large 呼应。他对人表示（付出）善意，上天也以同样丰厚（as largely）的报酬答谢他。第 121～122 两行又与第 123～124 两行呼应。
116. Misery：受苦难的一切。
117. a tear：同情心、博爱、人道的象征，不可作为"仅仅一滴眼泪"解；同情心是他全部的人格。
118. seek：命令式；该行正常的顺序是 Seek to disclose his merits no farther (no more)。
119. dread abode：指死后所居之所（即第 128 行 bosom）；dread 是过去分词（dreaded），因为是弱点，所以怕上帝惩罚。
120. they：指 merits 和 frailties。人死后居留一地，等候上帝的末日审判，行善（merits）的人有希望（hopes）上天堂，有罪（frailties）的人唯恐（trembling）下地狱。

Text Analysis

Graveyard School of poetry is noted for the melancholic democratic feelings, and this characterizes this poem as well. The poem's gentle melancholy and its reflective, calm and stoic tone are typical of all early romantic poetry which also appeal for democratic spirits and equal rights for all levels of people, including the lower classes.

The poem is a perfect combination of Romanticism and Neoclassicism. While its call for democracy and equality reminds us of the rising English bourgeoisie, its nostalgic tone, restraint and grace of writing display features of classicism. It is noted especially for its beauty and skill. It employs a lot of long vowels and diphthongs, to indicate sense of nostalgia and looking back into the past, especially in the beginning stanzas, where the sense is intensely conveyed. The rhyme scheme varies to achieve artistic diversity, such as alliteration in "herd winds" and "homeward" (lines 2-3), "droning flight" and "distant folds" (lines 7-8); internal rhyme in"slowly o'er the lea" (line 2) or "And all the air... / Save where" (lines 6-7); initial assonance or consonance in "Beneath… / Where heaves" (lines 13-14), and "The cock's shrill… / No more shall" (lines 19-20).

Gray adopts and refines a regular poetics typical of his period. His iambic pentameter quatrains are self-contained and end-stopped. They do not enjamb with the next stanza but close with terminal punctuation, except for two passionate sequences. Stanzas 16-18 express the narrator's crescendo of anger at the empowered proud whose virtues go hand-in-hand with crimes: slaughter, mercilessness, and lying. Stanzas 24-25 introduce the dead youth who probably narrates the poem. Quatrains also regularly consist of end-stopped lines, equally self-contained and even interchangeable. When required, parallel syntactic construction across line and stanza boundaries links sequences of larger units, and thus builds symmetry at all levels. Semantically, the poem reads like a collage of remembered experiences. Some are realized in both image and sound. "The swallow twittering from the straw-built shed" (line 18) vividly and sharply conveys one instant in the awakening process on a farm. At other times, the five senses blur, as in "the madding crowd's ignoble strife" (line 73), or "This pleasing anxious being" (line 86), but these remain snapshots, though of feelings, not images. They flow from a lived life remembering its keenest moments in tranquility. Some of these moments are literary.

These formal elements in Gray's poetics beautifully strengthen the poem's content. This "Elegy" gives us a ghost's perspective on his life, and ours. The old swain describes him as a melancholic loner who loved walking by hill, heath, trees, and stream. The epitaph also reveals that he was a well-educated youth who died unknown. These are the very qualities we might find in the writer from the style of his verse. Gray does not just give his readers succinct aphorisms about what Isaac Watt would term, "Man Frail, God Eternal", but recreates a lost human being. In reading this poem, we find a melancholy that so many share in a person who is too kind and who dies too young.

Samuel Johnson had the following to say about the poem: "The Churchyard abounds with images which find a mirror in every mind, and with sentiments to which every bosom returns an echo. The four stanzas beginning 'yet even these bones' are to me original: I have never seen the motions in any other place; yet he that reads them here, persuades himself that he has always felt them. Had Gray written often thus, it had been vain to blame, and useless to praise him."

Questions

1. What is the function of the final "Epitaph"? Should Gray have added it to this poem?

2. How does the elegy show the poet's democratic thoughts? Please illustrate your viewpoints.

3. Who, in your understanding, is the speaker of the poem?

4. The poem is very popular and has versions in different languages. Try to find its different Chinese versions from the one given below, and compare them.

Chinese Translation

墓园挽歌

晚钟响起来一阵阵给白昼报丧，
牛群在草原上迂回，吼声起落，
耕地人累了，回家走，脚步踉跄，
把整个世界留给了黄昏与我。

苍茫的景色逐渐从眼前消退，
一边肃穆的寂静盖遍了尘寰，
只听见嗡嗡的甲虫转圈子纷飞，
昏沉的铃声催眠着远处的羊栏。

只听见常春藤披裹的塔顶底下
一只阴郁的鸱枭向月亮诉苦，
怪人家无端走近它秘密的住家，
搅扰它这个悠久而僻静的领土。

峥嵘的榆树底下，扁柏的荫里，
草皮鼓起了许多零落的荒堆，
各自在洞窟里永远放下了身体，
小村里粗鄙的父老在那里安睡。

香气四溢的晨风轻松地呼召，
燕子从茅草棚子里吐出的呢喃，
公鸡的尖喇叭，使山鸣谷应的猎号，
再不能唤醒他们在地下的长眠。

在他们，熊熊的炉火不再会燃烧，
忙碌的管家妇不再会赶她的夜活；
孩子们不再会“牙牙”地报父亲来到，
为一个亲吻爬到他膝上去争夺。

往常是：他们一开镰就所向披靡，
顽梗的泥板让他们犁出了垄沟；
他们多么欢欣地赶牲口下地！
他们一猛砍，树木就一棵棵低头！

“雄心”别嘲讽他们实用的操劳，
家常的欢乐、默默无闻的运命；
“豪华”也不用带着轻蔑的冷笑
来听讲穷人的又短又简的生平。

门第的炫耀，有权有势的煊赫，
凡是美和财富所能赋予的好处，
前头都等待着不可避免的时刻：
光荣的道路无非是引导到坟墓。

骄傲人，你也不要怪这些人不行，
“怀念”没有给这些坟建立纪念堂，
没有让悠久的廊道、雕花的拱顶
洋溢着宏亮的赞美歌，进行颂扬。

栩栩的半身像、铭刻了事略的瓮碑，
难道能恢复断气，促使还魂？

"荣誉"的声音能激发沉默的死灰?
"谄媚"能叫死神听软了耳根?

也许这一块地方，尽管荒芜，
就埋着曾经充满过灵焰的一颗心;
一双手，本可以执掌到帝国的王笏
或者出神入化地拨响了七弦琴。

可是"知识"从不曾对他们展开
它世代积累而琳琅满目的书卷;
"贫寒"压制了他们高贵的襟怀，
冻结了他们从灵府涌出的流泉。

世界上多少晶莹皎洁的珠宝
埋在幽暗而深不可测的海底:
世界上多少花吐艳而无人知晓，
把芳香白白地散发给荒凉的空气。

也许有乡村汉普顿在这里埋身，
反抗过当地的小霸王，胆大，坚决;
也许有缄口的弥尔顿，从没有名声;
有一位克伦威尔，并不曾害国家流血，

要博得满场的元老雷动的鼓掌，
无视威胁，全不管存亡生死，
把富庶、丰饶遍播到四处八方，
打从全国的笑眼里读自己的历史——

他们的命运可不许:既不许罪过
有所放纵，也不许发挥德行;
不许从杀戮中间涉登宝座，
从此对人类关上仁慈的大门;

不许掩饰天良在内心的发作，
隐瞒天真的羞愧，恬不红脸;
不许用诗神的金焰点燃了香火
锦上添花去塞满"骄""奢"的神龛。

远离了纷纭人世的钩心斗角，
他们有清醒的愿望，从不学糊涂，
顺着生活的清凉僻静的山坳，
他们坚持了不声不响的正路。

可是叫这些尸骨免受到糟蹋，
还是有脆弱的碑牌树立在近边，
点缀了拙劣的韵语、凌乱的刻划，
请求过往人就便献一声惋叹。

无文的野诗神注上了姓名、年份，
另外再加上地址和一篇诔词；
她在周围散播了一些经文，
教训乡土道德家怎样去死。

要知道谁甘愿舍身喂哑口的"遗忘"，
坦然撇下了忧喜交织的此生，
谁离开风和日暖的明媚现场
而能不依依地回头来顾盼一阵？

辞世的灵魂还依傍钟情的怀抱；
临闭的眼睛需要尽哀的珠泪，
即使坟冢里也有"自然"的呼号
他们的旧火还点燃我们的新灰。

至于你，你关心这些陈死人，
用这些诗句讲他们质朴的故事，
假如在幽思的引领下，偶然有缘分，
一位同道来问起你的身世——

也许会有白头的乡下人对他说，
"我们常常看见他，天还刚亮，
就用匆忙的脚步把露水碰落，
上那边的高处的草地去会晤朝阳；

"那边有一棵婆娑的山毛榉老树，
树底下隆起的老根盘错在一起，

他常常在那里懒躺过一个中午，
悉心看旁边一道涓涓的小溪。

“他转游到林边，有时候笑里带嘲，
念念有词，发他的奇谈怪议，
有时候垂头丧气，像无依无靠，
像忧心忡忡或者像情场失意。

“有一天早上，在他惯去的山头，
灌木丛、他那棵爱树下，我不见他出现；
第二天早上，尽管我走下溪流，
上草地，穿过树林，他还是不见。

“第三天我们见到了送葬的行列，
唱着挽歌，抬着他向坟场走去——
请上前看那丛老荆棘底下的碑碣
（你是识字的）请念念这些诗句”：

墓　铭

这里边，高枕地膝，是一位青年，
生平从不曾受知于“富贵”和“名声”；
“知识”可没有轻视他生身的微贱，
“清愁”把他标出来认作宠幸。

他生性真挚，最乐于慷慨施惠，
上苍也给了他同样慷慨的报酬：
他给了“坎坷”全部的所有，一滴泪；
从上苍全得了所求，一位朋友。

别再想法子表彰他的功绩，
也别再把他的弱点翻出了暗窨
（它们同样在颤抖的希望中休息），
那就是他的天父和上帝的怀抱。

（卞之琳　译）

THE ROMANTIC PERIOD

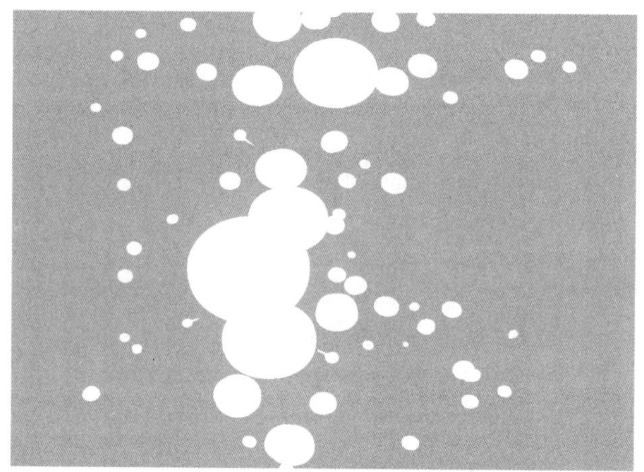

Unit 6 Robert Burns

Introduction to the Author

Robert Burns (1759-1796), Scottish poet and songwriter, is known as a ploughman poet and one of the important pioneers of the British Romantic movement. He is regarded as the national poet of Scotland and is recognized as a great lyricist of the world. Burns was born in Ayrshire, Scotland. His childhood and teenage were spent in poverty and hard manual labour of a common Scottish peasant family life. Burns didn't receive much regular school education except a short time learning at Dalrymple Parish School and a summer with a tutor at Kirkoswald, mostly being taught when he was young by his father and a school teacher at home.

Hard life did not depress Burns' enthusiasm in poetry. From 1775 on, Burns began to write poetry. He worked as a ploughman to make a living and to support his family, while he kept on writing poetry and collecting folksongs from the countryside. Many of his best poems were written in such a condition, like "The Twa Dogs", "Halloween" and "To a Mouse".

In 1786, Burns decided to immigrate to Jamaica to make a better living. To get enough money for the trip, Burns sent his poems to a publisher. The first published volume with the title *Poems, Chiefly in Scottish Dialect*, being known as the Kilmarnock volume for the place where it published, proved to be a big success and brought fame to the poet. In 1788, Burns was given a job as a tax inspector. Then he could spare some time to poetry from his work of official duties and farming.

Burns had participated in the collection of the Scottish folk songs in 1787 for an anthology called *The Scots Musical Museum* and soon became its real editor. He devoted almost all his spare time to the collection and edition of Scottish folk songs or to the composition of his own poems by following the traditional tunes. Most of his creative writings in the later part of life had been contributed to *The Scots Musical Museum* and *A Select Collection of Original Scottish Airs for the Voice*.

Burns' best poems were written in Scots, an English spoken dialect by the Scottish in his time, branded with clear identity of his nationality. The spirit expressed in these poems is with natural Scottish color. The common Scottish people, their lives, their feelings, their hopes and their disillusion are the subjects and themes of Burns' poetry. He comes from the most common people and sings for them in a way they are familiar with, that is, the folk songs composed in Scots. The style of his writing is marked for its directness, sincerity and spontaneity.

A Red Red Rose

O my Luve's[1] like a red, red rose,
    That's newly sprung in June;
O my Luve's like the melodie
    That's sweetly play'd in tune[2].

As fair art thou, my bonnie[3] lass,
    So deep in luve am I;
And I will luve thee still, my dear,
    Till a' the seas gang[4] dry.

Till a' the seas gang dry, my dear,
    And the rocks melt wi'[5] the sun:
O I will luve thee still, my dear,
While the sands o' life[6] shall run.

And fare thee weel[7], my only Luve!
And fare thee weel, a while[8]!
And I will come again, my Luve,
Tho'[9] it were ten thousand mile!

1. Luve：爱人，爱（love）。
2. in tune：合拍，合调，和谐。
3. bonnie：美丽的（pretty，beautiful）。
4. Till a' the sea gang dry：直到大海全部干涸。till：to；a'：all；gang：to go.

5. wi'：with.

6. sands o' life：生命的时钟。sands：沙漏；o'：of。

7. fare thee weel：再见（fare you well）。

8. a while：暂时（for a while）。常有人将此诗与中国汉乐府短诗《上邪》比较，认为有异曲同工之妙。细心的读者会在这里发现两者的差别，彭斯诗里有对生活困顿的隐忧。（附《上邪》全文："上邪！/我欲与君相知，/长命无绝衰。/山无陵，江水为竭，/冬雷震震夏雨雪，/天地合，/乃敢与君绝！"后人以"君"推断此歌为女子所唱，寄语予她的爱人，誓言忠贞。诗中叙述者为女子说存疑。）

9. tho'：though.

Written with the tune of a traditional Scottish folk song, the poem simply but effectively expresses the theme of fresh but ever lasting love. In the first stanza, the speaker compares his love with a red rose, "That's newly sprung in June" and with a melody, "That's sweetly play'd in tune". By these two similes, the speaker describes his love with vivid images, thus well explaining the abstract qualities of personality that his love possesses: she is with vigorous youth, attractive and refreshing. Then in the second and third stanzas, the speaker swears his loyalty to his sweetheart. He exaggerates in hyperbole that his love to his "bonnie lass" is eternal as those eternally existing things on earth. But the tone in the last stanza reveals the speaker's light sadness. Although he is longing for staying with his love forever, he has to leave her for "a while!" Burns projects too much of his feelings onto this "a while!" Hard life of Scottish people from the bottom of the society forces them to leave reluctantly their love and their most cherished things, roaming around the world with worries.

1. Please explain the lines "O my Luve's like the melodie, / That's sweetly played in tune".

2. It seems that the poem ends with a tone of melancholy. Do you agree or disagree with this judgment? Please give your reason(s).

Chinese Translation

一朵红红的玫瑰

呵，我的爱人像朵红红的玫瑰，
六月里迎风初开；
呵，我的爱人像支甜甜的曲子，
奏得合拍又和谐。

我的好姑娘，你有多么美，
我的情也有多么深。
我将永远爱你，亲爱的，
直到大海干枯水流尽。

直到大海干枯水流尽，
太阳把岩石烧作灰尘，
我也永远爱你，亲爱的，
只要我一息犹存。

珍重吧，我唯一的爱人，
珍重吧，让我们暂时别离，
我准定回来，亲爱的，
哪怕跋涉千万里！

（王佐良 译）

Auld Lang Syne

Should auld acquaintance[1] be forgot
And never brought to min'[2]?
Should auld acquaintance be forgot,

And auld lang syne[3]!

Chorus—For auld lang syne my jo,
For auld lang syne,
We'll tak[4] a cup o' kindness yet
For auld lang syne.

We twa hae run about the braes[5],
And pou'd the gowans fine[6];
But we've wander'd mony a weary fitt[7],
Sin[8] auld lang syne.
For auld, &c.

We twa hae paidl'd in the burn[9],
Frae morning sun till dine[10];
But seas between us braid hae roar'd[11]
Sin auld lang syne.
For auld, &c.

And there's a hand, my trusty fiere[12]!
And gie's a hand o' thine[13]!
And we'll tak a right gude-willie-waught[14],
For auld lang syne.
For auld, &c.

And surely ye'll be your pint stowp[15]!
And surely I'll be mine!
And we'll tak a cup o'kindness yet,
For auld lang syne.
For auld, &c.

1. auld acquaintance：老朋友。auld：old；acquaintance：熟人，朋友，相识。
2. min'：脑海，mind。
3. auld lang syne：从很久以来。lang：long；syne：since, then。
4. tak a cup o' kindness：举起友谊的酒杯。tak：to take。

Notes

5. We twa hae run about the braes：我们两个曾经跑遍山岗。twa：two；hae：have；brae：the slope of a hill。
6. pou'd the gowans fine：采摘美丽的雏菊。pou'd：to pull，to gather；gowan：the daisy，喻极美好的事物。
7. But we've wander'd mony a weary fitt：但我们已在满怀疲惫四处流浪。mony：many；fitt：foot。
8. sin'：从此，since。
9. We twa hae paidl'd in the burn：我们两个曾经一起趟过溪流。paidle：to paddle；burn：stream。
10. dine：晚饭时间，dinner time。
11. seas between us braid hae roar'd：我们远隔宽阔又汹涌的海洋。braid：broad。
12. my trusty fiere：我忠诚的伙伴。fiere：friend，companion。
13. gie's a hand o' thine：伸出你的手。gie's：give us。
14. a right gude-willie waught：正好一个开怀痛饮。gude：good；willie：will；waught：a big drink。
15. surely ye'll be your pint stowp：你一定会买你一大杯。pint：品脱，(Scots) three imperial pints；stowp：cup。

Text Analysis

The title of the poem is literally equal to the English "old long since", meaning "very long ago", "old days gone by" or "old times", etc. Set to the tune of a traditional Scottish folk song, the poem is popularly sung when people celebrate the beginning of a new year at the midnight when the bell rings, or when people are on the occasion of a farewell.

The speaker in the poem recalls in detail the good time he had passed with his friend in their homeland: running around the slopes of the hills and picking beautiful flowers commonly seen in their countryside, and paddling in the stream all day long. Then they have to part for seeking each one's fortune far away from their homeland, experiencing weary journey over the seas. When old friends meet, the speaker sings loudly of a heavy drink to celebrate the rare reunion. The happy and careless life at home, the happy and noisy revelry of old friends' meeting, all these are presented with the life scenes familiar to common people, touching the tender heart of the readers.

Questions

1. What may you imagine about the Scottish people's life from the lines "But we've wander'd mony a weary fit" and "But seas between us braid hae roar'd"?

2. What effect(s) may be achieved with the repetition of "auld lang syne"?

Chinese Translation

往昔的时光

老朋友哪能遗忘，
哪能不放在心上？
老朋友哪能遗忘，
还有往昔的时光？
（合唱：）
为了往昔的时光，老朋友，
为了往昔的时光，
再干一杯友情的酒，
为了往昔的时光。

你来痛饮一大杯，
我也买酒来相陪。
干一杯友情的酒又何妨？
为了往昔的时光。
（合唱：）
为了往昔的时光，老朋友，
为了往昔的时光，
再干一杯友情的酒，
为了往昔的时光。

我们曾遨游山，
到处将野花拜访。
但以后走上疲惫的旅程，
逝去了往昔的时光！

（合唱：）
为了往昔的时光，老朋友，
为了往昔的时光，
再干一杯友情的酒，
为了往昔的时光。

我们曾赤脚蹚过河流，
水声笑语里将时间忘。
如今大海的怒涛把我们隔开，
逝去了往昔的时光！
（合唱：）
为了往昔的时光，老朋友，
为了往昔的时光，
再干一杯友情的酒，
为了往昔的时光。

忠实的老友，伸出你的手，
让我们握手聚一堂。
再来痛饮一杯欢乐酒，
为了往昔的时光！
（合唱：）
为了往昔的时光，老朋友，
为了往昔的时光，
再干一杯友情的酒，
为了往昔的时光。

（王佐良　译）

（说明：译文依据因与课文中原作版本不同，诗节排序略有出入）

Unit 7 William Blake

Introduction to the Author

William Blake (1757-1827) is an English poet, painter, and printmaker. He was born in London in a family of hosier. Most of his youth was spent in a life of vision, which potentially influenced his later career. He was rebellious to the rationalism of Neoclassicism in the 18th century, writing with a style of lyrical vision.

Blake's first collection of poems is *Poetical Sketches* (1783), a collection of his apprentice verse. He published his *Songs of Innocence* (1789) and *Songs of Experience* (1793) with illuminations. These two volumes were jointly published as *Songs of Innocence and Experience* in 1794, making clearer the contradictory themes of the conflicts between nature and human being's society, between the innocence of a child and social experience that he has to get. *The Marriage of Heaven and Hell* (1790-1793) is Blake's influential prose work, expressing his personal romantic beliefs by imitating the biblical prophecy. From 1802 on, Blake kept on writing and improving his last great prophetic works, *The Four Zoas*, *Milton*, and *Jerusalem* till about 1820 when he finally had them published.

Blake's works are full of symbolic visions, some of which are directly illustrated, either through the innocent children's description of the world or through the images of the natural things such as lambs, flowers and scenes in different seasons, etc. Some visions are difficult to interpret, for they suggest Blake's own mythological world and his philosophy. *Songs of Innocence and Experience* centers upon images of children. Blake expresses his disappointment in the adults who mercilessly exploit naïve children while at the same time cheating them with phony hopes. Poems of innocence express Blake's belief in the power of natural beings and their unstained feelings, while poems of experience show the poet's dissatisfaction of the worldly society symbolized by the industrial city in which innocence eventually becomes corrupted. The conflicting states of human beings' innocence and experience are displayed in pairs with poems of the same titles. Blake explores psychologically and philosophically the growth of us human beings in our spiritual world in a notably modern way.

In his lifetime Blake failed to achieve much fame for his avantgarde poetry. Only a few talented people, Coleridge, Wordsworth and Lamb for instance, acclaimed Blake "a man of Genius". He believed that his poetry could be understood by people, and he refused to give up his symbolic visions. His poetic talents were fully recognized in the 20th century with the rise of modernism.

The Sick Rose

O Rose, thou art sick.
The invisible worm[1]
That flies in the night
In the howling storm[2]

Has found out thy bed[3]
Of crimson joy[4],
And his dark secret love[5]
Does thy life destroy.

1. invisible worm：看不见的虫子，喻隐藏的危害者。
2. howling storm：暴风雨。howling：（拟声词）嚎叫，指凄婉的哀嚎（the uttering of a prolonged wailing cry; or a similar sound by the wind）。
3. bed：花心，喻令人愉快的栖息地，安乐窝（delightful resting place）。
4. crimson joy：血腥的欢乐。crimson：紫红色，血色。
5. dark secret love：阴险的寻欢。dark：阴险（insidious，sinister）; secret：偷偷的（stealthy）。

The poem can be interpreted in at least two ways. Literally, the speaker in the poem tells the readers one incident. In a storming night, a worm creeps into the flower, biting the flower from the bottom and making the flower sick. The speaker declares the incident in a definitive tone, "O Rose thou art sick". He states this with the strong passion which is expressed through the exclamation "O", an apostrophe. "Rose" here is personified and addressed with "thou", suggesting the speaker's respect and friendliness. Then he explains the reason why the rose is sick: in a stormy night, a worm creeps into the bed of the flower, and destroys the flower by eating her from the inside. The incident is described as a terrible murder. The "invisible worm" is dangerous, vicious and hideous because it is not easily found; it "flies in the night" so boldly and arrogantly when it can hide in the night, a time of disorder. Because of the howling storm, the worm can fly by the wind. When the worm finds the rose, it takes the flower as its bed of pleasure. Crimson refers to a bloodily red color, therefore, "crimson joy" implies here a criminal joy which the worm enjoys by killing the rose. In the end, the speaker affirms that it is the worm's insidious and stealthy rape ("dark secret love") that destroys the rose's life.

Metaphorically, Blake's composition can easily lead the readers to understand the verse in this way: the incident of the rose's being killed by the worm may hint at a tragic love affair in which a beautiful maiden becomes a victim to some evil and brutal man; the cruel and bloody illustration of the crime committed in the dark night intensifies the tragic atmosphere, evoking the readers' deep sympathy. A meditative reader may further dig out meanings of the poem. A rose in the English context often represents a beautiful thing, then the poem is possibly interpreted as the speaker's wailing accusation against a criminal murder of the beauty.

Questions

1. The poem begins with a brief statement, proceeding with an explanation. What effect(s) would be achieved in the arrangement of the structure of the poem?

2. Why the "invisible worm" "flies in the night" in "the howling storm"?

Chinese Translation

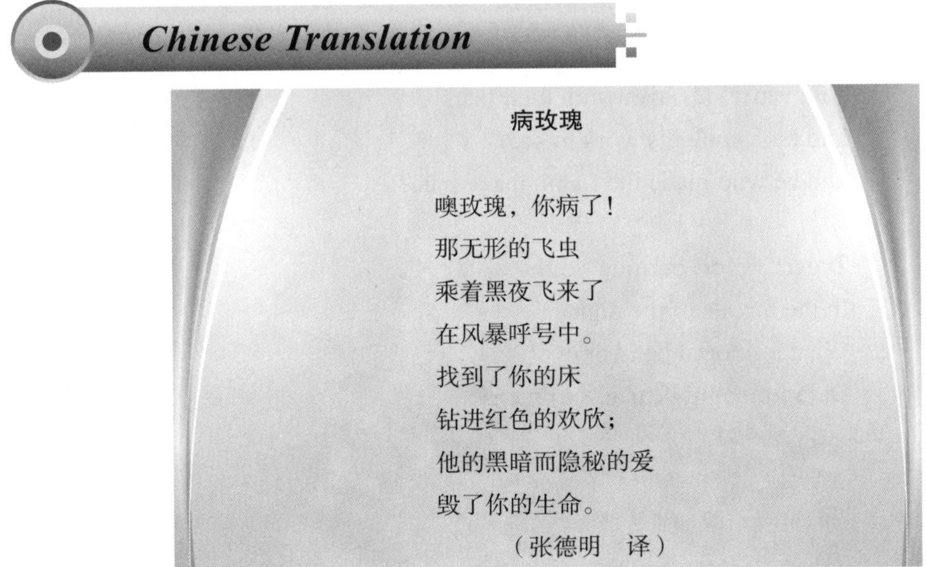

病玫瑰

噢玫瑰，你病了！
那无形的飞虫
乘着黑夜飞来了
在风暴呼号中。
找到了你的床
钻进红色的欢欣；
他的黑暗而隐秘的爱
毁了你的生命。

（张德明　译）

Text 2

The Tyger

Tyger! Tyger! burning bright[1]
In the forests of the night[2],
What immortal[3] hand or eye
Could frame thy fearful symmetry[4]?

In what distant deeps[5] or skies
Burnt the fire of thine eyes?
On what wings dare he aspire[6]?
What the hand dare sieze the fire?

And what shoulder, & what art,
Could twist the sinews[7] of thy heart?
And when thy heart began to beat,
What dread hand? & what dread feet?

What the hammer? what the chain?
In what furnace was thy brain[8]?
What the anvil? what dread grasp[9]
Dare its deadly terrors clasp[10]?

When the stars threw down their spears[11],
And water'd heaven with their tears[12],
Did he[13] smile his work to see?
Did he who made the Lamb make thee?

Tyger! Tyger! burning bright
In the forests of the night,
What immortal hand or eye
Dare frame thy fearful symmetry?

Notes

1. burning bright：炽烈的明亮。
2. the forests of the night：黑夜的森林里。
3. immortal：不朽，暗指神明。
4. fearful symmetry：令人惊恐的匀称。fearful 在此处用于强调，意思是非常，极其（enormous in quantity）；symmetry：匀称，有和谐美之意。
5. deeps：深渊。
6. On what wings dare he aspire：凭借什么样的翅膀他敢于飞升。aspire：上升（ascend, rise up）。乘着翅膀飞升是一个用典（allusion）：古希腊神话传说中，雅典的能工巧匠代达罗斯（Daedalus）为克里特国王米诺斯（Minos）建造迷宫。工程完成后，克里特国王担心代达罗斯泄露迷宫的秘密，便把代达罗斯及其儿子伊卡鲁斯（Icarus）囚禁在克里特岛。没有船只可以用来逃跑，代达罗斯用蜡把鸟的羽毛粘在一起做成两对翅膀，带着儿子飞离克里特岛。父亲在出逃前曾告诫儿子不要飞得太高，以免翅膀被太阳烤化。伊卡鲁斯飞上天空以后，产生了飞得更高的冲动。他忘却父亲的告诫，不断向更高的天空飞升，结果因为飞得离太阳太近，翅膀被烤化，跌落海中淹死了。伊卡鲁斯在欧美文化中因此成为大胆和鲁莽的代名词。这里，诗中叙述者意指谁会冒着生命危险飞到那么高的天上。
7. sinews：筋腱。
8. In what furnace was thy brain：你的头脑在什么样的熔炉锻造。
9. what dread grasp：多么可怕的把握。
10. deadly terrors clasp：钳住死亡般的恐惧。
11. When the stars threw down their spears：当星星丢弃他们的枪矛。
12. watered heaven with their tears：他们的眼泪在天庭流淌。一种传说是英国中世纪时，人们相信流星是天使的眼泪。诗中描绘的景象是，当上帝造出老虎时，天庭里的众天使都心惊胆战，丢掉手中的投枪，吓得泪飞如雨。
13. he：伟大的神明，上帝（God）。

Text Analysis

The poem displays William Blake as a religious poet. It is a eulogy of the tiger as well as its creator. The archaic spelling "tyger" is used, endowing the poem with some alien and exotic qualities. The tiger is described as a newly created mighty thing by the almighty divinity from the furnace, still brightly burning when it walks "in the forests of the night". A series of rhetoric questions is employed, from classical Greek mythologies and the Holy Bible, to denote the divine quality of the tiger.

God's role in the creation is like a blacksmith, and his workshop is the vast universe. This idea of the poet reflects his conflicting view of the industrial era which often is attacked by him as the "experienced". The hammering rhythm, combining with the compactly rhetoric questions, forms the tension of the verse from the beginning to the end, with one exceptionally leisure relieve in rhythm at the climax part of the fifth stanza, achieving a marvelous musical effect.

Questions

1. What are the effects of the hammering rhythm of the verse?
2. What functions do the allusions play in the poem? Please interpret Blake's symbolic usage of the allusions.

Chinese Translation

老虎

老虎！老虎！黑夜的森林中
燃烧着的煌煌的火光，
是怎样的神手或天眼
造出了你这样的威武堂堂？

你炯炯的两眼中的火
燃烧在多远的天空或深渊？
他乘着怎样的翅膀搏击？
用怎样的手夺来火焰？

又是怎样的膂力，怎样的技巧，
把你的心脏的筋肉捏成？
当你的心脏开始搏动时，
使用怎样猛的手腕和脚胫？

是怎样的槌？怎样的链子？
在怎样的熔炉中炼成你的脑筋？
是怎样的铁砧？怎样的铁臂
敢于捉着这可怖的凶神？

群星投下了他们的投枪。
用它们的眼泪润湿了穹苍，
他是否微笑着欣赏他的作品？
他创造了你，也创造了羔羊？

老虎！老虎！黑夜的森林中
燃烧着的煌煌的火光，
是怎样的神手或天眼
造出了你这样的威武堂堂？

（郭沫若　译）

Unit 8 William Wordsworth

Introduction to the Author

William Wordsworth was born on 7 April 1770 in Cockermouth, Cumberland. Wordsworth's deep love for the "beauteous forms" of the natural world was established early. In 1787, Wordsworth went up to Cambridge. During his last summer as an undergraduate, he and his college friend decided to make a tour of the Alps; his poetic career began with this first trip to France and Switzerland. During this period he also formed his early political opinions—especially his hatred of tyranny. Wordsworth was intoxicated by the combination of revolutionary fervor he found in France and the impressive natural beauty of the countryside and mountains. But he later changed his views and became conservative and moved to the countryside.

The years between 1797 and 1800 mark the period of Wordsworth and Coleridge's close collaboration, and also the beginning of Wordsworth's mature poetic career. Their cooperative endeavour—*Lyrical Ballads*, marks a revolutionary moment in English poetry. Its second edition, appearing in 1800, includes an extended preface by Wordsworth, setting out a personal poetics that has remained influential and controversial to the present day. In the preface, Wordsworth proposed a famous definition of poetry, by seeing poetry, to be written in "the real language of men", as "the spontaneous overflow of feelings: it takes its origin from emotion recollected in tranquility". Wordsworth made an explicit connection between a plain poetic diction and a proper relationship to nature and society; that is, he made the issue of a poetic diction a moral one. The preface was a fount of wisdom for Victorian readers such as Matthew Arnold, but the modernists were deeply suspicious of Wordsworth's reliance on feeling: poets such as T. S. Eliot and Ezra Pound, while they could accept the strictures on poetic diction, found the underlying theory unacceptable. Subsequent critics have focused on the literary and historical sources of Wordsworth's ideas, demonstrating that, while the poet certainly reinvented English poetic diction, his theories were deeply rooted in the practice of earlier poets, especially John Milton.

Wordsworth was concerned with the common people; he wrote about them using their own language. Influenced by Neoplatonism, his poetry presents a fully developed, yet morally flexible, picture of the relationship between human beings and the natural world.

Wordsworth is prolific, attempting different poetic forms. The autobiographic epic *The Prelude* records the poet's life and development of his mind; philosophical lyrics of intermediate length, such as "Tintern Abbey", fuses the poet's philosophy and poetics; some narratives like "Michael" and "The Ruined Cottage" are in blank verse, and present the poet's thoughts on the countryside in an age of industrialization. Like many poets, Wordsworth is a good sonneteer with more than 500 sonnets, and his sonnets display his observations of some important historical events. *Lyrical Ballads* is another achievement of Wordsworth, who had such masterpieces as "The Solitary Reaper", "I Wondered Lonely as a Cloud", etc. Wordsworth is not remembered as a prose writer but as a poet of spiritual and epistemological speculation, a poet concerned with the human relationship to nature. Wordsworth's prose, while not extensive and often difficult, reveals the poet's historical context. A careful reading of his prose will lead, perhaps, to a clearer understanding of the path he traveled from the 18th century to the Victorian age, and modern readers will recognize the origins of their own literary and political culture. Wordsworth also has numerous political prose writings which are crucial to an understanding of his entanglement in local and national politics. Besides, Wordsworth is also a prolific correspondent throughout his life, and his letters provide a useful prose fabric to trace the embroidery of the poems upon.

In 1843, Wordsworth was named Poet Laureate of England, though by this time he had for the most part quit composing verse. When he died in 1850, he had for some years been venerated as a sage, though his most ardent detractors were glossing over the radical origins of his poetics and politics.

Lines Composed a Few Miles above Tintern Abbey on Revisiting the Banks of the Wye During a Tour, July 13, 1798[1]

Five years have past; five summers, with the length
Of five long winters! and again I hear
These waters, rolling from their mountain-springs
With a soft inland murmur. —Once again
Do I behold these steep and lofty cliffs,
That on a wild secluded scene impress

Thoughts of more deep seclusion; and connect
The landscape with the quiet of the sky[2].
The day is come when I again repose
Here, under this dark sycamore, and view
These plots of cottage-ground, these orchard-tufts,
Which at this season, with their unripe fruits,
Are clad in one green hue, and lose themselves
'Mid groves and copses[3]. Once again I see
These hedge-rows, hardly hedge-rows, little lines
Of sportive wood run wild[4]: these pastoral farms,
Green to the very door: and wreaths of smoke
Sent up, in silence, from among the trees[5]!
With some uncertain notice, as might seem[6]
Of vagrant dwellers in the houseless woods,
Or of some Hermit's cave, where by his fire
The Hermit sits alone.

These beauteous forms,
Through[7] a long absence, have not been to me
As is a landscape to a blind man's eye:
But oft, in lonely rooms, and 'mid the din[8]
Of towns and cities, I have owed to them
In hours of weariness, sensations sweet,
Felt in the blood, and felt along the heart;
And passing even into my purer mind,
With tranquil restoration[9]:—feelings too
Of unremembered pleasure: such, perhaps,
As have no slight or trivial influence
On that best portion of a good man's life,
His little, nameless, unremembered, acts
Of kindness and of love[10]. Nor less, I trust,
To them I may have owed another gift,
Of aspect more sublime; that blessed mood,
In which the burthen of the mystery,
In which the heavy and the weary weight
Of all this unintelligible world,
Is lightened[11]: —that serene and blessed mood,
In which the affections gently lead us on, —

Until, the breath of this corporeal frame
And even the motion of our human blood
Almost suspended, we are laid asleep
In body, and become a living soul[12]:
While with an eye made quiet by the power
Of harmony, and the deep power of joy,
We see into the life of things[13].

If this
Be but a vain belief[14], yet, oh! how oft —
In darkness and amid the many shapes[15]
Of joyless daylight; when the fretful stir
Unprofitable, and the fever of the world[16],
Have hung upon the beatings of my heart —
How oft, in spirit, have I turned to thee,
O sylvan[17] Wye! thou wanderer thro' the woods,
How often has my spirit turned to thee!

And now, with gleams of half-extinguished thought[18],
With many recognitions dim and faint,
And somewhat of a sad perplexity[19],
The picture of the mind revives again:
While here I stand, not only with the sense
Of present pleasure, but with pleasing thoughts
That in this moment there is life and food
For future years[20]. And so I dare to hope[21],
Though changed, no doubt, from what I was when first
I came among these hills; when like a roe
I bounded o'er the mountains, by the sides
Of the deep rivers, and the lonely streams,
Wherever nature led: more like a man
Flying from something that he dreads than one
Who sought the thing he loved. For nature then
(The coarser pleasures of my boyish days,
And their glad animal movements all gone by[22])
To me was all in all[23]. — I cannot paint
What then I was. The sounding cataract
Haunted me like a passion: the tall rock,

The mountain, and the deep and gloomy wood,
Their colours and their forms, were then to me
An appetite; a feeling and a love,
That had no need of a remoter charm,
By thought supplied, nor any interest
Unborrowed from the eye[24]. — That time is past,
And all its aching joys[25] are now no more,
And all its dizzy raptures. Not for this
Faint[26] I, nor mourn nor murmur, other gifts
Have followed; for such loss, I would believe,
Abundant recompence. For I have learned
To look on nature, not as in the hour
Of thoughtless youth; but hearing oftentimes
The still, sad music of humanity,
Nor harsh nor grating, though of ample power
To chasten and subdue[27]. And I have felt
A presence[28] that disturbs me with the joy
Of elevated thoughts; a sense sublime[29]
Of something far more deeply interfused,
Whose dwelling is the light of setting suns,
And the round ocean and the living air,
And the blue sky, and[30] in the mind of man:
A motion and a spirit, that impels
All thinking things, all objects of all thought,
And rolls through all things. Therefore am I still
A lover of the meadows and the woods,
And mountains; and of all that we behold
From this green earth; of all the mighty world
Of eye, and ear, — both what they half create[31],
And what perceive; well pleased to recognise
In nature and the language of the sense,
The anchor[32] of my purest thoughts, the nurse,
The guide, the guardian of my heart, and soul
Of all my moral being.

Nor perchance[33],
If I were not thus taught, should I the more
Suffer my genial spirits[34] to decay:

For thou[35] art with me here upon the banks
Of this fair river; thou my dearest Friend,
My dear, dear Friend[36]; and in thy voice I catch
The language of my former heart[37], and read
My former pleasures in the shooting lights
Of thy wild eyes. Oh! yet a little while
May I behold in thee what I was once,
My dear, dear Sister! and this prayer I make,
Knowing that Nature never did betray
The heart that loved her; 'tis her privilege,
Through all the years of this our life, to lead
From joy to joy: for she can so inform[38]
The mind that is within us, so impress[39]
With quietness and beauty, and so feed
With lofty thoughts, that neither evil tongues,
Rash judgments, nor the sneers of selfish men,
Nor greetings where no kindness is, nor all
The dreary intercourse of daily life,
Shall e'er prevail against us, or disturb
Our cheerful faith, that all which we behold
Is full of blessings. Therefore let the moon
Shine on thee in thy solitary walk;
And let the misty mountain-winds[40] be free
To blow against thee: and, in after years,
When these wild ecstasies[41] shall be matured
Into a sober pleasure; when thy mind
Shall be a mansion[42] for all lovely forms,
Thy memory be as a dwelling-place
For all sweet sounds and harmonies; oh! then,
If solitude, or fear, or pain, or grief,
Should be thy portion, with what healing thoughts
Of tender joy wilt thou remember me,
And these my exhortations! Nor, perchance—
If I should be where I no more can hear
Thy voice, nor catch from thy wild eyes these gleams
Of past existence[43] —wilt thou then forget
That on the banks of this delightful stream
We stood together; and that I, so long

A worshipper of Nature[44], hither came
Unwearied in that service: rather say
With warmer love—oh! with far deeper zeal
Of holier love. Nor wilt thou then forget,
That after many wanderings, many years
Of absence, these steep woods and lofty cliffs,
And this green pastoral landscape, were to me
More dear, both for themselves and for thy sake[45]!

1. 华兹华斯 1793 年 8 月曾去英格兰西部的蒙茅斯郡（Monmouthshire）徒步旅行，游历了怀河河谷（Wye Valley）和丁登寺（Tintern Abbey）遗址，时年 23 岁。5 年后，他和妹妹多萝西（Dorothy Wordsworth）故地重游，有了不同的感受，于是发出深远的幽思。眼下景致与记忆中“头脑中的景象”（picture of the mind）的区别，使他产生了种种思绪，既有对少年时代的留恋缅怀，又有对现在的评价和对未来的期待。一种淡淡的忧伤和对人生恬然自适的静观态度与诗人对自然的渴求和信念完美地糅合在一起，使这首诗成为展现华兹华斯艺术风格与思想观念最典型的作品之一。

   华兹华斯在《抒情歌谣集》的序言中提出了一个著名的诗歌定义，强调诗歌需有感而发，朴实自然。这首诗虽长达 160 余行，却也是在美景和诗情的激发下一气呵成的，流畅而幽婉，无斧凿痕迹。诗人如此描述该诗的创作过程：“No poem of mine was composed under circumstances more pleasant for me to remember than this. I began it upon leaving Tintern, after crossing the Wye, and concluded it just as I was entering Bristol in the evening, after a ramble of 4 or 5 days, with my sister. Not a line of it was altered, and not any part of it written down till I reached Bristol.”

2. 全诗虚实结合，以虚导实：先言五年已逝，五年后重临故地的欣喜跃然纸上；再描摹一幅立体的画面：垂危峭拔的悬崖连接着遥远的天际，内河潺潺的溪流映衬出天际的辽阔以及景色的隐幽，而这些更加衬托出观景者内心的平静安详。在语言表现方面，five 和 again 的反复使用，长元音和双元音为主的音韵，加上句间停顿（caesura）的间或使用（如在第 1、2、4 行中），无不舒缓了语言的节奏，营造出时光漫长、阔别已久的效果。过去的五年对诗人来说尤其漫长，因为他对法国资产阶级革命曾有的澎湃激情，由于对雅各宾派激进主义的不满和英法战争的爆发而消失。

   第 5~8 行的大意为：在一片幽静的野外风景里，河岸两旁的峭壁激起人更为幽远的思绪，河谷中的景色与浩浩长空的静穆融为一体。第 3 行中的 mountain-springs 指山间的溪流；第 7 行中的 Thoughts of more deep seclusion：眼前的景致已然清幽静谧，而由此激起的思想更隐秘自适，这是天人合一思想的反映。

3. 第 9～14 行，描写眼前山上的果木葳蕤的景象。请注意，诗人一路写来，笔触由远及近，由抽象到具体。该节中 green 一词出现两次（第 13、17 行），诗人在此描摹的是自然景色，而在诗的后面部分，诗人又赋予大自然某种想象的色彩，如第 158 行中出现的 green 便可作此理解。
4. These hedge-rows，hardly hedge-rows：这种写法反映了诗人的思想变化，是诗人情感和思想的自然流露，同时给人以即兴赋诗的印象。sportive wood run wild：sportive 即 playful；这里是拟人（personification）的用法。
5. wreaths of smoke / Sent up, in silence, from among the trees：反复出现的“s”音强化了炊烟丛林中袅袅升起的声音效果。炊烟与前面提及的流水一起，更添境界之幽静，以及此中人之怡然自得。
6. With some uncertain notice, as might seem：诗人对炊烟的来源不敢肯定，因为周围无人迹。notice 意为 sign 或 indication。as might seem：诗人猜想，炊烟可能源于流浪者（第 20 行中的 vagrant dwellers）的住处，或出自隐居者（第 21 行的 Hermit）的洞穴。流浪者暗指吉普赛人，“吉普赛人”和“隐居者”的意象早已通过意大利绘画进入英国诗歌，都属于传统意象。
7. Through：throughout, during.
8. oft：often. din：喧嚣，嘈杂，这里指城镇（towns and cities）的喧嚣和对人的心灵的搅扰。华兹华斯所熟悉的唯一的大城市就是伦敦，而诗中的 town 可能指巴塞洛缪基石；在《序曲》（*The Prelude*）第 7 卷中，它是城市生活的象征：“what anarchy and din，/ Barbarian and infernal”（第 686～687 行）。
9. 第 25～31 行的大意是：自然界的美景（即第 23 行中的 These beauteous forms，这里特指第 1 节所描写的风景），在诗人蛰居都市期间，依然通过回忆发挥作用，抚慰诗人寂寥的心情，在其疲累困顿之时提供源源不竭的灵感。这是本诗的主导性思想，也是华兹华斯诗歌的一个重要思想，可参见《水仙花》（“The Daffodils”）一诗。
10. （1）第 23～36 行是一个复合长句，分 3 部分：第 23～25 行是第 1 部分，第 26～31 行是第 2 部分，也是主要部分，其主语是 I，谓语是 have owed，to them（指第 23 行中的 These beauteous forms；第 37 行中的 them 同此）是补语，In hours of weariness 是状语，宾语是 sensations（第 28 行，sweet 和其后的 3 行修饰限定中心词 sensations）和 feelings（第 31 行）；第 32～36 行是第 3 部分。这是从句法上来说。（2）第 33 行中的 no slight or trivial influence 的用法是 litotes 或称 understatement，语轻意重，意思是：不是轻微的或琐碎的影响（no slight or trivial influence），而是强烈的和重要的影响（intense and significant influence）。（3）从内容上来看，第 2 部分中，sensation 的限定语值得关注，具体说来，是其形成的顺序：先 blood，继而 heart，最后是 mind，这是从低级到高级的发展，是不可逆的（blood 是纯粹生理的，mind 是精神的和心灵的，而 heart 介乎二者之间；从位置上而言，三者也是按照由

低到高的顺序排列，俨然是形而下与形而上的呼应)。(4)从诗学观念分析，第31行中的With tranquil restoration反映了诗人的诗学主张：他在《抒情歌谣集》的序言中，指出诗是强烈情感的自然流露，但需要创作者事发之后在静谧的回忆中将心境记录下来，这是对当时情感的沉淀和升华(Poetry is the spontaneous overflow of powerful feelings: it takes its origin from emotion recollected in tranquility)。

11. 第38行中的sublime指从自然美景得到的另一馈赠(gift，第37行)，这是从上文绵延而来的顺序发展，是在感官冲击、情感体验之后的美感享受，是自然界对人的心灵的提升，因此有崇高(sublime)一说。在这一部分，诗人将凡俗之人的躯体之滞重(第39行中的burthen of the mystery；burthen指burden，负载；mystery可指life，生活，人生)与大自然之空灵形成对照，二者高下立见；在自然美景的烛照之下，人生的负载和疲累皆变得轻柔，瞬间升腾起来。
12. 第42～50行，诗人的情绪变得激越，由于自然景致的启迪，诗人从感官的愉悦到美感的体验再向更高的层级发展(lead us on，第43行)。在美景的感召之下，诗人变得安详，受到庇佑(serene and blessed，第42行)，此时物质的躯体之呼吸(第44行)以及血液之流动(第45行)几乎停顿下来，于是，人陷入昏睡并渐成一副鲜活的灵魂(living soul，第47行)。这是人对大自然认知的高度的发展，由低到高，渐次过渡到宗教的层面，这是美感体验的最高层级。living soul的出现令我们想到美国哲人和文学家爱默生在《论自然》("Nature")中的著名意象——透明的眼球："In the woods, we return to reason and faith. There I feel that nothing can befall me in life, —no disgrace, no calamity, (leaving me my eyes,) which nature cannot repair. Standing on the bare ground, —my head bathed by the blithe air, and uplifted into infinite space, —all mean egotism vanishes. I become a transparent eyeball. I am nothing. I see all. The currents of the Universal Being circulate through me; I am part or particle of God."，这里体现出华兹华斯的自然观。需要指出的是，从诗的开始诗人沉浸于对往昔的回忆，到直面美景，再到透过美景而生发的昂扬情绪，诗人对自我的信心被逐渐激发出来。
13. 第48～50行承上而来，继续解说大自然对于人类的力量(power)：它使人和谐(harmony)，给人愉悦(joy)，人因此得以深入事物，并借此对万物诸象有更深刻的体察。人与自然融为一体，人以平和安详的心态洞察事物的本质。
14. If this / Be but a vain belief：这是一个让步(concession)的表达，在结构和形式上是一种缓冲(recoil)。内容方面，这一节(第3节)并未增加新的思想，主要是承前启后，为上一小节(23～50行)做小结，并为下一节的发展打下基础。this指与自然的对话(即诗歌的此前部分，主要是36～50行)。
15. shapes：manifestations，experiences，白日所见或经历。
16. fretful stir / Unprofitable，and the fever of the world：Unprofitable fretful stir，无益的

焦躁烦扰，与 fever of the world 内涵接近；stir 有“搅动思绪的平静”之意。此句似化用莎士比亚的名句：How weary，stale，flat and unprofitable / Seem to me all the uses of the world!

17. sylvan：多树木的，来自拉丁文 silva（树林）。该行中的轻柔舒缓的“w”音（Wye, wanderer, woods）的反复出现暗示自然的和谐流畅，与第 54～55 行中的具有滞涩凝重感的“f”音的重复（fretful, unprofitable, fever）形成对比。
18. And now：承上而来，具有转折功能，仿佛诗人蓄势待发。gleams of half-extinguished thought：往事在回忆中如半灭的灰烬，重又燃烧起来。
19. 对往事的回忆模糊不清，诗人又极力希望廓清迷茫；当下的景致令诗人朦胧地忆起五年前首次造访的情景，但眼前所见与前又有所不同，因此产生了伤感、迷茫和困惑。
20. 第一次，诗人将现在与未来联系了起来。当下的愉悦（present pleasure，第 65 行）来自于自然美景，而对未来的愉快的思想（pleasing thoughts，第 65 行）则由此而激发。对当下美丽景致有所感知（sense），而对于未来则上升为思想（thoughts），其间有一种顺序的延展和程度的递进。
21. 从第 66 行到第 113 行，诗人从对自然界的认知的演变入手，揭示了自身成长的三个阶段：第 75～76 行为第一阶段，写少年纯粹基于身体的感官感受的阶段；第 67～74 行，以及第 76～85 行为第二阶段，描写青年时期对大自然的迷茫、困顿及不知其所以然的状态；第 85～113 行为第三阶段，揭示较成熟时期的状况，对应当下的状态。叶维廉在《中国古典诗中山水美感意识的演变》一文中对此有精彩的论述，他引用禅宗《传灯录》中一段著名的公案，“老僧三十年前参禅时，见山是山，见水是水，及至后来亲见知识，有个入处，见山不是山，见水不是水，而今得个体歇处，依然见山只是山，见水只是水”，来诠释华兹华斯对自然认知的三个阶段：第一阶段“见山是山，见水是水”，以素朴之心或未进入认识论的哲学思维之前的素心感应山水，即对于美景的动物似的感官反应；第二阶段“见山不是山，见水不是水”，以无智的素心进入认识论的哲学思维去感应山水，力图理解美景何以产生美感；第三阶段“见山只是山，见水只是水”，是对自然现象“即物即真”的感悟，全盘接受山水自然自主的原始存在，而这要求我们摒弃语言和心智活动，返归事物之本来面目。我们认为，华兹华斯与自然美景对话的三个阶段，可以在王国维《人间词话》中的三境界中得到很好的解释。王国维《人间词话》的“三境界”，本是对治学之道的论述：“古今成大学问者，必经过三种境界：昨夜西风凋碧树。独上高楼，望尽天涯路。此第一境也。衣带渐宽终不悔，为伊消得人憔悴。此第二境也。众里寻他千百度，蓦然回首，那人却在，灯火阑珊处。此第三境也。”三境界也可用来解说华兹华斯在该诗中所描摹的对自然认知的三个发展阶段。
22. 第 75～76 行是对第一阶段的描写，记述诗人年少时期对自然美景“粗浅的愉悦”（coarser pleasures），仿佛动物似的单纯的身体反应（animal movements）。

23. all in all: everything. 这一短语出自《新约 · 哥林多书》(15: 28):"… that God may be all in all"。
24. 第 82～85 行为双重否定。诗人用 passion(第 79 行)和 appetite(第 82 行)等词，强调上述第一阶段对自然的感观上的享受，与第二阶段不是单纯由眼睛观察而来(unborrowed from the eye，第 85 行)，而是由沉思而来的长远的雅兴(remoter charm)(第 83 行)相对照。
25. aching joys : 矛盾修饰法(oxymoron)，下一行中的 dizzy raptures 同；两处都表达给人强烈的痛感(因此是"痛快")。这些表达的另一层意思是说，弄清楚自然山水何以产生美感，何以给人灵感和精神慰藉是一个含有痛楚(需要巨大的智力消耗)及令人眩晕的过程，但一旦明了这个过程，便可以给人带来巨大的喜悦。
26. Faint: lose heart，沮丧。
27. 第 92～95 行，诗人把人性比拟为音乐，形象地解释了本来很抽象的概念。still: 寂静，安详。人性之音乐优雅悦耳，却富有净化和克制的力量。
28. A presence: something presents in nature，自然界中的存在之物。
29. a sense sublime: sublime(崇高)一词此前出现过，如在第 38 行中。a sense sublime(一种崇高或升华了的意念)可以看作 A presence(第 96 行)的同位语，是对这种自然中存在之物的解释。在华兹华斯的自然观中，人与自然相互交融，成为一个有机的整体，他似乎感到一种宇宙中的精神运行在人与自然的王国。参见《序曲》:"I felt the sentiment of Being spread / O'er all that moves and all that seemth still."(Ⅱ. 401-402)这可以看作自然神论的一种体现。
30. 第 100～101 行中连续 4 次出现 and，旨在强调人的思想与自然界的统一性。
31. what they half create: 华兹华斯曾说此行是套用爱德华·扬(Edward Young)《静夜思》(*Night Thoughts*)中的一行诗，人的感觉"half create the wondrous world they see"。人的感官不仅被动地接受，而且还主观地选择，因此从一定意义上说也是在创造。
32. anchor: 支撑。
33. perchance: perhaps. 从该行到诗的结尾(即诗的第 5 节)，诗人引入他的妹妹多萝西。华兹华斯认为大自然中一切造物之间互为伙伴，正如怀河(the Wye)象征着整个大自然，他和多萝西之间也是伙伴的关系，他视之为人类之间的关系。
34. genial spirits: genial 为形容词，源于名词 genius(意思是 native powers，自然的、天性的力量)。
35. thou: you. 诗人在第 5 节中直接和他的妹妹对话。
36. My dear，dear Friend: 试比较莎士比亚《理查德二世》(*King Richard Ⅱ*)中的诗行:"This land of such dear souls，this dear dear land"(第 2 幕第 2 场，第 57 行)。
37. in thy voice I catch / The language of my former heart: 第 119～124 行的大意是: 诗人自己的第二发展阶段已经过去，但却存在于他的妹妹多萝西身上，因此他把多萝西看成自己的昨日，而自己就是多萝西的明天。

38. inform：animate, give life to, give form to. 试比较诗人在另一作品中对该词的用法："I raise my thoughts，inform my deeds and words"［《意大利纪行》(*Memories of a Tour of Italy*)，第 21 节第 7 行］。第 128～141 行的大意：人和自然通常是和谐的，二者之间的冲突只是暂时脱离常规；二者之间的和谐，在此表现为多萝西和怀河之间的和谐相处。
39. impress：其宾语为该行中的 the mind。
40. mountain-winds：比较莎士比亚《暴风雨》(*The Tempest*，第 2 幕第 2 场，第 498～499 行)"Thou shalt be as free / As mountain winds."。另参见华兹华斯《序曲》("The Prelude")的开头一行"O there is blessing in this gentle breeze."
41. wild ecstasies：狂喜，即第 86～87 行中的 aching joys 和 dizzy raptures。第 141～149 行说明当多萝西从第 2 阶段转向第 3 阶段，即从狂喜（wild ecstasies）转向平静的欢乐（sober pleasure，第 142 行）时，她狂野的眼睛（wild eyes，第 151 行）将因美妙动听的乐声（sweet sounds and harmonies，第 145 行）而变得柔和。
42. mansion：宅邸；源于拉丁文 manere, to dwell，与下一行中的 dwelling-place 同义（dwelling 也出现于第 99 行）。
43. past existence：指诗人自己此前五年（1793—1798 年）的第二发展阶段。
44. worshipper of Nature：大自然的崇拜者。第 155～158 行，诗人更明确地把自然界看成带有神性的，是神性在自然界中的具体显现。
45. both for themselves and for thy sake：该诗的结束部分中，诗人暗示，只有当大自然与人类和谐相处、融合为一时，才具有神性，成为诗人的一种宗教。最后一节中，人类以其代表多萝西的面目出现。

Text Analysis

Nature and its relation with man is a central theme of English romantic poetry, and it is also an explicit theme of this poem by Wordsworth, as well as of its sequence *The Prelude*: they deal with the influence of Nature in forming and sustaining human mind and character. As elsewhere in his poetry, at least three meanings of nature can be distinguished here: external nature, here the scenery of Wye Valley; all existence, a harmonious, integrated and living whole; a "presence" or divine life that informs the whole and every part. When speaking of Nature, Wordsworth involves all these meanings at the same time and maintains that they interfuse each other; this goes consistent with his philosophy of organism. Hence he can assert that "the language of the sense" —sensory awareness of nature is "the guide, the guardian of my heart, and soul / Of all my moral being" (lines 112-113) simultaneously; he recognizes that in perception the senses are not passive, but can themselves "half-create". This means that the mind may have already modified or endowed the impressions it receives, and which it interprets as coming solely from without. Following Coleridge, Wordsworth soon begins to call this active and creative process "imagination". Besides, Wordsworth argued that the troubles of society were specifically urban in nature. This view finds eloquent expression in this poem, arguably Wordsworth's most powerful early poem. It concludes with a meditation on the power of nature to prevail against the false and superficial "dreary intercourse of daily life" that Wordsworth associated with city life, especially literary life in London.

Usually a poem has only one persona or, if there is dialogue within the poem, it is the persona speaking to himself, thus forming a dialogue. In this poem, we have two personas—William Wordsworth and his sister Dorothy Wordsworth, who actually functions as his past and who will develop herself tomorrow into what he is today. Between the brother and sister is the closest dramatic bond. Wordsworth needs somebody to guarantee (sponsor) his belief. He projects into his sister the negative of continuity, as he looks at her as his past. What happens here has great pathos, idea of natural covenant (religious agreement). The sister here serves as a sort of agent between nature and the brother poet.

The poem is in blank verse and in iambic pentameter, which was popular in poets like Shakespeare and Milton when they wrote epics. However, heroic couplet took the place and became the major poetic form in the hands of the Neoclassical poets. In the age of Romanticism, blank verse revived again to lead the fashion. Together with some other Romantic poets, Wordsworth has quite some masterpieces using the form of blank verse. One feature of this poem is its enjambment with sentences often running across the lines, to match the poet's passionate and sustainable thinking.

Questions

1. This poem is sometimes entitled "Tintern Abbey" which serves as abbreviated form of the original long title. However, Tintern Abbey actually is nowhere in the poem. What is your understanding of this?

2. In this poem, what is the function of Dorothy Wordsworth, the poet's sister?

3. William Wordsworth is often compared with some classical Chinese poets, such as Tao Yuanming, for their treatment of nature. In your understanding, what are their major similarities and differences in depicting nature?

Chinese Translation

丁登寺旁

五年过去了，五个夏天，加上
长长的五个冬天！我终于又听见
这水声，这从高山滚流而下的泉水，
带着柔和的内河的潺潺。
——我又一次
看到这些陡峭挺拔的山峰，
这里已经是幽静的野地，
它们却使人感到更加清幽，
把眼前景物一直挂上宁静的高天。
这个日子又来到了，我能再一次站
在这里，
傍着这棵苍翠的槭树，俯览脚下，
各处村舍的园地，种满果树的山坡，
由于季节未到，果子未结，
只见果树一片葱绿，
隐没在灌木和树林之中。我又一次
看到了树篱，也许称不上篱，
而是一行行活泼顽皮的小树精；
看到了田园的绿色，一直绿到家门；
一片沉寂的树林里升起了袅袅炊烟，
烟的来处难定，或许是
林中有无家的流浪者在走动，
或许是有隐士住在山洞，现在正
独坐火旁。

　　　　　　这些美好的形体
虽已久别，倒从来不曾忘怀，
不是像盲人看不见美景，
而是每当我孤居喧闹的城市，
寂寞而疲惫的时候，
它们带来甜蜜的感觉，
让我从血液里心脏里感到，

甚至还进入我最纯洁的思想，
使我恢复了恬静：——还有许多感觉，
使我回忆起已经忘却的愉快，它们对
一个良善的人的最宝贵的岁月
有过绝非细微、琐碎的影响，
一些早已忘记的无名小事，
但饱含着善意和爱。不仅如此，
我还靠它们得到另一种能力，
更高的能力，一种幸福的心情，
忽然间人世的神秘感，
整个无法理解的世界的
沉重感疲惫感的压力
减轻了；一种恬静和幸福的心情，
听从温情引导我们前进，
直到我们这躯壳中止了呼吸，
甚至我们的血液也暂停流动，
我们的身体入睡了，
我们变成一个活的灵魂，
这时候我们的眼睛变得冷静，由于和谐的力量，
也由于欢乐的深入的力量，
我们看得清事物的内在生命。

也许这只是
一种错觉，可是啊，多少次
在黑暗中，在各色各样无聊的白天里，
当无益的纷扰和世界的热病
沉重地压在我的心上，
使它不住地狂跳，多少次
在精神上我转向你，啊，树影婆娑的怀河！
你这穿越树林而流的漫游者，
多少次我的精神转向了你！

而现在，依稀犹见昔日思想的余光，
带着许多模糊朦胧的记认，
还多少有一点怅然的困惑，
心里的图景回来了；
我站在这里，不仅感到

当前的愉快，而且愉快地想到
眼前这一刻包含了将来岁月的
生命和粮食。至少我敢这样希望，
虽然我无疑已经改变，早不是
我初来这山上的光景；那时节我像一头小鹿，
腾跳山岭间，遨游大河两岸，
徘徊在凄寂的溪水旁边，
去大自然指引的任何地方，与其说是
追求所爱的东西，更像是
逃避所怕的东西。因为自从
我儿童时代的粗糙的乐趣
和动物般的行径消逝了之后，
大自然成了我的一切。——我无法描画
当年的自己。瀑布的轰鸣
日夜缠住我，像一种情欲；大块岩石，
高山，深密而幽暗的树林，
它们的颜色和形体，当时是我的
强烈嗜好，一种体感，一种爱欲，
无需思想来提供长远的雅兴，
也无需官感以外的
任何趣味。——这个时期过去了，
所有它的半带痛苦的欢乐消失了，
连同所有它的令人昏眩的狂喜。我再也不为这些
沮丧，哀伤，诉怨，我得到了
别的能力，完全能抵偿
所失的一切，因为我学会了
怎样看待大自然，不再似青年时期
不用头脑，而且经常听得到
人生的低柔而忧郁的乐声
不粗厉，不刺耳，却有足够的力量
使人沉静而服帖。我感到
有物令我惊起，它带来了
崇高思想的欢乐，一种超脱之感，
像是有高度融合的东西
来自落日的余晖，
来自大洋和清新的空气，
来自蓝天和人的心灵，

一种动力，一种精神，推动
一切有思想的东西，一切思想的对象，
穿过一切东西而运行。所以我仍然
热爱草原，树林，山峰，
一切从这绿色大地能见到的东西，
一切凭眼和耳所能感觉到的
这个神奇的世界，既有感觉到的，
也像想象创造的。我高兴地发现：
在大自然和感觉的语言里，
我找到了最纯洁的思想的支撑，心灵的保姆，
引导、保护者，我整个道德生命的灵魂。

　　　　　　　　　　　　　　也许即使
我没有得到这种教育，我也不至于
遭受天生能力的毁蚀，
因为有你陪着我在这美丽的
河岸上，你呀，我最亲爱的朋友，
我的亲而又亲的朋友，在你的声音里
我听见了我过去心灵的语言，
在你那流星般的无畏的双眼里
我重温了我过去的愉快。但愿我能
在你身上多看一会儿我过去的自己，
我的亲而又亲的妹妹！我要祈祷，
我知道大自然从来不曾背弃
任何爱她的心，她有特殊的力量
能够把我们一生的岁月
从欢乐引向欢乐，由于她能够
充实我们身上的心智，用
宁静和美感来影响我们，
用崇高的思想来养育我们，使得
流言蜚语、急性的判断、自私者的冷嘲、
硬心汉的随口应对，日常人生里的
全部阴郁的交际
都不能压倒我们，不能扰乱
我们的愉快的信念，相信我们所见的
一切都充满幸福。因此让月光
照着你在路上独行吧，

让雾里的山风随意地
吹拂你吧，在以后的岁月里，
当这些按捺不住的狂喜变成了
清醒的乐趣，当你的心灵
变成了一切美好形体的大厦，
当你的记忆像家屋一般收容下
一切甜美的乐声和谐音；啊，那时候，
纵使孤独、恐惧、痛苦、哀伤
成为你的命运，你又将带着怎样亲切的喜悦
想起我，想起我今天的这番嘱咐
而感到安慰！即使我去了
不能再听到你的声音的地方，
不能再在你那无畏的眼里看见
我过去生活的亮光，你也不会忘记
我俩曾在这条可爱的河岸
并肩站着；不会忘记我这个长期崇拜
大自然的人，重来此地，崇敬之心
毫未减弱，而是怀着
更热烈的爱——啊，更深的热诚，
更神圣的爱；那时候你更不会忘记
经过多年的流浪，多年的离别，
这些高大的树林，耸立的山峰，
这绿色的田园景色，对我更加亲切
半因为它们自己，半因为你的缘故！

（王佐良　译）

Unit 9 Samuel Taylor Coleridge

Introduction to the Author

Samuel Taylor Coleridge (1772-1834), poet and critic, a leader of the British Romantic movement, was born in the family of a country vicar in Devonshire, England. Coleridge was a student at his father's school and an avid reader. After his father died in 1781, Coleridge attended Christ's Hospital School in London, where he met lifelong friend Charles Lamb (1775-1834).

On the way to Wales in June 1794, Coleridge met Robert Southey (1774-1843). Coleridge postponed his trip for several weeks, and the men shared their philosophical ideas. Influenced by Plato's *Republic*, they planned to construct a utopia called "Pantisocracy" in the New World of America. They envisioned the men sharing the workload, a great library, philosophical discussions, and freedom of religious and political beliefs in this utopia. However, their plan soon fell through when it came to the matter of ways and means.

At the beginning of 1797, Coleridge met William Wordsworth, a memorable encounter that marked the beginning of a memorable friendship. From 1797 to 1798 he lived near Wordsworth and his sister, Dorothy, in Somersetshire. This intimacy helped to mature his poetic genius and flowered in the planning and writing of *Lyrical Ballads*, in which Coleridge's share of work was to deal with supernatural subjects in a natural manner. The collection is considered the first great work of the Romantic School of poetry. Coleridge's best poems, "The Rime of the Ancient Mariner", "Kubla Khan", and "Christabel" all came out during the years when he was in close contact with the Wordsworths.

In the autumn of 1798, the two poets traveled to the Continent together. Coleridge spent most of the trip in Germany, studying German literature and German idealist philosophy. Great German thinkers such as Lessing, Kant, Schiller, and Schelling greatly influenced Coleridge's intellectual life. Following these thinkers, Coleridge believed that genius is organic, not so mechanical as mere talent is; genius arrives therefore by instinct at that harmonious blend of things which we call Art. Genius, like Nature, is self-organizing; and Art is the self-expression of the creative power of Nature. Coleridge was credited with introducing critical and transcendental philosophy to English audience, and helping shape the early

19th-century English thought on problems of science and method.

Back in England in 1800, Coleridge lived in the Lake District. Over the next two decades Coleridge lectured on literature and philosophy, wrote about religious and political theory, and spent two years on the island of Malta as a secretary to the governor in an effort to overcome his poor health and his opium addiction. Still addicted to opium, he moved in with the physician James Gillman in 1816. In 1817, Coleridge published *Biographia Literaria*, which contained his finest literary criticism. This prose work afforded the Romantic poetry a new principle of criticism, whose task was not to judge but to appreciate and interpret. He continued to publish poetry and prose, notably *Sibylline Leaves* (1817), *Aids to Reflection* (1825), and *Church and State* (1830). He died in London on July 25, 1834.

There are two outstanding characteristics in Coleridge's poetic works: the first a psychical, the second an intellectual quality. The psychical element lies in its pervading sense of mystery; the intellectual, in the crystalline simplicity with which this sense of mystery is expressed.

Kubla Khan[1]
Or a Vision in a Dream. A Fragment.

In Xanadu[2] did Kubla Khan
A stately pleasure-dome[3] decree:
Where Alph[4], the sacred river, ran
Through caverns measureless to man
    Down to a sunless sea.
So twice five miles[5] of fertile ground
With walls and towers were girdled round[6]:
And there were gardens bright with sinuous rills,
Where blossomed many an incense-bearing[7] tree;
And here were forests ancient as the hills,
Enfolding sunny spots of greenery.[8]

But oh! that deep romantic chasm which slanted
Down the green hill athwart[9] a cedarn cover[10]!

A savage place! as holy and enchanted
As e'er beneath a waning moon[11] was haunted
By woman wailing for her demon lover[12]!
And from this chasm, with ceaseless turmoil seething,
As if this earth in fast thick pants[13] were breathing,
A mighty fountain momently was forced[14]:
Amid whose swift half-intermitted burst[15]
Huge fragments vaulted like rebounding hail,
Or chaffy grain beneath the thresher's flail:[16]
And 'mid these dancing rocks[17] at once and ever
It flung up momently the sacred river.
Five miles meandering with a mazy motion[19]
Through wood and dale the sacred river ran,
Then reached the caverns measureless to man,
And sank in tumult to a lifeless ocean:
And 'mid this tumult Kubla heard from far
Ancestral voices prophesying war[20]!

The shadow of the dome of pleasure
Floated midway on the waves;
Where was heard the mingled measure[21]
From the fountain and the caves.
It was a miracle of rare device,
A sunny pleasure dome with caves of ice![22]

A damsel[23] with a dulcimer
In a vision once I saw:
It was an Abyssinian maid[24],
And on her dulcimer[25] she played,
Singing of Mount Abora[26].
Could I revive[27] within me
Her symphony and song,
To such a deep delight 'twould win me[28],
That with music loud and long,
I would build that dome in air,
That sunny dome! Those caves of ice!
And all who heard should see them there,
And all should cry, Beware! Beware!

His flashing eyes, his floating hair[29]!
Weave a circle round him thrice[30],
And close your eyes with holy dread,
For he on honey-dew hath fed,
And drunk the milk of Paradise[31].

1. 关于该诗的写作，有一个众所周知的故事：据说有一天晚上柯勒律治抽鸦片之后昏昏入睡，梦中他写了一首诗。醒来时他几乎能把全诗背诵出来，于是立即抄录。据诗人自己说，全诗约有二三百行，但写出来的只有所选这一段。之所以未能完成，是因为写到这一片断的最后一行时，有访客把他叫走。个把小时回来之后，其余的诗句都记不起来了。该篇短诗尽管不完整，但诗人独特的风格——奇特的想象，神秘的感觉，富于音乐性的文字，在这短短的五十余行尽显无余。Kubla Khan 即中国元朝皇帝忽必烈汗，又称薛禅皇帝，汗即可汗的简称，意为“最高统治者”。至元元年（1264 年）迁都燕京，后改大都。至元八年（1271 年），始定国号为元。
2. Xanadu：又作 Xamdu，上都，在今内蒙古自治区内。忽必烈汗定都大都（北京）后，上都仍为行宫。
3. pleasure-dome：逍遥宫，是 decree（下令修建）的宾语。dome: stately building.
4. Alph：诗人梦中的河。
5. twice five miles：十英里。
6. girdle：surround，环绕。
7. incense-bearing：开着香花的。
8. 诗歌第一、二节描写忽必烈围圈三十余里的肥沃土地建造豪华的园林，园中有古老的树木，芬芳馥郁，绿荫投射出点点阳光。
9. athwart：passing through，穿过。
10. a cedarn cover：松林。cedarn 是诗的用语，即 cedar，雪松；cover，覆盖物，此处意为 wood。弥尔顿曾写过，“And west winds with musky wing / About the cedarn alleys fling / Nard and cassia's balmy smells”(*Comus*)；丁尼生也曾写过，“The carven cedarn doors”（“Arabian Nights”）。
11. a waning moon：下弦月，据迷信说法是不祥的征兆。
12. 第 15～16 行描写经常徘徊在下弦月下哭着等待冥界情人（demon-lover）的女人，增添了这片荒山野地（a savage place）的浪漫奇幻的（romantic，第 12 行）气氛。
13. thick pants：频频急促的喘息，指泉水好像是因大地急促呼吸而喷涌出来似的。
14. A mighty fountain momently was forced：每时每刻都喷出强有力的泉水，momently 即 every moment。
15. swift half-intermitted burst：几乎毫不间断地迸发。

16. 第 20～22 行描写急流有时受到乱石阻遏，流势稍缓，但忽然又浪涛汹涌，犹如猛烈的冰雹，或打谷时的谷壳飞扬。
17. 'mid：amid，第 29 行同。these dancing rocks 在喷涌的泉水冲击下，岩石看上去也像在跳跃。
18. It：主语 the sacred river 的重复，即 The sacred river it (flung up momently)。
19. Five miles meandering with a mazy motion：迷宫般蜿蜒曲折地流淌五英里。此行由于"m"音多而加强了溪水缓慢流淌的意味。
20. Kubla heard from far / Ancestral voices prophesying war：该句的意思是忽必烈汗从祖宗的声音中听到了战争的预言。
21. measure：rhythm，节奏。
22. 在第 31～36 行中，诗人想象豪华的宫殿在浪涛中浮现出倒影，他仿佛听到喷泉和洞穴发出交织在一起的共鸣声。
23. damsel：maiden 的古用法。自此行起，诗歌先后描写了一位操琴的少女和一位迷狂的诗人，虽与忽必烈汗毫无关联，但作为梦境的片断，在浪漫奇幻的情调上与诗的前一部分保持一致。
24. Abyssinian maid：阿比西尼亚女郎。Abyssinia 位于非洲东部，现称 Ethiopia（埃塞俄比亚）。
25. dulcimer：类似于扬琴的一种古乐器。
26. Mount Abora：诗人梦中的山。
27. Could I revive：If I could revive.
28. To such a deep delight 'twould win me：正常的结构是 'twould (it would) win me to (bring me) such a deep delight。
29. His flashing eyes，his floating hair：眼睛闪光，头发飘扬，如同神灵附体而发狂。相传这是诗人获得灵感时的表现。
30. Weave a circle round him thrice：巫师或女巫在施法时都以某种方式与"3"这个神秘的数字（mystic number）相联系。在《古舟之咏》中，柯勒律治为制造神秘气氛曾反复使用过这个数字，如"And he stopped one of three"（第 3 行），"And listens like a three years' child"（第 15 行），"Quoth she, and whistles thrice"（第 198 行），"I saw a third—I heard his voice"（第 508 行）。另外，3 的倍数 9 也是传统意义上所谓神秘的数，如莎士比亚《麦克白》中女巫的话："Thrice to thine，and thrice to mine, /And thrice again to make up nine."
31. the milk of Paradise：天堂的乳汁。据柏拉图《伊安篇》所说，有灵感的诗人如同酒神的狂女，从诗神（the Muses）的河里汲取乳蜜。

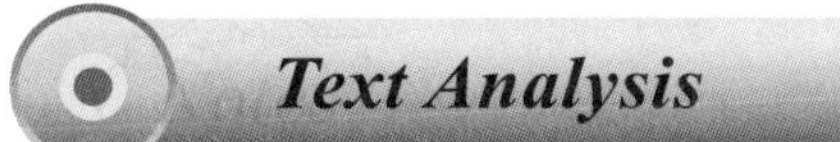

Text Analysis

The poem is written in iambic tetrameter and alternating rhyme schemes. The first stanza is written in tetrameter with a rhyme scheme of abaabccdede, alternating between staggered rhymes and couplets. The second stanza expands into tetrameter and follows roughly the same rhyming pattern, but expanded—abaabccddffgghiihjj. The third stanza tightens into tetrameter and rhymes ababcc. The fourth stanza continues the tetrameter of the third and rhymes abccbdedefgfffghhg. Coleridge's masterful use of meter and rhyme results in the chant-like, musical incantations of the text.

The first three stanzas of the poem are products of pure imagination: the pleasure-dome of Kubla Khan is not a useful metaphor for anything in particular (though in the context of the poem's history, it becomes a metaphor for the monument of imagination); however, it is a fantastically prodigious descriptive act. The poem becomes especially evocative when, after the second stanza, the meter suddenly tightens; the resulting lines are terse and solid, almost beating out the sound of the war drums ("The shadow of the dome of pleasure / Floated midway on the waves...").

The fourth stanza states the theme of the poem as a whole (though "Kubla Khan" is almost impossible to be considered as a unified whole, as its parts are so sharply divided). The speaker says that he once had a vision of the damsel singing of Mount Abora; this vision becomes a metaphor for Coleridge's vision of the 300-hundred-line masterpiece he never completed. The speaker insists that if he could only "revive" within him "her symphony and song", he would recreate the pleasure-dome out of music and words, and take on the persona of the magician or visionary. His hearers would recognize the dangerous power of the vision, which would manifest itself in his "flashing eyes" and "floating hair". But, awestruck, they would nonetheless dutifully take part in the ritual, recognizing that "he on honey-dew hath fed / And drunk the milk of Paradise".

Questions

1. A contrast is set up between the first stanza and the second. What is this contrast for?

2. In lines 37 to 41, why does the author suddenly focus on a girl, which seems incompatible to the poem? What is the function of this transformation?

3. Is the "pleasure-dome" in conflict with "caves of ice"? Why or Why not?

4. Could you tell the similarities and differences between "Kubla Khan" and "Tintern Abbey"?

Chinese Translation

忽必烈汗

忽必烈汗在上都曾经
下令造一座堂皇的安乐殿堂：
这地方有圣河亚佛流奔，
穿过深不可测的洞门，
直流入不见阳光的海洋。
有方圆五英里肥沃的土壤，
四周给围上楼塔和城墙：
那里有花园，蜿蜒的溪河在其间闪耀，
园里树枝上鲜花盛开，一片芬芳；
这里有森林，跟山峦同样古老，
围住了洒满阳光的一块块青草草场。

但是，啊！那深沉而奇异的巨壑
沿青山斜裂，横过伞盖的柏树！
野蛮的地方，既神圣而又着了魔——
好像有女人在衰落的月色里出没，
为她的魔鬼情郎而凄声嚎哭！
巨壑下，不绝的喧嚣在沸腾汹涌，
似乎这土地正喘息在快速而猛烈的悸动中，
从这巨壑里，不断迸出股猛烈的地泉；
在它那时断时续的涌迸之间，
巨大的石块飞跃着像反跳的冰雹，
或者像打稻人连枷下一撮撮新稻；
从这些舞蹈的岩石中，时时刻刻
迸发出那条神圣的溪河。
迷乱地移动着，蜿蜒了五英里地方，
那神圣的溪河流过了峡谷和森林，
于是到达了深不可测的洞门，
在喧嚣中沉入了没有生命的海洋；
从那喧嚣中忽必烈远远听到
祖先的喊声预言着战争的凶兆！

安乐的宫殿有倒影
宛在水波的中央漂动；
这儿能听见和谐的音韵
来自那地泉和那岩洞。
这是个奇迹呀，算得是稀有的技巧，
阳光灿烂的安乐宫，连同那雪窟冰窖！

有一回我在幻象中见到
一个手拿德西马琴的姑娘：
那是个阿比西尼亚少女，
在她的琴上她奏出乐曲，
歌唱着阿伯若山。
如果我心中能再度产生
她的音乐和歌唱，
我将被引入如此深切的欢欣，
以至于我要用音乐高朗而又长久
在空中建造那安乐宫廷，
那阳光照临的宫廷，那雪窟冰窖！
谁都能见到这宫殿，只要听见了乐音。
他们全都会喊叫：当心！当心！
他飘动的头发，他闪光的眼睛！
织一个圆圈，把他三道围住，
闭下你两眼，带着神圣的恐惧，
因为他一直吃着蜜样甘露，
一直饮着天堂的琼浆仙乳。

（屠岸 译）

Unit 10 George Gordon Byron

Introduction to the Author

George Gordon Byron was born on January 22, 1788 in Aberdeen, Scotland. He inherited his family's English title at the age of ten, becoming Lord Byron. He studied at Aberdeen Grammar School and then Trinity College in Cambridge. During this time Byron collected and published his first two volumes of poetry. The first, *Fugitive Pieces*, published anonymously, was printed in 1806 and contained a miscellany of poems, some of which were written when Byron was only fourteen. As a whole, the collection was poorly received. The next year Byron published his second collection, *Hours of Idleness*, dealing with childish recollections and early friendships, showing the influence of 18th century traditions.

By Byron's 20th birthday, he faced overwhelming debt. Though his second collection received an initially favorable response, a disturbingly negative review was printed in January, 1808, followed by harsh criticisms a few months later. His response was a satire, *English Bards and Scotch Reviewers*, which attacked all literary celebrities of the day including the Lake Poets. After enjoying the success of his counter-attack, Byron set out on a two-year tour, traveling to Europe. What he saw and did on the way provided him with rich writing materials and inspired his future writing.

Byron returned to England in the summer of 1811, having completed the opening cantos of *Childe Harold*'s *Pilgrimage*, a poem which tells the story of a world-weary young man looking for meaning in the world. The publication of the two cantos brought instant fame to Byron. His fame as a poet rose steadily in the ensuing years. Several narrative poems appeared: "Giaour" (1813), "The Bride of Abydos" (1813), "The Corsair" (1814), "Lara" (1814), "Parisina" (1816), and "The Siege of Corinth" (1816). With an oriental setting, these poems are sometimes called "Oriental Tales". In them appeared the "Byronic heroes", characterized by fiery passions, great talent, unbending will, and rebellion against tyranny and injustice.

After his rise to fame, Byron used his popularity to speak in favor of workers' rights and social reform. He also continued to publish romantic tales in verse. His personal life, however, remained unhappy. He was married and divorced. The divorce, together with the following love affairs, evoked a wholesale attack on him. He was forced to leave England for good on

April 25, 1816. Byron first went to Switzerland, where he met Shelley and made friends with him. In the autumn of 1816, Byron settled in Italy and began writing his masterpiece Don Juan, a narrative poem loosely based on a legendary hero. From 1816 to 1822, he finished several works, including the famous "Sonnet on Chillon", a narrative poem "The Prisoner of Chillon" (1816), two poetical dramas, "Manfred" (1817) and "Cain" (1821), and a long poem *The Age of Bronze* (1822). He also spent much of his time engaged in the Greek fight for independence and planned to join a battle against a Turkish-held fortress when he fell ill, becoming increasingly sick with persistent colds and fevers.

When he died on April 19, 1824, at the age of 36, *Don Juan* was yet to be finished, though 17 cantos had been written. Today, Byron's Don Juan is considered one of the greatest long poems in English since Milton's Paradise Lost.

She Walks in Beauty[1]

She walks in beauty, like the night
　　Of cloudless climes[2] and starry skies;
And all that's best of dark and bright[3]
　　Meet in her aspect[4] and her eyes:
Thus mellowed to that tender light[5]
Which heaven to gaudy day denies[6].

One shade the more, one ray the less[7],
　　Had half impaired[8] the nameless grace
Which waves in every raven tress[9],
　　Or softly lightens o'er her face[10];
Where thoughts serenely sweet express
　　How pure, how dear their dwelling place.

And on that cheek, and o'er that brow,
　　So soft, so calm, yet eloquent[11],
The smiles that win[12], the tints that glow[13],
　　But tell of days in goodness spent[14],
A mind at peace with all below[15],
　　A heart whose love is innocent[16]!

1. 此诗是拜伦早期的恋爱抒情诗，据说是青年拜伦在一次舞会之后写成的。在这次舞会上，他遇到了威尔莫夫人（Lady Wilmot Horton），当时夫人身着丧服，上面缀有许多金属小亮片。
2. clime：同 climate，多见于诗中。
3. all that's best of dark and bright：明与暗的精华。
4. aspect：面容，仪表。
5. Thus mellow'd to that tender light：由于明与暗的精华在她的面容与眼神中融合在一起，因此既不耀眼，也不暗淡，而是一片柔光。
6. Which heaven to gaudy day denies：which heaven denies to gaudy day，意思是明耀的白昼，怎能与这柔和之光相比。
7. One shade the more, one ray the less：与宋玉在《登徒子好色赋》中描述的类似："增之一分则太长，减之一分则太短，施朱则太赤，著粉则太白"。
8. Had half impaired：would have half impaired，古体英语中的虚拟语气形式。
9. raven tress：乌黑的长发。
10. softly lightens o'er her face：在她脸上布了一层淡淡的光晕。
11. So soft, so calm, yet eloquent：eloquent 在此处是"富有表现力的"之意。
12. The smiles that win：笑脸盈盈。
13. the tints that glow：容颜焕发。
14. But tell of days in goodness spent：But tell of days spent in goodness；but：only；goodness 指"善良的德行"。
15. A mind at peace with all below 是 tell of 的宾语。all below 指世上万物。
16. A heart whose love is innocent 也是 tell of 的宾语。

Text Analysis

This poem begins with the image of a woman who "walks in beauty like the night", which might arouse the readers to ask how she could be seen. That question is answered in the next line when the speaker says that it is a cloudless night with stars twinkling in the sky, thus bringing into focus the imagery of light and darkness. In the first four lines, the technique of enjambment is used, i.e., the first line is not punctuated and is followed by a line that clarifies the first statement.

In the next few lines the readers' attention is drawn to the word "meet": it stresses the contrasts in the woman being described. The imagery presented in the first two lines reappears in these lines, and the contrast of light and dark is again built up. The opposites "meet" in this woman: just as enjambment and a change in meter are joined as mechanisms in the poem, the unlikely pair of darkness and light meet in her. The light and dark appear in her face and in her eyes. Her face contains light alabaster skin, yet is engulfed in dark hair, and her eyes are dark in the iris, in contrast with their whites. This repeat of the contrast between light and dark reinforces the imagery introduced at the beginning of the poem. The poem goes on to say that if she were to have even one shade more darkness, or a bit less light, her beauty would be, though not wholly ruined, "half impair'd".

Towards the end of the poem, the narrator speaks of the woman's inner thoughts and how they are all good, which serves to convey the woman as pure, making her all the more beautiful. The reference to her angelic looks provides a window into her morality as a person, and enhances her beauty as a result. The last stanza consists of three lines of visage description and three lines of character description. Hence, the poem presents us a perfect lady who is not only endowed with a beautiful outer appearance but also with a pure and kind inner heart.

The rhythm and language of this poem also contribute to the theme of beauty. Composed of three six-line stanzas, the poem follows a basic iambic tetrameter with a rhyme scheme of ababab, cdcdcd, efefef. The alliteration and rhyme throughout the poem help to bring out the effect of a delightful melody. Meanwhile, the expressive and vivid language, the adjectives in particular, not only render a beautiful poetic atmosphere but also create a gentle, kind, and ideal image of beauty.

Questions

1. Why is the lady compared to the night in the first stanza?

2. Can you name at least three rhetorical devices applied in this poem? What is the function of each rhetorical device?

3. What is the connection between the rhythm of the poem and its mood and tone?

4. What do you think is the theme of the poem?

Chinese Translation

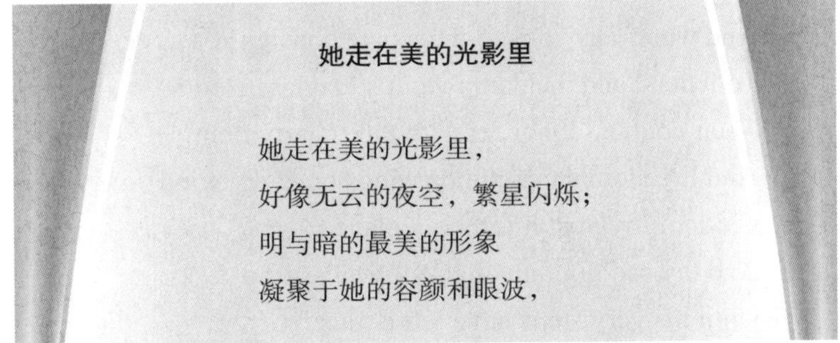

她走在美的光影里

她走在美的光影里，
好像无云的夜空，繁星闪烁；
明与暗的最美的形象
凝聚于她的容颜和眼波，

融成一片淡雅的清光——
浓艳的白天得不到的恩泽。

多一道阴影，少一缕光芒，
都会有损于这无名之美；
美在她缕缕黑发间飘带，
也在她颜面上洒布柔辉；
愉悦的思想在那里颂扬，
这种圣寓所的纯洁高贵。

安详，和婉，富于情态——
在那脸颊上，在那眉宇间，
迷人的笑容，照人的光彩，
显示温情伴随着芳年，
恬静的、涵容一切的胸怀，
蕴蓄着真纯爱情的心田！

（查良铮　译）

On the Castle of Chillon[1]

Eternal Spirit of the chainless Mind[2]!
Brightest in dungeons[3], Liberty! thou art[4],
For there thy habitation is the heart—
The heart which love of Thee alone can bind;
And when Thy sons to fetters are consign'd.
To fetters, and the damp vault's[5] dayless gloom,
Their country conquers with their martyrdom[6],
And Freedom's fame finds wings on every wind[7].
Chillon! thy prison is a holy place
And thy sad floor an altar—for 'twas trod[8],
Until his very steps have left a trace

Worn as if thy cold pavement were a sod,
By Bonnivard[9]! —May none those marks efface!
For they appeal from tyranny to God[10].

Notes

1. Castle Chillon，锡雍城堡，瑞士最著名的旅游观光点之一，位于日内瓦湖中的岛上，该湖处于法国、意大利北部和瑞士西部的交接点。锡雍城堡只有其大门通过一座桥与外界相连。它广为人所知的地牢，是由11世纪修筑完成的城堡的底部基石建成的[“锡雍”(chillon)在法文中是“石头”的意思]。它曾出现在卢梭、雨果和大仲马等作家的笔下，而最著名的当属拜伦的这首诗篇。
2. Eternal Spirit of the chainless Mind：指 Liberty。
3. dungeon：地牢。
4. art：are 的古用法。
5. the damp vault：潮湿的地窖。
6. conquers with their martyrdom：由于他们的殉难而获胜，with 指 on account of。
7. wind：读 /waind/，与第4行的 bind 押韵。
8. 'twas trod：it was trod；“it”指地牢的地面。
9. Bonnivard: Francois de Bonnivard，born in 1496, became prior of the monastery of St. Victor near Geneva，and conspired with a band of ardent patriots of that city to throw off the yoke of the Duke of Savoy and establish a free republic. For this he was twice imprisoned by the Duke；his second imprisonment was in the Castle of Chillon and lasted from 1530-1536.
10. appeal from tyranny to God: call on God in protest against tyranny.

Text Analysis

Lord Byron was a passionate advocator of freedom and liberty and died in Greek war for independence from the Ottoman Empire. The eternal and everlasting spirit of the chainless mind is free even when his body is in chains. The abode of liberty is the heart in which only love alone can bind together and unite the spirit of patriotism. This poem definitely reveals Byron's strong love of liberty.

When ardent patriots were captured or arrested they were sent to be imprisoned in the dungeons of Chillon indefinitely in the darkness of a cold prison house. The dirty floor of the dungeon has become an altar of prayer for the imprisoned patriots. The Castle of Chillon is a symbol of tyranny and oppression because in it many a fighter for freedom was condemned to live in fetters and die. Bonnivard who rose against tyranny was imprisoned there. But Bonnivard has turned the prison into a church by his sacred presence. The lover of freedom remains free even when in prison because the seat of freedom is the heart which nothing but the love of God can ever bind. The spirit of freedom burns brightest when the body is in chains and the nation gains freedom through the martyrdom of chained patriots. T. S. Eliot once asserted that the image of Byron shares, to some extent, Shelley's Promethean attitude, and the Romantic passion for liberty.

Questions

1. How do you understand the Castle of Chillon symbolically?
2. Do you think the character of Bonnivard is a "Byronic hero"?
3. What should a man fight for according to the speaker?
4. What is the difference between Bonnivard and a hero in your mind?

Chinese Translation

咏锡雍

你磅礴的精神之永恒的幽灵！
　　自由呵，你在地牢里才最灿烂！
　　因为在那儿你居于人的心间——
那心呵，它只听命对你的爱情；
当你的信徒们被戴上了枷锁，
　　在暗无天日的地牢里牺牲，
　　他们的祖国因此受人尊敬，
自由的声誉随着每阵风传播。
锡雍！你的监狱成了一隅圣地，
　　你阴郁的地面变成了神坛，
因为博尼瓦尔在那里走来走去，
　　印下深痕，仿佛你冰冷的石板
是生草的泥土！别涂去那足迹！
　　因为它在暴政下向上帝求援。

（查良铮　译）

Unit 11　Percy Bysshe Shelley

Introduction to the Author

Percy Bysshe Shelley (1792-1822), one of the most well-known English Romantic poets, was born in the year. Considered as too radical in his poetry and his political and social views, Shelley did not achieve fame during his lifetime; recognition of his status as a poet has been gradually grown after his death.

The "Bysshe" is from his grandfather, a Peer of the Realm. As the eldest son among the six children, Percy was beloved and admired by his family. At the age of twelve, he entered Eton College where he stayed for six years. Dr. James Lind, the physician to the royal household at Windsor, idealized as a kind of substitute father figure, shadowed strong influence upon young Percy for his wide knowledge and free spirit. Dr. Lind's library enabled him to read extensively ranging from science and magic to philosophy and literature. Though he gained his fame mainly in poetry, his first publication was a Gothic novel *Zastrozzi* (1810), followed by some poems he had written at Eton in *Original Poetry*. Early reviews considered his works sentimental and absurd for his enthusiasm in horror. The later subject matters of the typical Shelley grew from these doggerel verses: poetry, love, sorrow, hope, nature and politics.

In 1810, Shelley entered Oxford; There he met another freshman, Thomas Jefferson Hogg, and they shared common interests in various fields with each other. During his brief stay in Oxford, he published three volumes, among which their joint collection of poems, *Posthumous Fragments of Margaret Nicholson* (1810, the title character taken from "that noted female who attempted the life of the King [George Ⅲ] in 1786"), including Gothic and melancholy lyrics as well as some political ones, notably as the beginning of Shelley's lifelong attack on monarchy and authority. Shelley was expelled from Oxford for his *The Necessity of Atheism*. The insistence to the belief led to his break away from his father, which entailed financial distress for Shelley. The resulting estrangement from his father was completed when Shelley eloped with Harriet Westbrook, a 16-year-old daughter of a coffee-house keeper. Thus early in his life Shelley demonstrated his idealism by his willingness to sacrifice comfort and security rather than compromise his principles or beliefs.

Throughout Shelley's short and dramatic life, the major themes include: rebellion against authority, interchange with nature, power of visionary imagination and of poetry, pursuit of ideal love, and the untamed spirit ever in search of freedom. Though he shared many basic themes and symbols with his great contemporaries, he has unique contribution to Romanticism: the creation and fashion of powerful symbols in his visionary pursuit of the ideal, at the same time maintaining a deep sense of skepticism. His thought is characterized by his persistence in taking the controversial side of issues, even risking being unpopular and rebellious. His works are known for being enigmatic and inspiring, and for their restlessness and brooding.

On July 8, 1822, shortly before his 30th birthday, Shelley was drowned in a storm while attempting to sail from Leghorn to La Spezia, Italy.

Ode to the West Wind[1]

I

O wild West Wind[2], thou breath of Autumn's being[3],
Thou, from whose unseen presence the leaves dead
Are driven, like ghosts from an enchanter fleeing[4],

Yellow, and black, and pale, and hectic red,
Pestilence-stricken multitudes[5]: O thou,
Who chariotest[6] to their dark wintry bed

The wingèd seeds, where they lie cold and low,
Each like a corpse within its grave, until
Thine azure sister of the Spring shall blow

Her clarion o'er the dreaming earth, and fill
(Driving sweet buds like flocks to feed in air)
With living hues and odours plain and hill:[7]

Wild Spirit, which art moving everywhere;
Destroyer and preserver; hear, oh hear[8]!

II

Thou on whose stream, mid the steep sky's commotion,

Loose clouds like earth's decaying leaves are shed,
Shook from the tangled boughs of Heaven and Ocean,

Angels of rain and lightning:[9] there are spread
On the blue surface of thine aëry surge,
Like the bright hair uplifted from the head

Of some fierce Maenad, even from the dim verge
Of the horizon to the zenith's height,
The locks of the approaching storm.[10] Thou dirge

Of the dying year, to which this closing night
Will be the dome of a vast sepulchre,
Vaulted with all thy congregated might

Of vapours, from whose solid atmosphere
Black rain, and fire, and hail will burst：oh hear![11]

Ⅲ

Thou who didst waken from his summer dreams
The blue Mediterranean, where he lay,
Lulled by the coil of his crystàlline streams[12],

Beside a pumice isle in Baiae's bay,
And saw in sleep old palaces and towers
Quivering within the wave's intenser day,

All overgrown with azure moss and flowers
So sweet, the sense faints picturing them![13] Thou
For whose path the Atlantic's level powers

Cleave themselves into chasms, while far below[14]
The sea-blooms and the oozy woods which wear
The sapless foliage of the ocean, know

Thy voice, and suddenly grow grey with fear,
And tremble and despoil themselves：oh hear![15]

Ⅳ

If I were a dead leaf thou mightest bear;
If I were a swift cloud to fly with thee;
A wave to pant beneath thy power, and share

The impulse of thy strength, only less free
Than thou, O uncontrollable![16] If even
I were as in my boyhood, and could be

The comrade of thy wanderings over Heaven,
As then, when to outstrip thy skyey speed
Scarce seemed a vision;[17] I would ne'er have striven

As thus with thee in prayer in my sore need.
Oh, lift me as a wave, a leaf, a cloud[18]!
I fall upon the thorns of life! I bleed!

A heavy weight of hours has chained and bowed
One too like thee: tameless, and swift, and proud.[19]

Ⅴ

Make me thy lyre, even as the forest is:
What if my leaves are falling like its own![20]
The tumult of thy mighty harmonies

Will take from both a deep, autumnal tone,
Sweet though in sadness.[21] Be thou, Spirit fierce,
My spirit! Be thou me, impetuous one![22]

Drive my dead thoughts over the universe
Like withered leaves to quicken a new birth![23]
And, by the incantation of this verse,

Scatter, as from an unextinguished hearth
Ashes and sparks, my words among mankind![24]
Be through my lips to unawakened earth

The trumpet of a prophecy[25]! O Wind,
If Winter comes, can Spring be far behind[26]?

1. 这首诗构思于 1819 年秋的一天，当时雪莱正在意大利佛罗伦萨（Florence）附近的阿诺（Arno）河畔的一片树林里散步，遭遇雨雹交加的风暴，有感而发写成此诗。第三节结尾处所提到的是博物学家十分熟悉的现象。如同陆上植物，海洋、河流和湖泊底部的水生植物同样感受到季节的交换，因此受到随着季节变化而变化的风的影响。

    这首诗是雪莱著名的抒情诗，是人类诗歌史上的珍品。全诗共五节，每节由十四行诗组成。从形式上看，五个小节格律完整，相对独立；前三节均以“oh hear!”结尾，语气上各节之间相互照应。从内容看，它们由中心统领，相互交融。第一节描写西风扫除林中残叶，吹送生命的种子，点出了西风既是毁灭者又是保护者的主题。第二节写西风在空中扫荡残云，呼唤暴雨雷电的来临。第三节表现西风掀起大海的汹涌波涛，摧毁海底花树。每节各有意境，诗人幻想的翅膀飞翔在树林、天空和大海之间，歌唱西风摧枯拉朽、鼓舞新生的强大威力。第四节起由写景转向抒情，抒发诗人对西风的热爱和向往，和愿随西风而舞的心愿。最后，第五节中发出了愿与西风合二为一的澎湃情怀。
2. O wild West Wind：诗人在第一节中四次呼唤西风，心中沸腾的激情一触即发。
3. Autumn’s being：秋天的生命，拟人的修辞手法。being: existence，life.
4. Are driven, like ghosts from an enchanter fleeing：like a magician banishing ghosts or evil spirits, the West Wind sweeps away the dead leaves，像巫师驱鬼般，西风扫除了这些枯死的落叶。
5. These dead leaves are multicolored，but not beautiful in the way we usually think of autumn leaves. 这里诗人将不同颜色的叶子比作得了瘟疫的成堆的枯叶。
6. chariotest：spread，send，驱车送往。wintry：cold，寒冷的。
7. 第 7～12 行：西风将这些种子吹落地面，经过寒冷的冬天，当春风吹响她的喇叭，便会苏醒。这里多处用到了明喻和拟人的手法，如墓中的死尸，羊群的觅食等，既传神又达意。azure：blue，天蓝色；clarion：a kind of trumpet，喇叭。
8. Destroyer and preserver：it brings the death of winter，but also makes possible the regeneration of spring，破坏者兼保护者。hear, oh hear：此处表明说话者希望西风聆听正在发生的一切。
9. 第 15～18 行：诗人继续描绘西风。这一时段西风冲入云霄，将朵朵白云吹散得如溪流上漂浮的枯叶。树叶从树枝上坠落，云朵从天空和海洋的“树枝”（boughs）吹落，与“雨和电的使者”（Angels of rain and lightening）一道组成了天气系统。暴风骤雨即将来临。
10. 第 18～23 行：雪莱在此处精心设计了一个复杂的明喻描写西风带来的狂风巨浪。西风席卷的乌云（The locks of the approaching storm），已经布满蔚蓝色的水面（the airy “blue surface”），如同女祭司飘扬的头发（the bright hair uplifted from the head），从最低点（the dim verge of the horizon）到最高处（the zenith’s height）。Maenad：one of the wild, savage women who hang out with the god Dionysus in Greek mythology,

Notes

希腊神话中酒神狄俄尼索斯的女祭司，性格以狂野、不拘一格著称。诗人用狂野的女祭司四处飘扬的头发来形容密布的乌云，动感十足。

11. 第 23～28 行：这里用了一个恐怖的暗喻来显示西风可怕的力量。西风成了一曲挽歌（dirge: funeral songs），来标记过去一年的结束。残年的最后一夜（this closing night）像是巨大墓穴的拱顶，笼罩在密集的蒸汽之中。congregate：come together，聚集。might：power，力量。vapour：蒸汽，比 stream 含义广，常指由于温度变化而产生的气体。hail：precipitation of ice pellets when there are strong rising air currents，冰雹。此节末尾再次呼唤西风，但是其真正意图仍未表明。
12. 第三节起诗人继续展示西风的巨大威力。地中海的夏天以其宁静闻名，巴亚海湾是古罗马人的度假胜地。但是西风唤醒了沉睡的地中海，掀起了壮阔的波澜。lull：使入睡；coil：曲折的波漩。地中海在此拟作男性。
13. 第 33～36 行：在地中海的睡梦中，"他"梦见了巴亚海湾边古老的宫殿和楼阁已为青苔和花朵所覆盖，香气四溢，好一幅迷人的场景！ intenser：波浪在阳光的映射下色彩更加浓艳；the sense faints：宜人的香气把人的感觉器官也醉倒了。
14. 第 37、38 两行诗意地表现西风如何在地中海兴风作浪，同时也暗示地中海在西风的巨大力量下俯首称臣。level：the surface of the ocean，海平面；cleave：分开；chasm：深渊，峡谷。
15. 第 38～42 行：在大西洋的底部，不同的海洋植物听到西风的咆哮声瑟瑟发抖、自动消亡 (suddenly grow grey with fear，/ And tremble and despoil themselves)。sapless：withered，枯萎的；despoil：destroy and strip of its possession，夺取。
16. 第 43～47 行：从第四节起诗人更为明确地表达自己的意图。他期望自己是西风能够托起的一片枯叶（a dead leaf）或是一朵浮云（a swift cloud），甚至是能够感受到西风威力的波浪（a wave）。一系列的假设让他如西风般徜徉在想象的世界，无拘无束（uncontrollable）。
17. 第 47～51 行：诗人的妥协——即便成不了落叶和浮云，那让"我"回到我的少年时代，因为那时"我"和西风是"同志"[comrade(s)]，"我们"曾一道在天空漫步（thy wanderings over heaven）。诗人认为"我"在年少时期身体更为快捷，身形更为矫健，这样才能与凌厉的西风相匹配（outstrip thy skyey speed: keep up with the speedy pace of the West Wind）。
18. 第 51～53 行：sore need: the need / thought causing misery or pain or distress，恼火的。"我"若是更年轻、更有活力，便不至于像如今祈求西风的帮助：将我如水波、落叶和浮云一般举起（lift me as a wave, a leaf, a cloud!）。
19. 第 54～56 行：A heavy weight of hours has chained and bowed: the passage of time has weighed him down and bowed (but not yet broken) his spirit. 随着时间的流逝，"我"多次受挫，但是"我"依旧如西风般"骄傲、轻捷和不驯"（tameless, and swift, and proud）。
20. 第 57～58 行：最后，诗人终于向西风表达了自己的意愿——想成为它的竖琴。

lyre: the aeolian harp，竖琴，浪漫主义诗歌中常见的比喻，风吹竖琴琴弦时能发出自然之声。此处诗人自比竖琴，向往西风的弹奏，如同西风吹落了树叶，树枝依旧能发出声音。

21. 第 59～61 行：“我”和森林里的树木都在老去——树木正在掉叶子，不过当西风将“我”和树木都当作乐器，我们便能一起演奏甜蜜而忧伤的曲子（sweet though in sadness）。
22. 第 61～62 行：诗人开始转变策略，不再要求西风与其一同演奏，而是让二者合二为一（Be thou）。他希望西风狂野的力量能够加诸其身，甚至替代自己。
23. 第 63～64 行：将他的想法比作枯叶，希望西风将他的思想如同它吹扫落叶般吹向世界的各个角落，再像枯叶一样催生新的生命在春天到来。
24. 第 65～67 行：incantation of this verse—another metaphor to describe what he wants the wind to do to his thoughts, his own words—perhaps the words of this very poem，这一篇符咒般的诗歌如同还未熄灭的炉火中的灰烬向人间散播。
25. 第 68～69 行：诗人又回到之前乐器的比喻，但这一次他成了向世人宣讲预言的喇叭（trumpet），与第一节中 clarion 相呼应。
26. 第 69～70 行：全诗以一个看似非常简单的问题结尾。这是个设问句，诗人要表达的意思已然隐含在其中，不需要回答。诗人将象征的意义附加到季节的更替上，让读者意识到这不仅仅是年轮的问题，其真实意图在于点明在死亡或者腐朽即将到来之际，重生就在眼前。当然，他本人对此持积极的态度。

Text Analysis

Shelley develops the poem with terze rime in Dante's *Divine Comedy* and Shakespearean sonnet. Each stanza has fourteen lines, with four terze rima and a couplet. The run-on lines apply iambic pentameter rhyming aba, bcb, cdc, ded, ee. The sublime ideal, conspicuous natural images, changing musical effects and strict rhyming scheme win harmonious unification in the poem.

This is an ode, a choral celebration, and the tone of the speaker understandably includes excitement, pleasure, joy, and hope. Shelley draws a parallel between the seasonal cycles of the wind and that of his ever-changing spirit. Thematically, then, this poem is about the inspiration Shelley draws from nature. The “breath of autumn being” is Shelley's atheistic version of the Christian Holy Spirit. Instead of relying on traditional religion, Shelley focuses his praise around the wind's role on the various cycles in nature—death, regeneration, “preservation”, and “destruction”. The speaker begins by praising the wind, using anthropomorphic techniques (wintry bed, chariots, corpses, and clarions) to personalize the great natural spirit in hopes that it will somehow heed his plea. The speaker is aware of his own mortality and the immortality of his subject. This drives him to beg that he too can be inspired ("make me thy lyre") and carried ("be through my lips to unawakened earth") through space and time.

Shelley, like all the other Romantic poets, constantly tries to achieve a transcendence to the sublime. In "Ode to the West Wind", Shelley uses the wind as a power of change that flow through history, civilization, religions and human life itself. In poems such as "Stanzas Written in Dejection Near Naples" Shelley uses images of "lightning" and "flashing" to help demonstrate that he can only attain a partial sublime unlike the poet William Wordsworth. Perhaps that's why he tries to give rebirth to his individual imagination. Even the trees that will grow from "the winged seeds" are not totally new, but that is the point Shelley is trying to make. He feels himself to be part of a continuing cycle. Since Shelley is an atheist the only way his soul can live on is through the "incantation" of his words. It seems that it is only in his death that the "Wild Spirit" could be lifted "as a wave, a leaf, a cloud" to blow free in the "Wild West Wind".

Questions

1. Is the speaker in "Ode to the West Wind" a representative of all mankind, or is he unique or special in some way?

2. The poem itself ends with a question: "If Winter comes, can Spring be far behind?" Can it? Can we assume that every kind of decay and death that we compare to the desolation of winter will always result in a rebirth?

3. Why is wildness so important here? The West Wind is wild, the clouds it blows around are like the hair of crazy Maenad, and the speaker wishes he were also "uncontrollable". What can be created through wildness that isn't possible to be within control? Why does a poem that stresses wildness have such a controlled form and meter?

4. Why the West Wind is so important according to Shelley? Why not the East Wind or the Winter Wind?

Chinese Translation

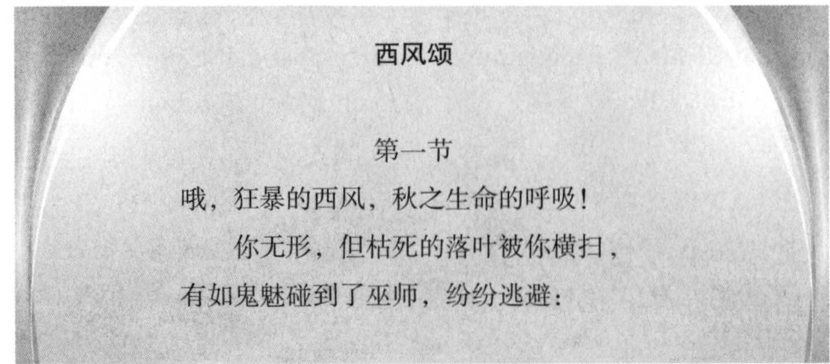

西风颂

第一节

哦，狂暴的西风，秋之生命的呼吸！
　　你无形，但枯死的落叶被你横扫，
有如鬼魅碰到了巫师，纷纷逃避：

黄的，黑的，灰的，红得像患肺痨，
　　呵，重染疫疠的一群：西风呵，是你
以车驾把有翼的种子催送到

黑暗的冬床上，它们就躺在那里，
　　像是墓中的死尸，冰冷，深藏，低贱，
直等到春天，你碧空的姊妹吹起

她的喇叭，在沉睡的大地上响遍，
　　（唤出嫩芽，像羊群一样，觅食空中）
将色和香充满了山峰和平原：

不羁的精灵呵，你无处不远行；
破坏者兼保护者：听吧，你且聆听！

第二节

没入你的急流，当高空一片混乱，
　　流云像大地的枯叶一样被撕扯

脱离天空和海洋的纠缠的枝干，

成为雨和电的使者：它们飘落
　　在你的磅礴之气的蔚蓝的波面，
有如狂女的飘扬的头发在闪烁，

从天穹的最遥远而模糊的边沿
　　直抵九霄的中天，到处都在摇曳
欲来雷雨的卷发。对濒死的一年

你唱出了葬歌，而这密集的黑夜
　　将成为它广大墓陵的一座圆顶，
里面正有你的万钧之力的凝结；

那是你的浑然之气，从它会迸涌
黑色的雨、冰雹和火焰：哦，你听！

第三节

是你，你将蓝色的地中海唤醒，
　　而它曾经昏睡了一整个夏天，
被澄澈水流的回旋催眠入梦，

就在巴亚海湾的一个浮石岛边，
　　它梦见了古老的宫殿和楼阁
在水天辉映的波影里抖颤，

而且都生满青苔，开满花朵，
　　那芬芳真迷人欲醉！呵，为了给你
让一条路，大西洋的汹涌的浪波

把自己向两边劈开，而深在渊底
　　那海洋中的花草和泥污的森林
虽然枝叶扶疏，却没有精力；

听到你的声音，它们已吓得发青：
一边颤栗，一边自动萎缩：哦，你听！

第四节

哎，假如我是一片枯叶被你浮起，
　　假如我是能和你飞跑的云雾，
是一个波浪，和你的威力同喘息，

假如我分有你的脉搏，仅仅不如
　　你那么自由，哦，无法约束的生命！
假如我能像在少年时，凌风而舞

便成了你的伴侣，悠游于天空
　　（因为呵，那时候，要想追你上云霄，
似乎并非梦幻），我就不致像如今

这样焦躁地要和你争相祈祷。
　　哦，举起我吧，当我是水波、树叶、浮云！
我跌在生活的荆棘上，我流血了！

这被岁月的重轭所制伏的生命
原是和你一样的：骄傲、轻捷而不驯。

第五节

把我当作你的竖琴吧，有如树林：
　　尽管我的叶落了，那有什么关系！
你巨大的合奏所振起的乐音

将染有树林和我的深邃的秋意：
　　虽忧伤而甜蜜。呵，但愿你给予我
狂暴的精神！奋勇者呵，让我们合一！

请把我枯死的思想向世界吹落，
　　让它像枯叶一样促成新的生命！
哦，请听从这一篇符咒似的诗歌，

就把我的话语，像是灰烬和火星
　　从还未熄灭的炉火向人间播散！
让预言的喇叭通过我的嘴唇

把昏睡的大地唤醒吧！西风啊
如果冬天来了，春天还会远吗？

（查良铮　译）

Ozymandias[1]

I met a traveller from an antique land[2]
Who said：“Two vast and trunkless legs of stone
Stand in the desert… Near them, on the sand,
Half sunk, a shattered visage lies, whose frown,

And wrinkled lip, and sneer of cold command[3],
Tell that its sculptor well those passions read[4]
Which yet survive, stamped on these lifeless things[5],
The hand that mocked them, and the heart that fed:
And on the pedestal[6] these words appear:
My name is Ozymandias, king of kings[7]:
Look on my Works, ye Mighty, and despair!
Nothing beside remains[8]. Round the decay
Of that colossal wreck, boundless and bare
The lone and level sands stretch far away[9]".

1. 该诗写于1817年12月或1818年1月，题目取自奥西曼德斯，即公元前13世纪的埃及王拉米西斯二世（Rameses Ⅱ，公元前1304—公元前1227）的希腊名字。拉米西斯二世是《圣经》中的人物。据《出埃及记》，摩西曾与他进行过不懈的斗争。公元前1世纪古希腊历史学家狄奥多如斯·西库鲁斯（Diodorus Siculus）曾提到过他，说他为自己建造了埃及最大的陵墓，底座上镌刻着文字："我是奥西曼德斯，万王之王；若有人想知道我是谁以及我躺在哪里，就让他在某些功绩上胜过我。"他在平沙无垠的大漠建立巨大的狮身人面像，以纪念自己的威权和业绩。历史上的奥西曼德斯是一位专横暴虐的帝王。雪莱的诗歌取材于此，但是诗歌的内容是一位旅行者讲述他在埃及的荒漠里所见到的残存的雕像以及底座上镌刻的文字，指出其所谓盖世神功早已为时间所吞没，而匠人所刻的雕像作为艺术却流传千古。
3. "旅行者"对奥西曼德斯雕像残存物进行了细致的描写：两只巨大的没有身躯的石腿矗立在一望无垠的沙漠中，附近有一张破碎残缺的面庞半埋在黄沙里。他那紧锁的额头，满是皱纹的嘴唇和漠视前方的神色一览无余，再次暗示古埃及曾经的辉煌历史。vast legs 突出奥西曼德斯时期埃及领土之辽阔，"腿"在古代埃及象征着神圣的力量。shattered visage：破碎残缺的面庞。展现力量的"腿"成了"没有身躯的腿"；象征着权力和尊严的"脸"已残缺不全，且半埋黄沙。至此，古代埃及的风采已经被荒漠所吞噬，但是这并不意味着万事万物就此消亡。
4. Tell that its sculptor well those passions read: that its sculptor understood and represented those passions of the king well or faithfully. 雕刻家对这类情欲的表现有深刻的了解。而如今，奥西曼德斯和"了解"这些情绪的雕刻家们都已不复存在。
5. survive 和 stamped on：然而，雕刻家在石头上留下的痕迹却依旧历历在目。后人对远古的了解很有限，但是艺术的存续让我们对有限的历史有着更深入的认识。这里，雪莱隐喻了艺术的永恒性。雕刻家当年或许只是为了颂扬暴君的威严和他漠视一切的神态，现在他的作品却成了嘲讽历史上一切暴虐的证物。
6. pedestal：基座。

7. king of kings：奥西曼德斯这个不可一世的暴君，这个自称为“众王之王”的人，除了在《圣经》和西库鲁斯仅有的史料中零星的记载，后人再也看不到他的任何“丰功伟业”，而且在这些少量的记载中，他只是一个暴君。
8. Nothing beside remains：正如雪莱此处所言，奥西曼德斯除了这座雕像的残骸之外，“再也没有留下什么”。
9. Round the decay of that colossal wreck，boundless and bare, the lone and level sands stretch far away：残骸的周围，寂寞、荒凉、无边的平沙漫延向远方。despair, decay, bare 和 away，最后四行结尾押韵的长元音在声音效果上产生了一种悠长和延续的感觉，一望无垠的平沙和悠长的声音效果消解了读者脑海里作为历史人物的奥西曼德斯，留下的只有作为雕塑和诗歌的艺术，在时间的长河里永恒不朽。

“Ozymandias” is a sonnet metered in iambic pentameter. It is frequently anthologized and considered to be Shelley’s most famous short poem. It was written in competition with his friend Horace Smith. The poem is notable for its virtuosic diction and unusual rhyme scheme creating a sinuous and interwoven effect.

Essentially “Ozymandias” is devoted to a single metaphor：the shattered, ruined statue in the desert wasteland, with its arrogant, passionate face and monomaniacal inscription (“Look on my Works, ye Mighty, and despair!”). It is obsessed with transience；the very fact that the statue is a “colossal wreck” implies that there are things that will not last forever. But the poem is not just about how really “vast” statues eventually decay；the statue is a symbol of Ozymanidas’s ambition, pride, and absolute power. However, the once-great king’s proud boast is ironically disproved: Ozymandias’s works have crubled and disappeared, and his civilization is gone；all is turned to dust by the impersonal and destructive power of history. The ruined statue is now merely a witness to one man’s hubris, and a powerful statement about the insignificance of human beings to the passage of time. Ozymandias is first and foremost a metaphor for the ephemeral nature of political power, and in that sense the poem is Shelley’s most outstanding political sonnet, trading the specific rage of a poem like “England in 1819” for the crushing impersonal metaphor of the statue. But Ozymandias symbolizes not only political power—the statue can be a metaphor for the pride and hubris of all humanity, in any of its manifestations. It is significant that all that remains of Ozymandias is a work of art and a group of words；as Shakespeare does in the sonnets, Shelley demonstrates that art and language long outlast the other legacies of power.

Questions

1. Where do you think the encounter between the speaker and the traveller takes place? What does this vagueness contribute to the poem?

2. There are a lot of alliterations and rhymings in the sonnet. How do you understand this repetition? Does it suggest some kind of cyclical history-repeats-itself idea?

3. What do you think Ozymandias would say if he could see what has happened to his crumbling statue? Would he be humble or would he find some other way to boast?

4. How does the poem view the permanence of art? Do artistic "works" necessarily "decay" like the statue of Ozymandias? Is the poem's view of transience and impermanence hopeful or despairing?

Chinese Translation

奥西曼德斯

我遇见一个来自古国的旅客，
　　他说：有两只断落的巨大石腿
站在沙漠中……附近还半埋着
　　一块破碎的石雕的脸；他那皱眉，
那瘪唇，那威严中的轻蔑和冷漠，
　　在表明雕刻家很懂得那迄今
还留在这岩石上的情欲和愿望，
　　虽然早死了刻绘的手，原型的心；
在那石座上，还有这样的铭记：
"我是奥西曼德斯，众王之王。
强悍者呵，谁能和我的业绩相比！"
　　这就是一切了，再也没有其他。
在这巨大的荒墟四周，无边无际，
只见一片荒凉而寂寥的平沙。

（查良铮　译）

Unit 12　John Keats

Introduction to the Author

John Keats (1795-1821), English Romantic poet, was born in Moorgate, London, on October 31, 1795. When he was eight years old, his father, a liver-stable keeper, was killed in an accident. In the same year, his mother married again, but separated from her husband later and took her family to live with her mother. Keats received good education at John Clarke's school in Enfield, where he met an important mentor and friend, the headmaster's son, Charles Cowden Clarke, who introduced the Renaissance to Keats and acquainted him with classic and contemporary literature. In 1810, Keats' mother died of consumption, leaving her children to their grandmother. Keats was sent to be an apprentice to a surgeon named Thomas Hammond instead of continuing his schooling in Clarke's. But Keats finally sacrificed his medical ambition to literature in 1814 when he wrote his first poem "Lines in Limitation of Spenser".

In May 1816, Leigh Hunt, a close friend of Byron and Shelley and later a great friend of Keats, agreed to publish Keats' sonnet "O Solitude" in his magazine *The Examiner*, a leading liberal magazine of that time. But it wasn't till later in the year when his poem "On First Look on Chapman's Homer" was published, that his talent and potential as a poet was recognized. However, five months later, the first volume of Keats' poetry *Poems* turned out to be a critical failure. Despite the bad reviews of *Poems*, Hunt introduced Keats to many prominent men in his circle, including William Wordsworth, Charles Lamb, Thomas Barnes and the poet John Hamilton Reynolds. It was the turning point for Keats, establishing him in the public eyes as a figure of a new important poet.

Keats continued writing and Shelley then challenged him to an epic poetry competition over the summer. "Endymion", a four-thousand-line erotic and allegorical romance based on the Greek myth of the same name, appeared in 1818. He finished some of the finest poems between 1818 and 1819 and mainly worked on "Hyperion", a Miltonic blank-verse epic of the Greek creation myth. That same year he contracted tuberculosis, and by the following February he knew that death was not far from him, referring to the present as his "posthumous existence".

In July 1820, Keats published his third and best volume of poetry, *Lamia*, *Isabella*, *The*

Eve of St. Agnes, and Other Poems. The three title poems, dealing with mystical and legendary themes of the ancient, medieval, and Renaissance times, are rich in imagery and phrasing. The volume also includes the unfinished "Hyperion", and other poems considered among the finest in the English language, "Ode on a Grecian Urn", "Ode on Melancholy", and "Ode to a Nightingale". The volume received wide recognition and enthusiastic praise among poets and critics.

Under the doctor's orders to seek a warm climate for the winter, Keats went to Rome with his friend, the painter Joseph Severn. On the 23rd of February 1821, he died there at the age of 25. He requested that on his tombstone all that would be written was "Here lies one whose name was writ in water". However, Charles Brown thought that this was too short and had this carved into the tombstone: "This Grave contains all that was mortal of a YOUNG ENGLISH POET who on his Death Bed, in the Bitterness of his Heart at the Malicious Power of his Enemies, Desired these words to be engraved on his Tomb Stone 'Here lies One Whose Name was writ in Water.' "

Ode on a Grecian Urn[1]

Thou still unravished bride of quietness,
    Thou foster child of silence and slow time,
Sylvan historian[2], who canst thus express
    A flowery tale more sweetly than our rhyme:
What leaf-fringed legend haunts about thy shape
    Of deities or mortals, or of both,
        In Tempe or the dales of Arcady[3]?
    What men or gods are these? What maidens loath?
What mad pursuit? What struggle to escape[4]?
        What pipes and timbrels[5]? What wild ecstasy?

Heard melodies are sweet, but those unheard
    Are sweeter; therefore, ye soft pipes, play on;
Not to the sensual ear[6], but, more endeared[7],
    Pipe to the spirit ditties of no tone:
Fair youth, beneath the trees, thou canst not leave

Thy song, nor ever can those trees be bare;
Bold Lover, never, never canst thou kiss,
Though winning near the goal—yet, do not grieve;
She cannot fade, though thou hast not thy bliss,
Forever wilt thou love, and she be fair!

Ah, happy, happy boughs! that cannot shed
Your leaves, nor ever bid the Spring adieu[8];
And, happy melodist, unweariѐd,
Forever[9] piping songs forever new;
More happy love! more happy, happy love!
Forever warm and still to be enjoyed,
Forever panting, and forever young;
All breathing human passion far above,
That leaves a heart high-sorrowful and cloyed,
A burning forehead, and a parching tongue[10].

Who are these coming to the sacrifice?
To what green altar, O mysterious priest,
Lead'st thou that heifer lowing at the skies,
And all her silken flanks with garlands dressed[11]?
What little town by river or sea shore,
Or mountain-built with peaceful citadel,
Is emptied of this folk, this pious morn?
And, little town, thy streets for evermore
Will silent be; and not a soul to tell
Why thou art desolate, can e'er return.

O Attic shape! Fair attitude! with brede[12]
Of marble men and maidens overwrought[13],
With forest branches and the trodden weed;
Thou, silent form, dost tease us out of thought
As doth eternity: Cold Pastoral[14]!
When old age shall this generation waste,
Thou shalt remain, in midst of other woe
Than ours, a friend to man, to whom thou say'st,
"Beauty is truth, truth beauty," [15]—that is all
Ye know on earth, and all ye need to know.

Notes

1. 该诗创作于1819年5月，出版于1820年1月。它与《怠惰颂》（"Ode on Indolence"）、《忧郁颂》（"Ode on Melancholy"）、《夜莺颂》（"Ode to Nightingale"）、《赛姬颂》（"Ode to Psyche"）和《秋颂》（"To Autumn"）并称为济慈传世的六大颂诗。济慈不满足于早期的诗歌体例，发展出全新的颂体，以其六首颂诗为代表。本诗源于济慈阅读英国作家及画家本杰明·罗伯特·海登（Benjamin Robert Haydon）的两篇文章。济慈十分钟爱古希腊艺术品，曾以埃及金石雕之名作诗；他对古希腊艺术的理想主义哲学的信仰，以及对希腊古风之美的刻画，构成此诗的基础。浪漫主义时期的颂诗源于古希腊时代的颂歌，以严肃的曲调庆祝节日或者歌颂个人，诗人品达（Pindar）创作了一系列颂歌，赞美参加奥林匹克比赛的运动员们。济慈则试图在结构对称的古典诗歌和不对称的浪漫主义诗歌中寻找一种平衡。本诗共五小节，每小节包括十个诗行，每行十个音步；每小节的前四行采用莎士比亚四行体 abab 的尾韵，后六行则以弥尔顿式六行诗 cdecde 的韵脚结束。相同的句式结构和平行结构反复出现，增加了诗歌的气势。
2. still：一语双关，既表示"仍然"（作副词）又表示"安宁"（作形容词），既说明了时间的永恒，也渲染了宁静的氛围。unravished：依旧完好的。Sylvan：pretaining to or living in the woods，森林的；不仅唤起了读者对远离现代社会的嘈杂喧嚣，进入古代田园牧歌宁静生活的向往，还在形式上与"sylph"（窈窕淑女）一词相似。"sylvan history"肩负着记录林中历史的重任。
3. Tempe：滕佩河，位于希腊的一个美丽山谷，是司掌艺术的太阳神阿波罗的圣地；Arcady：即 Arcadia，是田园牧歌的理想国度，有版本称为宙斯的出生地，暗示乡村的宁静和民风的淳朴。
4. mad pursuit，struggle to escape：忘情地追逐、藏躲，让人联想起阿波罗和达芙妮以及河神阿尔菲俄斯和山林仙女阿瑞托萨的故事，隐射古瓮的世界与现实世界的差距。济慈在此连用七个 what 引导的疑问句，实为感叹句，且句型由第一个断断续续的长句变为非常简短的名词短语，既简练又强调，使读者有如闻其声、如临其境的感觉。另外，what 和 or 的重复，句型短而多停顿，排比的运用，节奏明快且有变化，加之头韵（alliteration）的使用（leaf / legend, deities / dales 等），凸显诗句的音乐感和节奏感。
5. timbrels：ancient tambourines，小手鼓，铃鼓，古代祭祀时演奏的乐器。
6. sensual ear：ear of the senses，他们的耳朵。
7. endeared：亲切的，把感情赋予"心灵"，只有面对激情四射的心灵，古瓮所传达的音乐才会更美妙。
8. adieu, bid adieu：say goodbye，告别。
9. Forever：永恒，该词在第三节出现六次，happy 也出现六次。forever 和 happy 的重复叠加使用，强化了瓮所代表的想象世界和神话世界，同时将视觉艺术的静态特征转化成诗歌的声音效果。
10. cloyed：发腻，倒胃口；parching：thirsty，焦干的。

Notes

11. heifer：小母牛；flank：腰腹，腰腹肉；garland：wreath，花环。
12. Attic：古希腊地名，位于希腊中部雅典所在地。brede：embroidery，镶嵌。
13. overwrought：covered with，被覆盖。
14. Cold Pastoral：pastoral story in marble，以大理石记载的田园历史故事。pastoral 有两层含义：一指牧羊人的栖息地，暗指简单、宁静的乡村生活以及与此生活相关的特质，如自然与天真；另一层则是歌颂乡村生活品质的诗歌，即田园牧歌。
15. 最后两行，想象瓮向人类传达"美即是真，真即是美"的信息，被认为是济慈诗行中最难阐释的。

Text Analysis

"Ode on a Grecian Urn" is a detailed description of an urn, a vessel traditionally used for a variety of ceremonial purposes. The urn is the star of the show, and it is described in several different ways. At the beginning of the poem, it is a married bride, but still virginal. Then the speaker looks more closely at the specific scenes depicted on its sides. He praises its shape and its decoration. Finally, he treats it like a sage with wisdom to impart. The poem is based on a series of paradoxes and opposites：the discrepancy between the urn with its frozen images and the dynamic life portrayed on the urn；the mortal and the changeable versus the immortal and the permanent；participation versus observation；life versus art. Therefore, it has two settings：the speaker's intimate world and the pastoral world of the urn.

The first stanza describes the urn as an "unravish'd bride of quietness", "foster child of silence and slow time", and "sylvan historian" because it has existed for centuries remaining intact. Using oxymoron and paradox in the beginning, the second stanza compares the silent music from the pipes and timbrels to the audible music of real life, since music from the urn is for the spirit. In the third stanza the speaker looks at the trees surrounding the lovers and feels happy that they will never shed the leaves. In the fourth stanza, another picture on the urn is examined：the images of people approaching an altar to sacrifice a "lowing" (mooing) cow, one that has never borne a calf, on a green alter. The empty streets of the little town will "for evermore" be silent, for those who have left it, and who were frozen in time, will never escape the urn and return to their homes. The final stanza addresses the urn itself, an "attic shape". Attic refers to a region of east-central ancient Greece of which Athens was the chief city. The urn is a beautiful one, adorned with "brede". As people look upon the scene, they try to grasp its meaning so that they exhaust themselves of thought. The poet thinks that when his generation is long dead, the urn will remain, telling future generations its enigmatic lesson："Beauty is truth, truth beauty". With this the poem goes beyond its seemingly mere description of scenes and turns to ponder

over some comprehensive issues and is thus tinted with metaphysical speculations.

Questions

1. Why is the urn called an "unravished bride"? What implications does the phrase suggest?

2. Do you think the men depicted on the urn would still be in love with the maidens if they recognize that their love would never be consummated?

3. The first four lines of the second stanza contrast the ideal (in art, love, and nature) and the real; which does Keats prefer to at this point? What is the paradox of unheard pipes? Is this an oxymoron?

4. How do you think of the relationship among love, truth and beauty? What do other Romantic poets prefer?

Chinese Translation

希腊古瓮颂

你委身"寂静"的、完美的处子，
　　受过了"沉默"和"悠久"的抚育，
啊，田园的史家，你竟能铺叙
　　一个如花的故事，比诗还瑰丽：
在你的形体上，岂非缭绕着
　　古老的传说，以绿叶为其边缘；
　　　　讲着人，或神，敦陂或阿卡狄？
　　啊，是怎样的人，或神！在舞乐前
多热烈的追求！少女怎样地逃躲！
　　怎样的风笛和鼓铙！怎样的狂喜！

听见的乐声虽好，但若听不见
　　却更美；所以，吹吧，柔情的风笛；
不是奏给耳朵听，而是更甜，
　　它给灵魂奏出无声的乐曲；
树下的美少年啊，你无法中断

你的歌，那树木也落不了叶子；
鲁莽的恋人，你永远、永远吻不上，
虽然够接近了——但不必心酸；
她不会老，虽然你不能如愿以偿，
你将永远爱下去，她也永远秀丽！

呵，幸福的树木！你的枝叶
不会剥落，从不曾离开春天；
幸福的吹笛人也不会停歇，
他的歌曲永远是那么新鲜；
啊，更为幸福的、幸福的爱！
永远热烈，正等待情人宴飨，
永远热情地心跳，永远年轻；
幸福的是这一切超凡的情态：
它不会使心灵餍足和悲伤，
没有炽热的头脑，焦渴的嘴唇。

这些人是谁啊，都去赶祭祀？
这作牺牲的小牛，对天鸣叫，
你要牵它到哪儿，神秘的祭司？
花环缀满着它光滑的身腰。
是从哪个傍河傍海的小镇，
或哪个静静的堡寨的山村，
来了这些人，在这敬神的清早？
啊，小镇，你的街道永远恬静；
再也不可能回来一个灵魂
告诉人你何以是这么寂寥。

哦，希腊的形状！唯美的观照！
上面缀有石雕的男人和女人，
还有林木，和践踏过的青草；
沉默的形体呵，你像是“永恒”
使人超越思想：啊，冰冷的牧歌！
等暮年使这一世代都凋落，
只有你如旧；在另外的一些
忧伤中，你会抚慰后人说：
“美即是真，真即是美，”这就包括
你们所知道、和该知道的一切。

（查良铮　译）

THE VICTORIAN AGE

Unit 13 Elizabeth Barrett Browning

Introduction to the Author

Elizabeth Barrett Browning (1806-1861) was one of the most prominent women poets of the Victorian age. Born at Coxhoe Hall, Durham, England, Elizabeth was the eldest of twelve children of the family. She studied Latin and Greek under her brother's tutorials and she read voraciously in history, philosophy, and literature. By her 12th year she had written her first "epic" poem.

In 1826, Elizabeth anonymously published her collection *An Essay on Mind and Other Poems*. In 1832, Elizabeth's father moved his family to a coastal town and Elizabeth published her translation of *Prometheus Bound* (1833), by the Greek dramatist Aeschylus. Gaining fame for her work in the 1830s, Elizabeth continued to live in her father's London house under his tyrannical rule. During this time, she wrote *The Seraphim and Other Poem*s (1838), expressing Christian sentiments in the form of classical Greek tragedy. She continued writing, and in 1844 produced a collection entitled simply *Poems*. This volume gained attention of the poet Robert Browning, whose works Elizabeth had praised in one of her poems, and he wrote her a letter. Elizabeth and Robert, who was six years her junior, exchanged 574 letters over the next twenty months. Their romance was bitterly opposed by her father, who did not want any of his children to marry. In 1846, the couple eloped and settled in Florence, Italy, where Elizabeth's health improved and she bore a son, Robert Wideman Browning. Elizabeth's *Sonnets from the Portuguese*, dedicated to her husband and written in secret before her marriage, was published in 1850. Critics generally consider the volume—one of the most widely known collections of love lyrics in English—to be her best work.

Elizabeth's poetry is also characterized by a fervent moral sensibility. Her early poems lament the fallen state of humanity and look forward in Christian hope to redemption. Furthermore, she expressed her intense sympathy for the struggle for the unification of Italy in *Casa Guidi Windows* (1848-1851) and *Poems Before Congress* (1860). In 1857, she published her verse novel *Aurora Leigh*, which portrays male domination of a woman. In her poetry she also addressed the oppression of the Italians by the Austrians, the child labor in mines and mills of England, and slavery, among other social injustices. Elizabeth died in Florence on June 29, 1861.

Sonnets from the Portuguese (21)

Say over again, and yet once over again,
That thou dost love me[1]. Though the word repeated
Should seem "a cuckoo-song"[2], as thou dost treat it.
Remember, never to the hill or plain
Valley and wood, without her cuckoo strain[3]
Comes the fresh Spring in all her green completed.[4]
Beloved, I, amid the darkness greeted
By a doubtful spirit voice, in that doubt's pain
Cry, "Speak once more—thou lovest! [5]" Who can fear
Too many stars, though each in heaven shall roll[6],
Too many flowers, though each shall crown the year?
Say thou dost love me, love me, love me—toll
The silver[7] iterance!—only minding, Dear,
To love me also in silence with thy soul.

1. thou dost love me: you do love me.
2. a cuckoo-song：杜鹃的歌声，重复单调的声音。
3. strain：乐曲。
4. never... to the hill or plan... completed: the fresh Spring in all her green completed never comes to the hill or plain, valley or wood, without her cuckoo strain. in all her green completed：全身披上绿装。
5. thou lovest: you love.
6. roll:（星星）循环运行。
7. silver：表示声音如银铃般清脆。

Text Analysis

For many years Elizabeth Barret Browning was best-known for her *Sonnets from the Portuguese* (1850), in which she recorded the stages of her love for Robert Browning. The above is a classical love poem and the speaker is behaving rather giddily, imploring her beloved to keep repeating that he loves her. Therefore, she is transforming from the timid, little doubter to a rather self-assured woman.

In the first quatrain, the speaker requests her lover to tell her "over again, and yet once over again / That thou dost love me". Yet she admits that repeating the same phrase over and over again might sound silly as the cuckoo bird's song. But then she asserts that nature is full of repetition. She reminds her lover and herself that spring never comes without the hills and plains being greeted with the same greens, as the valley and woods resound with the crazy cuckoo's repetition. In the second quatrain, the speaker compares the human world with the world of nature to justify or correct sometimes human nature's, or at least, her own fastidiousness. She simply has grown in delight, hearing her lover tell her he loves her, and she has finally accepted it as truth. She thus cannot stop her giddiness as she asks him to repeat the love declaration.

But she then tells him that during the night, her old demons caused her again to doubt, and "in that doubt's pain", she felt compelled to request that he speak those words of love to her once more. Thus, she emphatically calls, "Speak once more—thou lovest!" The speaker is emphasizing that no one would fear "too many stars" nor "too many flowers"; therefore, she insists that there is nothing to fear from repeating the love declaration so she may hear it again and again, then "Say thou dost love me, love me, love me—toll". In the final tercet, she dramatizes the repetition by repeating it herself: "Say thou dost love me, love me, love me", and she calls the repetition a "silver iterance", suggesting that it has the quality of a bell sound; she craves hearing the "toll" of the "silver iterance"!

But the speaker also offers an addition to her insist on the audible reiteration of the love proclamation; she also requests her lover "to love me also in silence with thy soul". She knows that her final demand is even more vital than hearing the words, for words without soul are like husks without grain.

In conclusion, this sonnet is so much more than these lines. It is a work of passion, doubt, fear, and most importantly, a work of love.

Questions

1. How does the speaker in the poem express her love?
2. What does the "cuckoo-song" imply?

3. How does the speaker liken the human world to the world of nature?
4. What does the "toll" refer to?
5. How do you think of the last line "To love me also in silence with thy soul"?

Chinese Translation

葡萄牙十四行诗（第21首）

请说了一遍再向我说一遍，
　　说“我爱你！”即使那样一遍遍重复，
　　你会把它看成一支“布谷鸟的歌曲”；
可是记着，在那青山和绿林间，
那山谷和田野中，纵使清新的春天，
　　披着全身绿装降临、也不算完美无缺，
　　要是她缺少了那串布谷鸟的音节。
爱，四周那么黑暗，耳边只听见
惊悸的心声，处于那痛苦的不安中，
　　我嚷道：“再说一遍：我爱你！”谁嫌
太多的星，即使每颗都在太空转动；
　　太多的花，即使每朵洋溢着春意？
说你爱我，你爱我，一声声敲着银钟！
　　只是记住，还得用灵魂爱我，在默默里。

（方平　译）

Unit 14 Alfred Tennyson

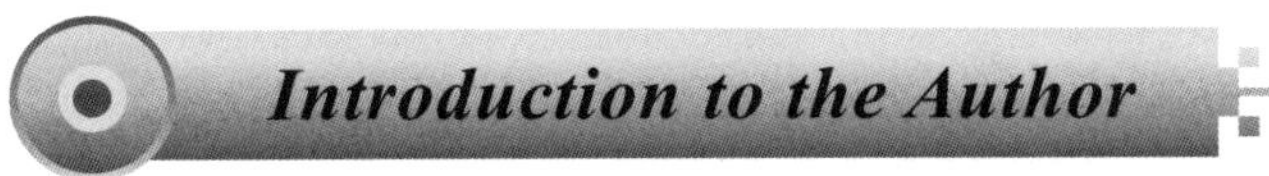

Introduction to the Author

Alfred Tennyson (1809-1892) is recognized as the greatest poet of Victorian England. He was made Poet Laureate in 1850 after William Wordsworth.

Tennyson was born in the village of Somersby, Lincolnshire, and was the fourth of twelve children. His father was an intelligent and cultivated but very unhappy man given to periods of severe depression. He educated his children himself in classical and modern languages. Tennyson grew up as a sensitive and well-read but often melancholy boy. He enjoyed the companionship of his brothers and sisters, but he also spent long time by himself, roaming the countryside both day and night. He began writing poetry before he was ten, and in 1827, he and his brother Charles published anonymously *Poems by Two Brothers*. More than half of the poems are strongly influenced by Byron and Scott.

In 1827, Tennyson went to study at Cambridge University and the poems he had published drew him to the attention of a small group of brilliant undergraduates. In 1830, he published his first volume of verse. In 1831, Tennyson had to leave Cambridge without a degree because of financial difficulties and family dissension. Discouraged and uncertain of his future, Tennyson remained silent for ten years. He published nothing during this time but he spent these years privately revising his published poems and working on new and more ambitious projects. It was during these years that he perfected his art.

Tennyson returned to public attention in 1824 with the publication of poems in two volumes. This collection firmly established his reputation and made him the major figure in Victorian poetry. He was made Poet Laureate in 1850. In 1883, he was made Peer of the Realm and was thus accorded the title of Lord. He died at 81.

Tennyson's major works are *The Princess*, *Maud*, *In Memoriam A. H. H.* and *Idylls of the King*. Tennyson has a total mastery of the sounds and rhythms of the English language. He has a genius for evoking moods and states of mind in his poems. He is able to create a sense of nostalgia, a wistful longing for the past or for remote experiences. No other English poet surpasses Tennyson at linking descriptions of nature or setting to the state of mind of the speaker. Some of his poems deal with the main political, religious and scientific issues of his day. His poems reflect his conservative ideas and idealization of the bourgeois social reality.

Ulysses[1]

It little profits that an idle king[2],
By this still hearth, among these barren crags,
Matched with an agéd wife[3], I mete and dole
Unequal laws unto a savage race,
That hoard, and sleep, and feed, and know not me.

I cannot rest from travel: I will drink
Life to the lees[4]; all times I have enjoyed
Greatly, have suffered greatly, both with those
That loved me, and alone; on shore, and when
Through scudding drifts the rainy Hyades[5]
Vext the dim sea: I am become a name;
For always roaming with a hungry heart
Much have I seen and known; cities of men
And manners, climates, councils, governments,
Myself not least, but honoured of them all[6];
And drunk delight of battle with my peers[7],
Far on the ringing plains of windy Troy,
I am a part of all that I have met;
Yet all experience is an arch wherethrough
Gleams that untravelled world[8], whose margin fades
For ever and for ever when I move.
How dull it is to pause, to make an end,
To rust unburnished[9], not to shine in use!
As though to breathe were life. Life piled on life
Were all too little, and of one to me
Little remains: but every hour is saved
From that eternal silence, something more,
A bringer of new things; and vile it were[10]

For some three suns[11] to store and hoard myself,
And this gray spirit yearning[12] in desire
To follow knowledge like a sinking star,
Beyond the utmost bound of human thought.

This is my son, mine own Telemachus[13],
To whom I leave the scepter and the isle[14]—
Well-loved of me, discerning to fulfill
This labor, by slow prudence to make mild
A rugged people, and through soft degrees
Subdue them to the useful and the good.
Most blameless is he, centered in the sphere
Of common duties, decent not to fail
In offices of tenderness, and pay
Meet[15] adoration to my household gods,
When I am gone. He works his work, I mine.

There lies the port; the vessel puffs her sail:
There gloom the dark, broad seas. My mariners,
Souls that have toiled, and wrought, and thought with me—
That ever with a frolic welcome took
The thunder and the sunshine, and opposed[16]
Free hearts, free foreheads[17]—you and I are old;
Old age hath yet his honour and his toil;
Death closes all: but something ere[18] the end,
Some work of noble note[19], may yet be done,
Not unbecoming men that strove with Gods[20].
The lights begin to twinkle from the rocks:
The long day wanes; the slow moon climbs; the deep[21]
Moans round with many voices. Come, my friends,
'Tis not too late to seek a newer world.
Push off, and sitting well in order smite
The sounding furrows; for my purpose holds
To sail beyond the sunset, and the baths
Of all the western stars[22], until I die.
It may be that the gulfs will wash us down:
It may be we shall touch the Happy Isles[23],
And see the great Achilles, whom we knew.

Though much is taken, much abides; and though
We are not now that strength which in old days
Moved earth and heaven; that which we are, we are,
One equal temper of heroic hearts[24],
Made weak by time and fate, but strong in will
To strive, to seek, to find, and not to yield.

Notes

1. 丁尼生此诗取材于但丁的《地狱篇》第 26 章。特洛伊战争结束后，尤利西斯在海上飘泊十年，历经千辛万苦，经受种种曲折，回到家乡伊萨卡（Ithaca），和忠实等待他的妻子佩涅罗庇（Penelope）和儿子堤莱莫克斯（Telemachus）团聚。但是，不久之后尤利西斯就感到百无聊赖，又想重返西方冒险。本诗描绘他的最后一次探险。
2. an idle King：指伊萨卡岛的国王尤利西斯，《荷马史诗》中的主角，他参加了著名的特洛伊战争。
3. an agéd wife：指尤利西斯的妻子。mete and dole / Unequal laws: measure out rewards and punishments，指赏罚伊萨卡岛上未开化的居民。
4. drink / Life to the lees：把生命之酒一饮而尽。lees：sediment or dregs of liguor，杯里的沉淀物。
5. scudding drifts：狂风暴雨。Hyades：（位于金牛星座中的）毕（宿）星团，传说该星团在日出时出现，天就会下雨，所以说 rainy Hyades。
6. Myself not least, but honoured of them all：myself 与 manners 等并列，意为"我"在其中并不是最微不足道的，而是颇受尊敬的一人。
7. drunk delight of battle with my peers：和我的朋友同享战斗的乐趣。
8. Yet all experience is an arch wherethrough / Gleams that untravelled world whose margin fades：经验就像一扇门，由此可以看见远方那模糊的未曾涉足的世界。wherethrough: through which.
9. To rust unburnished：比喻人生如不外出探险就像金属器具一样会生锈，失去光彩。
10. vile it were：it would be vile.
11. three suns：三年，一般作三日解。
12. this grey spirit yearning：with this grey head yearning，尤利西斯已经年老，故称白头，颇有老当益壮的精神。
13. Telemachus：尤利西斯之子堤莱莫克斯。
14. To whom I leave the scepter and the isle：尤利西斯准备把统治伊萨卡岛的权力交给儿子。scepter：节杖，象征国王的权力。
15. Meet：fitting.
16. with a frolic welcome took / The thunder and the sunshine，and opposed：以欢愉的心情迎接风雷和烈日。opposed：to resist, to contend with，和上文 took 并列，宾语为 the

thunder and the sunshine。

17. Free hearts, free foreheads：自由的心灵和头脑，指昔日和尤利西斯一起出海的水手们。
18. ere：before.
19. Some work of noble note：宏伟的大业。note: importance, significance.
20. Not unbecoming men that strove with Gods：（这种宏伟大业）和那些敢于和诸神一争高下的人是很相称的。
21. the deep：大海。
22. the baths / Of all the western stars：古希腊人认为平地的外面是一片汪洋，西下的星星将沉入海洋。
23. the Happy Isles：极乐岛。希腊神话传说人死后去极乐世界，后者又称 the Islands of the Blessed。据说这些岛屿在世界尽头以西的大洋里。
24. One equal temper of heroic hearts：同样气质的英雄胆略。temper: constitution of the body；temperament.

This is a moving and inspirational monologue by Ulysses, hero of the Trojan War, now admittedly aged. Initially, one thinks of the warrior hero as complaining about the lack of adventure that he has experienced for three years after his lengthy return from Troy. But then one realizes that it is not adventure but the acquisition of knowledge that the old man craves for. Throughout the poem the motif emerges again and again that he doesn't want "to rust unburnish'd" but "to shine in use".

The tone and pace quicken as Ulysses leaves consideration of his commonplace offspring and summons his fellow ancient mariners. "Souls that have toiled, and wrought, and thought with me—"：here again is that key verb prepared for by "free hearts, free foreheads".

The poem's final two lines are made up of single syllabic words joined with the infinitive particle "to". The commas call for caesuras or pauses which throw emphasis on the important verbs and the key word "not" so that the poem ends with a heroically defiant challenge. Note the speed and ease of "The lights begin to twinkle from the rocks" —a perfect iambic line with speed suggested particularly by "twinkle". Then comes the metrical variation or spondaic movement of "The long day wanes；the slow moon climbs；the deep / Moans round with many voice." Note the differences in sound and meaning between "moans" and "twinkle".

Questions

1. What general attitude and feeling does the poet picture Ulysses in his old age? In what situation does the poet dramatize the attitude and feeling?

2. The last line was once quoted by Winston Churchill in his speech. In what case and in what way does the line may inspire Churchill's audience or listeners?

3. Compare the character Ulysses here with that in James Joyce's novel *Ulysses*. Tell the differences between the characterization and their significance.

Chinese Translation

尤利西斯

这太无谓——当一个闲散的君主，
安居家中，在这个嶙峋的岛国，
我与年老的妻子相匹，颁布着
不公的法律，治理野蛮的种族，——
他们吃、睡、收藏，而不理解我。
我不能停歇我的跋涉；我决心
饮尽生命之杯。我一生都在
体验巨大的痛苦、巨大的欢乐，
有时与爱我的伙伴一起，有时却
独自一个；不论在岸上或海上，
当带来雨季的毕宿星团催动
我已经变成这样一个名字，——
激流滚滚，扬起灰暗的海波。
由于我如饥似渴地漂泊不止，
我已见识了许多民族的城
及其风气、习俗、枢密院、政府，
而我在他们之中最负盛名；
我和同僚们共饮战斗的欢欣，
在遥远而多风的特洛亚战场，
我自己是我全部经历的一部分；
而全部经验，也只是一座拱门，
尚未游历的世界在门外闪光，

而随着我一步一步地前进，
它的边界也不断向后退让。
最单调最沉闷的是停留，是终止，
是蒙尘生锈而不在使用中发亮！
难道说呼吸就能算是生活？
几次生命堆起来尚嫌太少，
何况我唯一的生命已余年无多。
唯有从永恒的沉寂之中抢救
每个小时，让每个小时带来
一点新的收获。最可厌的是
把自己长期封存、贮藏起来，
让我灰色的灵魂徒然渴望
在人类思想最远的边界之外
追求知识，像追求沉没的星星。

　　这是我的儿子忒勒玛科斯，
我给他留下我的岛国和王杖，
他是我所爱的，他有胆有识，
能胜任这一工作；谨慎耐心地
教化粗野的民族，用温和的步骤
驯化他们，使他们善良而有用。
他是无可指责的，他虽年少
在我离去后他会担起重任，
处理好那些需要谨慎应付的事务，
并对我家的佑护神表示崇敬。
他和我，将各做各的工作

海港就在那边，船儿已经扬帆，
大海黑暗一片。我的水手们——
与我同辛劳、同工作、同思想的人，
他们总是高高兴兴去迎接
雷电和阳光，
并用自由的心与头颅来抗争，
你们和我都已老了，但老年
仍有老年的荣誉、老年的辛劳；
死亡终结一切，但在终点前
我们还能做一番崇高的事业，

使我们配称为与神斗争的人。
礁石上的灯标开始闪光了：
长昼将尽，月亮缓缓攀登，
大海用无数音响在周围呼唤。
来呀，朋友们，探寻更新的世界
现在尚不是为时过晚。
开船吧！坐成排，划破这喧哗的海浪，
我决心驶向太阳沉没的彼方，
超越西方星斗的浴场，至死
方止。也许深渊会把我们吞噬，
也许我们将到达琼岛乐土，
与老朋友阿喀琉斯会晤。
尽管已达到的多，未知的也多啊，
虽然我们的力量已不如当初，
已远非昔日移天动地的雄姿，
但我们仍是我们，英雄的心
尽管被时间消磨，被命运削弱，
我们的意志坚强如故，坚持着
奋斗、探索、寻求，而不屈服。

（飞白　译）

Unit 15 Robert Browning

Introduction to the Author

Robert Browning (1812-1889), English poet and playwright, is probably the most important Victorian poet after Tennyson. His father was an official of the Bank of England, and a well-read and cultivated man. Browning attended a boarding school, and he was also tutored at home in ancient and modern languages, music and horsemanship. Browning began writing poetry at a very early age. His first book of poetry *Pauline* appeared when he was 21 years old. This book shows the influence of Byron and especially of Shelley.

Browning's major works are *The Dramatic Lyrics*, *The Ring and the Book* and *Paracelsus*. His mastery of dramatic verse, especially dramatic monologues, distinguished him a leading Victorian poet. In dramatic monologues, the words not only convey setting and action but also reveal the speaker's character. Unlike the soliloquy, the meaning in Browning's dramatic monologues is not what the speaker directly reveals but what he inadvertently "gives away" about himself in the process of rationalizing past actions, or "special-pleading" his case to a silent auditor in the poem. Rather than thinking out loud, the character composes a self-defense which the readers, as "jurors", are challenged to see through. The dramatic monologue greatly influences many high modernist poets, including T. S. Eliot and Ezra Pound.

Beside his long poems, Robert Browning is famous for his short poems as well. Unlike his long poems of obscurity and difficulty, his short lyrics are clear and accessible, full of passion and enthusiasm for life, such as his "Meeting at Night", "Parting at Morning", "Home-Thoughts, from Abroad" and so on. For the ten years between 1837 and 1847, Browning devoted himself to writing for theater.

Robert is also known for his romantic love story with his wife, poetess Elizabeth Browning, who is six years elder than him. Regardless of both parents' disapproval, the couple eloped to Italy and lived happily there for more than ten years. Their love brought forth the coming of many beautiful love verses, among which the collection *Sonnets from the Portuguese and Others* is the most famous. When Elizabeth Browning died in 1861, Robert returned to London. He enjoyed the life of a literary celebrity in his later years before his death at the age of 72.

Text 1

My Last Duchess

That's my last duchess painted on the wall,
Looking as if she were alive. I call
That piece a wonder, now: Frà Pandolf's[1] hands
Worked busily a day, and there she stands.[2]
Will't please you sit and look[3] at her? I said
"Frà Pandolf" by design, for never read
Strangers like you that pictured countenance,[4]
The depth and passion of its earnest glance,[5]
But to myself they turned (since none puts by
The curtain I have drawn for you, but I)[6]
And seemed as they would ask me, if they dust[7],
How such a glance came there; so, not the first
Are you to turn and ask thus. Sir, 'twas not
Her husband's presence only, called that spot
Of joy into the Duchess' cheek:[8] perhaps
Frà Pandolf chanced to say, "Her mantle laps
Over my lady's wrist too much,"[9] or "Paint
Must never hope to reproduce the faint
Half-flush that dies along her throat": such stuff
Was courtesy, she thought, and cause enough
For calling up that spot of joy.[10] She had
A heart—how shall I say? —too soon made glad,[11]
Too easily impressed; she liked whate'er
She looked on, and her looks went everywhere.[12]
Sir, 'twas all one! My favor at her breast,[13]
The dropping of the daylight in the West,
The bough of cherries some officious fool[14]
Broke in the orchard for her, the white mule
She rode with round the terrace—all and each
Would draw from her alike the approving speech,
Or blush, at least. She thanked men—good![15] but thanked

Somehow—I know not how—as if she ranked
My gift of a nine-hundred-years-old name[16]
With anybody's gift. Who'd stoop to blame
This sort of trifling?[17] Even had you skill
In speech—which I have not—to make your will
Quite clear to such an one[18] and say, "Just this
Or that in you disgusts me; here you miss,
Or there exceed the mark"[19] —and if she let
Herself be lessoned so, nor plainly set
Her wits to yours, forsooth,[20] and made excuse,
—E'en then would be some stooping; [21] and I choose
Never to stoop. Oh sir, she smiled, no doubt,
Whene'er I passed her; but who passed without
Much the same smile? This grew; I gave commands;[22]
Then all smiles stopped together.[23] There she stands
As if alive. Will't please you rise?[24] We'll meet
The company below, then. I repeat,
The Count your master's known munificence
Is ample warrant that no just pretence
Of mine for dowry will be disallowed;[25]
Though his fair daughter's self, as I avowed
At starting, is my object.[26] Nay, we'll go
Together down, sir. Notice Neptune, though,
Taming a sea-horse, thought a rarity,[27]
Which Claus of Innsbruck[28] cast in bronze for me!

1. I call / That piece a wonder：我认为这幅（公爵夫人的）画像是杰作。Frà Pandolf：Brother Pandolf，假想的画家。Frà 意为"教兄"，当时许多画家均为教士，故称。
2. there she stands：这幅画现在就挂在那里。
3. Will't：will it; sit and look：to sit and look.
4. by design：有意识地；意为知你必然要问画家是谁，故不等你发问，事先告诉你。read：主语是 strangers like you。read 意为观察，理解。pictured countenance：画像上的面容。
5. The depth and passion of its earnest glance：its 指 countenance，面容上的目光所流露的那深沉的情意。
6. But to myself they turned：意为像你这样的客人总是不能理解画像的表情，而总是转

过身来问我。since none puts by / The curtain I have drawn for you, but I：因为除我以外，无人可以为客人拉开遮盖画像的帷幕。暗示公爵爱护此画是因为它是一件艺术品而不是出于对夫人的怀念。

7. if they durst：如果他们有勇气（问我）。durst：dare 的过去式，主要在虚拟式中，现已不常用。
8. 'twas not... the Duchess, cheek：公爵夫人脸上之所以露出那片喜悦的红晕，不只是因为有丈夫在旁。'twas：it was. called：唤起，使露出，前面省略 that（关系代词）。
9. Her mantle laps / Over my lady's wrist too much：夫人的外套将她的手盖得太多了。Her 和 my lady 均指公爵夫人，用第三人称来称呼表示尊敬。
10. dies along her throat：（那片淡淡的红晕）沿着喉部逐渐消失。such stuff... that spot of joy：公爵夫人以为画家的那番话是礼貌的表示，因而值得为之（cause enough）感到高兴。此处讲夫人脸上红晕的来历，公爵认为她大可不必为这种恭维话激动，似乎有失尊严。
11. how shall I say：我该怎么说才好。too soon made glad：要使她心里高兴十分容易。
12. she liked whate'er / She looked on，and her looks went everywhere：她什么都爱看，看到了什么都喜欢。
13. 'twas all one：指以下列举的一切在公爵夫人的眼中都是同等之物。my favor at her breast：我送给她的胸饰。favor: a thing given or worn as a token of favour.
14. some officious fool：某个多事的蠢材。
15. She thanked men—good：她向人道谢——那好啊！语含讽刺。
16. a nine-hundred-years-old name：公爵家系有九百年的光荣历史。公爵不满意他夫人把普通人（anybody）的礼品和他名门望族的悠久历史的荣誉同等看待。
17. Who'd stoop to blame / This sort of trifling：谁能降低身份去指责这种鸡毛蒜皮的小事呢？
18. such an one：指公爵夫人。
19. here you miss, / Or there exceed the mark：这儿你做得不够，那儿你又太过分。mark 是 miss 和 exceed 的宾语。
20. be lessoned so：听从教训。plainly set / Her wits to yours：公然和你顶嘴。forsooth：in truth，certainly，确实是。
21. —E'en then would be some stooping：即使如此，也有点屈尊降格。E'en: even.
22. This grew：这种情况变本加厉，愈来愈严重。I gave commands：我下了命令。
23. Then all smiles stopped together：一般认为这是暗示公爵下令将其妻杀掉。布朗宁在答 Corson 问时说："Yes, I meant that the commands were that she be put to death." 停了会又说："Or he might have had her shut up in a convent."
24. Will't please you rise: will it please you to rise?

25. The Count... disallowed：你主人伯爵大人素以慷慨闻名（munificence），这可以保证（ample warrant）他不会拒绝我对于嫁妆的正当要求（just pretence）。刚说完杀死前妻之事，立即对来客提出嫁妆的要求。
26. Though his fair daughter's self, as I avowed / At starting, is my object：虽然我一开始就已申明，我所追求的是他美丽的女儿本人。
27. Notice Neptune, though, / Taming a sea-horse, thought a rarity：不过，请你看看海神驯服海马的铜像，据说是绝世的杰作。thought: which is thought.
28. Claus of Innsbruck：假想的雕刻家。因斯布鲁克（Innsbruck）在今奥地利境内，为当时蒂罗尔（Tyrol）邦的首府，以当地雕刻家著称。

Text Analysis

The most prominent contribution of Robert Browning to English poetry lies in his introduction of the dramatic monologue from play to poetic writing. The poem "My Last Duchess" is acknowledged as Browning's most skillful treatment of the dramatic monologue. By designing a visitor (a match-maker in fact), the poem successfully provides an opportunity for the readers / audiences to penetrate the inner heart of the Duke. By demonstrating the conflicts between what he says and what he thinks, the poem creates artistically an ironic effect in terms of characterization.

On the surface, the Duke is singing high prize of the skill of the painter in capturing the glimpse and countenance of the Duchess, whereas underneath, the Duke is expressing his strong resentment against his last wife's degeneration. On the surface, the Duke is showing proudly to the visitor his collection of arts and his high taste, while underneath the Duke's greed and hypocrisy is exposed clearly.

In terms of poetic form, on the surface the whole poem is narrative; essentially it is highly lyric by tearing the veil of cruelty and false. To some extent, the conflict between form and content offers dramatic tension in indicating the theme.

Questions

1. Why does the Duke want to show the guest his art collection?
2. Why was the Duke dissatisfied with his last Duchess? Was it merely sexual jealousy?
3. What can you characterize the Duchess' personality from the Duke's monologue?
4. How do you understand the line "I gave commands / Then all smiles stopped together"?

Chinese Translation

我的前公爵夫人

墙上的这幅画是我的前公爵夫人，
看起来就像她活着一样。如今，
我称它为奇迹：潘道夫画师的手笔
经一日忙碌，从此她就在此站立。
你愿坐下看看她吗？我有意提起
潘道夫，因为外来的生客（例如你）
凡是见了画中描绘的面容、
那真挚的眼神的深邃和热情，
没有一个不转向我（因为除我外
再没有别人把画上的帘幕拉开），
似乎想问我可是又不大敢问；
是从哪儿来的——这样的眼神？
你并非第一个人回头这样问我。
先生，不仅仅是她丈夫的在座
使公爵夫人面带欢容，可能
潘道夫偶然说过："夫人的披风
盖住她的手腕太多，"或者说：
"隐约的红晕向颈部渐渐隐没，
这绝非任何颜料所能复制。"
这种无聊话，却被她当成好意，
也足以唤起她的欢心。她那颗心——
怎么说好呢？——要取悦容易得很，
也太易感动。她看到什么都喜欢，
而她的目光又偏爱到处观看。
先生，她对什么都一样！她胸口上
佩戴的我的赠品，或落日的余光，
过分殷勤的傻子在园中攀折
给她的一枝樱桃，或她骑着
绕行花圃的白骡——所有这一切
都会使她同样地赞羡不绝，
或至少泛起红晕。她感激人，好的！

但她的感激（我说不上怎么搞的）
仿佛把我赐她的九百年的门第
与任何人的赠品并列。谁愿意
屈尊去谴责这种轻浮举止？即使
你有口才（我却没有）能把你的意志
给这样的人儿充分说明："你这点
或那点令我讨厌。这儿你差得远，
而那儿你超越了界限。"即使她肯听
你这样训诫她而毫不争论，
毫不为自己辩解，——我也觉得
这会有失身份，所以我选择
绝不屈尊。哦，先生，她总是在微笑，
每逢我走过；但是谁人走过得不到
同样慷慨的微笑？发展至此，
我下了令：于是一切微笑都从此制止。
她站在那儿，像活着一样。请你起身，
客人们在楼下等。我再重复一声：
你的主人——伯爵先生闻名的大方
足以充分保证：我对嫁妆
提出任何合理要求都不会遭拒绝；
当然，如我开头声明的，他美貌的小姐
才是我追求的目标。别客气，让咱们
一同下楼吧。但请看这海神尼普顿
在驯服海马，这是件珍贵的收藏，
是克劳斯为我特制的青铜铸像。

（飞白　译）

Meeting at Night

The grey sea and the long black land;
And the yellow half-noon large and low;
And the startled[1] little waves that leap

In fiery ringlets from their sleep,
As I gain the cove with pushing prow[2],
And quench its speed i' the slushy sand[3].

Then a mile of warm sea-scented beach,
Three fields to cross till a farm appears;
A tap at the pane, the quick sharp scratch
And blue spurt of a lighted match,[4]
And a voice less loud, thro' its joys and fears[5],
Than the two hearts beating each to each!

1. startled：惊醒的。此处为拟人手法，夜间小船将浪花从睡梦中惊醒。
2. gain the cove with pushing prow：驾着飞快的船到达海湾。cove：海湾。prow：船头。pushing prow 在声音效果上构成头韵，突出夜会男子的急迫心情。
3. quench its speed i' the slushy sand：在海岸的泥沙里把船停下来。
4. A tap at the pane, the quick sharp scratch / And blue spurt of a lighted match：连续的三个名词（tap, scratch, spurt）连贯地呈现出室外的男子与室内人接头的动作。
5. thro' its joys and fears：意为室内的爱人又惊又喜，发出低低的回应声，声音还不如两颗心紧贴在一起时心脏的跳动声。注意最后一行中比较级的运用，呈现出的形象生动真切。

The poem expresses the excitement and happiness of the lovers' meeting at night by depicting the details of environment and action. In diction, the poet prefers to use simple and concrete words, along with utilization of personification and alliteration to evoke the sensuous feelings in a tranquil but exciting night before meeting. In this way, the first stanza helps readers to understand the male's expectation and excitement before meeting his beloved.

However, the poem won't be called special without the last four lines, which are characterized by noun phrases instead of verbs, by fragmented phrases instead of complete sentences. The unique treatment and effect lie in the quick shifting from one to another, from one action to the next, which mimics the quick connection between excited but nervous lovers at night.

Questions

1. How do you comment on the successive four nouns (tap, scratch, spurt, voice) in the second stanza? How do the single nouns or fragmented phrases help to create the effect of movements and actions of the lovers?

2. Try to summarize the features of imagery in the poem. How do the different images help to evoke the sensations and passion in the readers to understand the lovers' meeting at night?

3. The occasion of the poem is a romantic one—a night meeting of the two lovers. Why does the poet select, by and large, such matter-of-fact details to fill out his poem? Why does not find the scent of blossoms, the song of nightingales, and the soft caress of the night breeze?

Chinese Translation

夜会

灰色的海，黑色的长岸：
半轮黄月大而低挂；
细碎的波浪从睡梦里惊觉，
溅出一道道火红的发鬈，
当急行的船头渐，止于松软的泥沙
我终于抵达了这个港湾。

接着是一哩海风温柔的沙滩；
再穿过三块田地，前面就是农庄；
轻叩小窗，急促的刮擦，
擦亮的火柴开一朵蓝花，
两颗心对跳时的响亮，
盖过了一声强抑惊喜的叫喊。

（卞之琳 译）

THE 20TH CENTURY

Unit 16　William Butler Yeats

Introduction to the Author

William Butler Yeats (1865-1939) was born in Sandy- mount, Dublin. His childhood and young manhood were spent between Dublin, London, and Sligo, and each of these places contributed something to his poetic development. He started to write poems around 20, and he continued to the day he died in 1939. He published thirteen volumes of 374 lyrics and eight narrative and dramatic poems recorded in *The Collected Poems of W. B. Yeats* (Definitive Edition, 1959). He suspended poetry writing around 1906 for his experiments in theater and absorbed the elements of the Japanese Noh and haiku into his works. Undoubtedly, the assistant work by Ezra Pound not only provided him with the new elements, but also helped him transform into a "modern" poet. The final phase of his poetry writing began with *The Tower* (1928) when the poet took a critical look at what he has written in his early age, publicly celebrating the Irish identity and culture which he endeavored to build through his life. He continued the themes of old age and death, and meditates on art and life in *The Winding Stairs and Other Poems* (1933), *From a Full Moon in March* (1935) and *Last Poems* (1939). Together with Lady Gregory, he founded the Irish theater later called the Abbey Theater. Throughout his life, he endeavored to seek a way to organize those events and his thoughts into a quasi-astrological system documented in *A Vision* (1st edition in 1925; 2nd edition in 1937).

Yeats is best remembered as a poet, however, he began his career as an apprentice in painting, following his Pre-Raphaelite father. He studied in Metropolitan School of Art, Dublin and later Royal Hibernian Academy School of London, from 1884 to 1886. He was never a satisfying student who followed teachers' instructions strictly and his artistic taste had inclinations to his father's. Yeats's acquaintance with visual arts, and his diligent exploration of the relationship between art and history, contribute to establish himself as one of the major poets of his age. Moreover, his poetry is not stagnant but dynamic, which would not stick to a certain period, but change with the social and historical environments. The greatness of his poetry lies in the combination of the artistic taste and the theory of culture and human history. He blends arts with his poetry writing to attain his ambitious intention—the cultural union of

Ireland, which is an outlet he searched for the salvation of his turbulent country and human beings as a whole. It is true that he is a poetic genius, and his outpourings are a brilliant record of the spiritual pains and pleasures he experienced in the process of searching.

Yeats's life and career spanned momentous literary, cultural, political and historical events. Yeats was drawn to mysticism as well as the cause for Irish independence. In the 1880s, he began to involve in the nationalist organization, the Irish Republican Brotherhood; in 1922, he was elected a Senate in the Irish Free Senator. Yet he is never simply a political propagandist or a radical poet.

The publication of *The Tower* in 1928 secured his status as one of the most talented lyrical poets and writers in Ireland. T. S. Eliot honored him as "the greatest poet of our age—certainly the greatest in this language". He was awarded the Nobel Prize in Literature in 1923.

The Lake Isle of Innisfree[1]

I will arise and go now, and go to Innisfree[2],
And a small cabin build there, of clay and wattles made[3]:
Nine bean-rows will I have there, a hive for the honey-bee,
And live alone in the bee-loud glade.[4]

And I shall have some peace there, for peace comes dropping slow,
Dropping from the veils of the mourning to where the cricket sings;
There midnight's all a glimmer, and noon a purple glow,
And evening full of the linnet's wings.[5]

I will arise and go now, for always night and day
I hear lake water lapping with low sounds by the shore[6];
While I stand on the roadway, or on the pavements grey,
I hear it in the deep heart's core[7].

1. 该诗作于1888年，最先发表于《全国观察家报》(*National Observer*)(1890)，1892年收录在《女伯爵和传奇及抒情诗》(*The Countess Kathleen and Various Legends and*

Lyrics）。作为叶芝早期试图区别于英诗传统的爱尔兰风格的代表，该诗在我国流传甚广，很多学者曾分析其中的隐逸向往。叶芝的早期诗歌作品深受前拉斐尔画派尤其是诗人、画家罗塞蒂（Dante Gabriel Rossetti）的影响，他回忆："我在前拉斐尔学派后期的氛围中学会了思考"。《茵尼斯弗里湖岛》集中地展现了绘画艺术，特别是前拉斐尔画派的风格对叶芝抒情诗创作的影响。叶芝怀着浓重的乡愁走在英国伦敦的舰队街上，抬眼看见商店橱窗里的一股喷泉，便勾起对故乡斯莱沟郡（Sligo）的思念，于是创作了这首名篇。全诗十二行，分为三节，韵脚为abab。第一节先用线条勾勒湖岛的大致轮廓，第二节以鲜艳的色彩展示了诗人对"光"和"色"的独特领悟，第三节借景抒情，抒发自己对城市生活的厌倦和对充满幻想的乌托邦式小岛的渴望。

2. Innisfree：一个虚构的湖岛。该词在盖尔语中意为heather island。值得注意的是该词拆分后的形式为Inn is free。这是个充满着自由的居所，诗人自称这个虚构湖岛的想法来自美国超验主义作家梭罗，他在信中回忆道："我父亲给我读过《瓦尔登湖》中的一些章节，我曾打算某天住在一个叫作Innisfree小岛上的小木屋里"。
3. 正常语序应为承接第一行的主语"I"。and build there a small cabin made of clay and wattles：在那里用树枝和泥土建起一间小屋。wattles：upright wooden poles or stakes through which sticks and branches are laced horizontally and daubed with clay to make weatherproof walls.
4. 第3—4行的正常语序应为：I will have there nine bean-rows，a hive for the honey-bee and live alone in the bee-loud glade。"九垄菜豆""一箱蜜蜂""林间空地"，一处幽居寥寥数笔便跃然纸上。整幅风景画的轮廓显现在读者的眼前，嗡嗡的蜜蜂和主人向往的独居形成一种巧妙的张力。
5. 第二节短短四行诗呈现了宁静的整体氛围，巧妙地描绘了一天四个时段不同的风景。细节描绘将景物有机地组合在一起，动静相宜，栩栩如生。半夜的湖面在月光的照射下"清波粼粼"，清晨的湖岛笼罩在薄雾中，俨然是烟水两茫茫的缥缈仙境。正午的太阳直射在湖岛的水面上，色彩混合成了紫色；黄昏时分的天空"织满了"正在扑腾的红雀的翅膀。该诗的取景效仿了受前拉斐尔画派影响的画家、编织工艺设计师莫里斯（William Morris），如同壁上挂毯一样，着眼于展现细节，湖岛景色仿佛壁毯编织而成。前拉斐尔画派强调运用光线和鲜艳色彩的对比来表达对象，这些在此诗中都得到完美表达：四幅强调光和色相互作用而产生的景物画，其一天之内的更迭似幻似真。叶芝很好地捕捉到各个时段不同的光的照射，展示了湖岛上宜人的风景。他找到了最适于表达光与色的明度差别变化的形式，并把光色明度的变化从绘画的其他因素中抽象出来。当然，这并不是一幅风景画，以上景物只是诗人"心眼"所见，并非眼前现实。叶芝从一开始写作诗歌便注重光线和色彩的作用，并产生了良好的审美效果。all a glimmer: shimmering starlight. purple glow: sunlight or flowers. glimmer and glow: alliteration. linnet：finch, a tiny seed-eating bird，红雀。

Notes

6. lake / lapping / low：这些都是头韵的例子。诗人的重心从视觉转向听觉，儿童时代在家乡爱尔兰南部斯莱沟郡的记忆在诗歌中回响。
7. roadway：refers to Fleet Street in London. pavements：实指城市。最后两行较之先前更为现实，诗人将他的读者从遥远的湖岛拉回充满喧嚣的都市。诗的结尾略显凄凉，起初诗人以一种欢快的口吻告诉读者他将起身前往一处平和、静谧的小岛，然而，诗人并未到达这个目的地，反而依旧伫立在都市的一隅黯然神伤。deep heart's core: a metaphor for the part of the speaker that feels and dreams deeply.

Text Analysis

"The Lake Isle of Innisfree" is one of the most popular poems of Yeats. It takes the readers to a tiny island in the middle of a lake—away from the hubbub of everyday life, from appointments and schedules—to live independently, alone, with a garden and a beehive for sustenance and a little cabin for shelter. Such an idyllic retreat is one that everyone dreams of from time to time, as Yeats did on busy London streets when he conceived the idea for the poem.

The poem is written mostly in hexameter, with six stresses in each line, and in a loosely iambic pattern. The last line of each four-line stanza shortens to tetrameter, with only four stresses, as in "And live alone in the bee-loud glade". Each of the three stanzas has the same abab rhyme scheme. Formally, this poem is somewhat unusual for Yeats: he rarely worked with hexameter, and every rhyme in the poem is usually a full rhyme; there is no sign of the half-rhymes Yeats often prefers in his later works. Yeats relies on alliteration and sounds of nature—the droning of bees, the chirping of crickets, and the flapping of birds' wings—to suggest peace and tranquillity. It appears that the stress pattern of the poem mimics the diastole-systole rhythm of the tranquil heartbeat—or the rise and fall of the ocean tides along the shore of County Sligo. A pause occurs in the middle of the first three lines of each stanza. The stress pattern before and after the pause is usually iambic, as in lines 1 and 2, with catalexis before the pause, hence the poem is silent for its musicality.

Questions

1. Do you think the speaker is really serious about going to Innisfree, or do you think this is just a passing daydream?

2. From the description of the ideal Innisfree, do you think the speaker has ever been

there? Why or why not?

3. What's the form of the poem? Do the quatrains (four-line stanzas) and rhymes contribute to the meaning in any way?

4. Why does the speaker want peace so badly? And why does peace come "dropping slow"? If he's so hungry for some quiet time, why can't he just make that happen in the city?

Chinese Translation

茵尼斯弗里湖岛

如今我要起身前去，前去茵尼斯弗里，
用树枝和泥土，在那里筑起小屋；
我要种下九垅菜豆，养一箱蜜蜂在那里，
在蜂吟嗡嗡的林间空地幽居独处。
我将得到些宁静，那里宁静缓缓降临，
从晨空的面纱上落到蟋蟀鸣响的地方；
那里的子夜水光粼粼，正午紫色辉映，
黄昏的天空中布满红雀的翅膀。
如今我要动身离去，因为每日每夜，
我总是听见湖水轻舐湖岸的幽音；
站在马路上，或踏着人行道的灰色，
我都能听见那水声萦回在我深心。

（傅浩　译）

Sailing to Byzantium[1]

I

That is no country for old men[2]. The young
In one another's arms, birds[3] in the trees
—Those dying generations[4]—at their song,
The salmon-falls, the mackerel-crowded seas,

Fish, flesh, or fowl, commend all summer long
Whatever is begotten, born, and dies.[5]
Caught in that sensual music[6] all neglect
Monuments of unageing intellect[7].

II

An aged man[8] is but a paltry thing,
A tattered coat upon a stick, unless
Soul clap its hands and sing, and louder sing
For every tatter in its mortal dress,
Nor is there singing school but studying
Monuments of its own magnificence;
And therefore I have sailed the seas and come
To the holy city of Byzantium.

III

O sages standing in God's holy fire
As in the gold mosaic[9] of a wall,
Come from the holy fire, perne in a gyre[10],
And be the singing-masters of my soul.
Consume my heart away; sick with desire
And fastened to a dying animal
It knows not what it is; and gather me
Into the artifice of eternity[11].

IV

Once out of nature I shall never take
My bodily form from any natural thing,
But such a form as Grecian goldsmiths make
Of hammered gold and gold enamelling
To keep a drowsy Emperor awake;[12]
Or set upon a golden bough[13] to sing
To lords and ladies of Byzantium
Of what is past, or passing, or to come.

1. 该诗创作于1926年，首先发表于杂志《十月的风》(*October Blast*)(1927)，后收录于诗集《塔堡》(*The Tower*，1928)。全诗共四节，循八音步抑扬格，韵脚为abababcc。《驶向拜占庭》一般被视为叶芝后期的巅峰之作，较完整地展现了其诗歌的艺术造诣。在1921年9月的一次BBC电台的采访中，叶芝谈到该诗的最初构想："最近我正在尝试着记录我灵魂的状态，因为这是作为一个迟暮的人对其灵魂的认识。我将我的这些关于这个主题的思想写入了这首诗——《驶向拜占庭》。"拜占庭，最早是古希腊的一个城市，是世界上唯一曾经拥有三个名字的著名国际大都市。公元330年，东罗马帝国君士坦丁大帝迁都于此，后来改名为君士坦丁堡。自此，拜占庭帝国持续了1100多年，直到1453年土耳其苏丹穆罕默德二世攻占此城，东罗马帝国灭亡，这里又成了奥斯曼帝国的首都，并再次改名为伊斯坦布尔，直至1923年土耳其共和国成立迁都安卡拉为止。公元4世纪后期起，基督教成为东罗马帝国的国教，大量以基督教为背景的意象充斥着这个城市的各个角落，无论是教堂还是家庭。这时出现了古希腊文化复兴的第一个浪潮，特别是6世纪时的文学和视觉艺术方面。早期拜占庭艺术将罗马文化、青铜器时期的拜占庭文化元素，以及凯尔特文化融为一体，这也成为后来吸引诗人叶芝的重要原因之一，他呼吁凯尔特文化在现代社会的复兴。此外，拜占庭独特的地理位置优势也使它成为叶芝关注的焦点。博斯普鲁斯海峡(Bosporus)从城中穿过，将这座城市一分为二，拜占庭是全世界唯一地跨亚欧两洲的城市。作为地中海到黑海的唯一通道，拜占庭也成了东西方地理和文化的重要交汇处。叶芝将"拜占庭"作为后期重要象征，认为它代表一座有着完美艺术成就并已获得永生的城市，在这座城市里，智慧和死亡的对立已经消解，人类的灵魂得到拯救并获得了永生。正如叶芝在后期重要作品《幻象》(*A Vision*，1937)中所称，在早期的拜占庭，作为其追寻精神生活的象征，历史、宗教、美学和生活都已合而为一。
2. no country for old men：不适合老年人的国度。此诗的巧妙之一在于其中的戏剧因素：一位老人认知的开始、发展、终结和起伏变化成为全诗的线索。一开头以肯定的语气指出这个充斥着感官刺激的世界并不适合老年人。那么老年人该何去何从呢？这为后来引向拜占庭打好伏笔。
3. 年轻的情侣拥抱，群鸟在树荫下歌唱，与老年人不同，他们尽情地享受着生命的乐趣。这些鸟儿与最后一节中栖息在"金枝"上的鸟儿形成呼应。
4. Those dying generations：前后两个破折号从形式上给读者一种空白的感觉，象征短暂的生命、虚无的人生。
5. salmon, mackerel, fish, flesh, fowl：这些动物象征着无知的生命，包括人类在内，竟然"commend all summer long"，为充满生机和活力的夏天唱赞歌，沉溺于感官的享受。诗人将源自盎格鲁-撒克逊语言的词汇和源于拉丁语的词汇并列，暗示其对人类肉体与灵魂、身体和冥想冲突的领悟(Whatever is begotten, born, and dies)。不管是多具有繁殖能力的物种，终究未能幸免死亡。

Notes

6. Caught in that sensual music：人类沉溺于感官的乐趣之中，最终在现代社会迷失了自我。
7. Monuments：这里指的是位于君士坦丁堡的圣索菲亚大教堂。从公元532年到537年，有艺术史上最大赞助人之称的东罗马帝国查士丁尼一世，为标榜自己的文治武功重建了圣索菲亚大教堂，它作为基督教的宫廷教堂，持续了9个世纪。作为拜占庭艺术和基督教文化的最大建筑物，圣索菲亚大教堂不仅是宗教的中心，更是当时西方文明的中心。叶芝将其视为象征着拜占庭文化的核心。
8. 老年人的意象在叶芝后期另一首诗歌《在学童中》(*Among School Children*)中再次出现。诗人将老年人比作一个衣衫褴褛的稻草人。
9. mosaic：镶嵌画，音译马赛克，是指将彩色块状的物质（如石头）拼贴成图画。此处为明喻，叶芝用圣索菲亚大教堂的镶嵌壁画上所展现的人物来模糊化真正的"圣人"与壁画人物之间的区别。同时，这也强化了上帝的圣火与艺术之间的关联。
10. perne in a gyre：turn in a vortex；spin around. 螺旋式的旋转，这也是叶芝后期诗歌中的一个重要象征，暗指人类文明呈螺旋式上升的态势。
11. the artifice of eternity：永恒的技艺。生命短暂，艺术永恒。千百年来诗人们久唱不衰的主题，叶芝也不例外。
12. 诗人想象他死后，他的灵魂脱离了肉体的束缚（out of nature），不需要任何的自然形式（natural thing），但是希望能附身于古希腊工匠锻造的金鸟（bodily form）。叶芝关于轮回、转世的理论源自他早期对印度教及玫瑰十字隐修会等宗教团体的兴趣。nature: natural being，residence of soul, the biological form and limitation of human being.
13. a golden bough：在维吉尔（Virgil）的《埃涅阿斯纪》(*Aeneid*)中，埃涅阿斯为去往冥府，必须先摘金枝。英国著名风景画家特纳（J. M. W. Turner）根据这个场景创作了名画《金枝》(Golden Bough)。叶芝对此画非常着迷，在回忆录中声称："我渴望模式，渴望前拉斐尔画派，渴望一种与艺术相连的诗歌。我一遍又一遍地去往我们的国家美术馆，观赏特纳的《金枝》。"金鸟和金枝的象征在后来的《拜占庭》一诗中再现。不过与本诗的线性结构相比，后者因其复杂的空间结构更戏剧化，也更难以描绘。

Text Analysis

The poem opens with a negative statement declaring that the sensual world of nature "is no country for old men". The apparent rejection moves to the conflicts between the transient but captivating stuff of physical living in the world of sexuality and the neglected "Monuments of unageing intellect". In the second stanza, the poet's agony of old age can be only redeemed if "Soul clap its hands and sing, and louder sing". A strong stress of the "soul" without definite article conveys its longing for spiritual life through the physical image of clapping and singing, and in this stanza "unageing intellect" is a natural force prompting the poet's voyage to Byzantium. The opposition of "sensual music" and "soul" has been set, hence, the third stanza comes to the core of the poem. The persona prays to the sages to spiral his way out of their domain and takes him up into theirs, however, it is his suffering heart that is "sick with desire", echoing Christ's words on the cross, "knows not what it is". The persona's torment moves on as the entrapment in the first stanza's "caught", while the act of prays indicates the poet's awareness of the limitations of an imagined permanence. "Soul", as well as "sages", has achieved the world of eternal artifice and transformed into what Byzantine goldsmiths made of enamels, the dazzling golden bird, which is representative of the "artifice" where "eternity" is "artificial" and also artistically shaped. In the final stanza, the poet offers an urbane diminuendo after his strong prayer; he imagines himself in the shape of the seeming ornamental golden bird, a trivial plaything to amuse the emperor, after which a strong sense of irony has been achieved. Thus, the inability of Yeats holy city to free itself from the dimension of time is reinforced by the syntactical chime across the poem between "Whatever is begotten, born, and dies" and the last line.

The themes in "Sailing to Byzantium" can be found in Yeats's ambitious work *A Vision* (1925), in which he develops his cyclical theory of human history, partly based on his understanding of the Hegelian dialectic and partly on his reading of Blake's prophetic poetry. In "Sailing to Byzantium", Yeats uses the symbol of the spiraling gyre to suggest that oppositions—such as youth and age, body and soul, nature and art, transience and immortality—are both antithetical to and dependent on each other. Motivated by the gyre and the poem itself, the mutually interpenetrating opposites thus produce a synthesis—unity of Being. In the poem, the golden bird contains elements of transitory nature, as seen in the song that the bird sings, with the transcendent qualities of timeless art.

Questions

1. Why does Yeats value art so highly in "Sailing to Byzantium"? Why did the poet abandon Ireland for Byzantium? What is his view of modern Ireland and its relation to Byzantine art?

2. How to understand Yeats' treatment of the typical Christian theme—immortality and eternity in the poem? What is the poet's attitude towards death as shown in the poem?

3. Work out the relation in the poem between the "birds in the trees" and the bird fashioned by "Grecian goldsmiths". What does the comparison stand for?

4. Yeats shows his oppositional views of the two extremities. Identify the opposite factors in the poem.

Chinese Translation

驶向拜占庭

一

那绝非老年人适宜之乡。青年人
互相拥抱着，树林中的鸟雀
——那些濒死的世代——在歌吟，
鲑鱼洄游的瀑布，鲭鱼麇集的海河，
水族、走兽、飞禽，整夏都在赞颂
萌发、出生和死亡的一切。
它们都沉溺于那肉感的音乐
而忽视了不朽的理性的杰作。

二

一个老人不过是无用的东西，
像一根竹竿上的破旧衣裳。
除非灵魂拍手歌唱，在凡胎肉体里
更高声地为每一件破旧衣裳歌唱，
而且没有一所歌唱学校不研习
自己的辉煌的不朽乐章；
因此我扬帆驶过波涛万顷，
来到这神圣之城拜占庭。

三

呵，伫立在上帝的圣火之中
一如在金镶壁画中的圣贤们，
走出圣火来吧，在旋锥中转动，
来教导我的灵魂练习歌吟。
耗尽我的心吧；它思欲成病，
紧附于一只垂死的动物肉身，
迷失了本性，请把我收集
到那永恒不朽的技艺里。

四

一旦超脱自然，我将绝不再采用
任何自然物做我身体的外形，
而只要那种古希腊金匠运用
鎏金和镀金法制作的完美造型，
以使睡意昏沉的皇帝保持清醒；
或栖止在一根金色的枝头唱吟，
把过去，现在，或将来的事情
唱给拜占庭的诸侯和贵妇们听。

（傅浩　译）

Unit 17 W. H. Auden

Wystan Hugh Auden (1907-1973), who publishes as W. H. Auden, is an Anglo-American poet, later an American citizen, regarded by many critics as one of the greatest writers of the 20th century. Auden was born in York and educated at Gresham's School, Holt, Norfolk, and Christ Church, Oxford. After leaving Oxford he taught at a school and later worked for the government. In 1935, he married Erika Mann, the daughter of the German novelist Thomas Mann. It was a marriage of convenience to enable Erika to gain British citizenship and escape Nazi Germany. Auden visited Germany, Iceland and China, and served in the Spanish Civil War; in 1939, he moved to the United States, which was considered a controversial move, and in the U.S. he met his lover Chester Kallman who would be his companion for the rest of his life. Auden taught at a number of American universities, and in 1946, he took US citizenship. His own beliefs changed radically from his youthful career in England, when he was an ardent advocate of socialism and Freudian psychoanalysis. His later phase in America witnessed his central preoccupation in Christianity and the modern Protestant theology.

Auden was a prolific writer, as well as a noted play-wright, librettist, editor, and essayist. Throughout his life, he published 27 volumes of poetry. The exciting collection *Poems* (1930) became a milestone for Auden to be the leading voice of a new generation. *Another Time* (1940) demonstrates greater control and less violence. Among his later phase, *Nones* (1951) shows distinctive ways of combining or alternating the grave and the flippant. His final works are increasingly personal in tone and combine an apparent air of offhand informality, which is hostile to the modern world and skeptical of all remedies for modern ills.

Early in his career Auden had intense interests in the poetry of Thomas Hardy, Robert Frost, William Blake, Emily Dickinson, Gerard Manley Hopkins, and Old English verse, and this helped to form his stylistic and technical achievements in writing poems in every imaginable verse form. Besides, he was admired for his engagement with moral and political issues, and for his incorporation of popular culture, current events and vernacular speech. He had a remarkable gift of mimicking the writing styles of other poets such as W. B. Yeats, Henry James and even Emily Dickinson. The major themes of his poetry are politics and citizenship, love, religion and morals, and the relationship between unique human beings and the anonymous, impersonal world of nature. Auden was the most active among the group of young English poets, who, in the late 1920s and early 1930s, saw themselves bringing new techniques and attitudes to English poetry.

Auden was a chancellor of the Academy of American Poets from 1954 to 1973. From 1956 to 1961, he worked as a professor of poetry at Oxford University. In the late 1950s, he bought a house in Austria, where he spent six months of every year and another half year in New York City. In 1972, with the declining health, he left the U.S. and moved back to Oxford. He died in Vienna on 29 September 1973. After his death, some of his poems, notably "Funeral Blues", "Musée des Beaux Arts", "Refugee Blues", "The Unknown Citizen" and "September 1, 1939" became widely known through films, broadcasts, and popular media.

Musée des Beaux Arts[1]

About suffering they were never wrong,
The Old Masters[2]: how well they understood
Its human position; how it takes place
While someone else is eating or opening a window or
just walking dully along;
How, when the aged are reverently, passionately waiting
For the miraculous birth, there always must be
Children who did not specially want it to happen, skating
On a pond at the edge of the wood:
They never forgot
That even the dreadful martyrdom[3] must run its course[4]
Anyhow in a corner, some untidy spot[5]
Where the dogs go on with their doggy life and the torturer's horse
Scratches its innocent behind[6] on a tree.

In Breughel's *Icarus*[7], for instance: how everything turns away
Quite leisurely from the disaster; the ploughman may
Have heard the splash, the forsaken cry[8],
But for him it was not an important failure[9]; the sun shone

As it had to on the white legs[10] disappearing into the green
Water; and the expensive delicate ship[11] that must have seen
Something amazing, a boy falling out of the sky,
Had somewhere to get to and sailed calmly on.

December, 1938

1. "Musée des Beaux Arts"(French for "Museum of Fine Arts",《美术馆》)创作于1938年，标题来自布鲁塞尔的比利时皇家美术馆 Musées Royaux des Beaux-Arts de Belgigue (Royal Museums of Fine Arts of Belgium)。本诗源自馆藏尼德兰画家老彼得·布吕赫尔(Pieter Bruegel de Oude)1558年的画作《伊卡鲁斯的堕落风景》(*Landscape with the Fall of Icarus*)，诗人在美术馆里看到这幅画，深有所感。后来美国诗人威廉斯(William Carlos Williams)在1960年也以此画为基础创作了同名诗《伊卡鲁斯的堕落风景》。根据希腊神话，灵巧的工匠代达罗斯曾为克里特国王建造迷宫，后来他自己和儿子伊卡鲁斯却被囚于此，代达罗斯用蜡和羽毛制成两副翅膀，和儿子一起逃离。但路上伊卡鲁斯忘了父亲的告诫，飞得离太阳过近，融化了翅膀，掉进了大海，丢了性命。
2. Old Masters：指文艺复兴及之前的画家。奥登此处援引早期画家及其画作，意图展示当时的人们对周围事物的人文关怀。紧接着，诗人描述了当今社会冷漠的现状，从一开始便展现了尖锐的冲突。该诗以对比的手法描绘了布吕赫尔的《伊卡鲁斯的堕落风景》和他的另外两幅画。第一节描述了"苦难"是如何发生的。
3. 奥登在此使用了两个例子"神异的降生"和"悲惨的殉道"引起读者的共鸣。批评家托马斯·迪尔沃斯(Thomas Dilworth)认为，这是出自布吕赫尔两幅画《屠杀无辜者》(*The Massacre of the Innocents*)和《伯利恒的户口调查》(*The Numbering at Bethlehem*)中的典故。诗人意图以此对比唤起读者如古代画家般对苦难的认知。"神异"指耶稣，耶稣的诞生为巨大的苦难所包围。耶稣降临两年之后，耶路撒冷的希律王下令杀死两岁以下的男婴，这些无辜孩童的家庭遭受了巨大的痛苦。"痛苦的殉难"指耶稣遇难，同样是多数人受苦。在这两个例子中，周围的人们都忽视了或者没有意识到身边所发生的事情。耶稣诞生的时候，多数人不知道这个消息，仍过着自己的生活，总有些孩子在"池塘上溜着冰"。同样，耶稣殉难的时候，仍有一些人不为所动，过着"狗"一般的日子。
4. run its course：经历，结束。叶芝在《踌躇》("Vancillation")一诗中写道："Between extremities, man runs its course"。
5. spot：catch sight of，看见。
6. scratches：scrape or rub as if to relieve itching，抓痒。behind：bottom，臀部。
7. Breughel's Icarus：指布吕赫尔的画作《伊卡鲁斯的堕落风景》。第二节描述了布吕赫尔《伊卡鲁斯的堕落风景》中的场景，当伊卡鲁斯掉入大海，农夫以及船上的人

们对此漠不关心。他们认为这是“怪事”一桩（something amazing）。

8. splash：水花四溅。forsaken cry：被遗忘的哭喊，这里使用了移就（transferred epithet）的修辞手法，伊卡鲁斯堕海，无人搭救，他发出了绝望的哭喊。

9. an important failure：了不得的失败。奥登认为伊卡鲁斯的堕海对于农夫而言不是一个了不得的失败，这与第一节描写的《屠杀无辜者》和《伯利恒的户口调查》中孩童、狗和马的活动一致。因此，该诗虽然在第二节中提到了伊卡鲁斯，但是诗人并不仅仅只停留在这一幅画。他将布吕赫尔的多幅画作联系起来说明“苦难”这一主题已为众人所忽视，他希望借此唤醒大众像早期画家那样洞察苦难和世情。

10. white legs：白腿，与后文中 green water（碧波）形成强烈的视觉冲突，反讽的语气跃然纸上，似乎诗人在质问：这么强烈的对比你们都视而不见吗？

11. the expensive delicate ship：华贵而精巧的船。诗人多次运用反讽的修辞手法，如后文中“Had somewhere to get to and sailed calmly on”似有某地要去，依旧静静地航行着。calmly 和前文中 splash，forsaken cry 形成对比，再次凸显主题。

Text Analysis

“Musée des Beaux Arts” was published in the collection *Another Time* (1940). Auden visited the museum in 1938 and viewed the painting by Brueghel. In this two-stanza poem that starts with “About suffering they were never wrong, / The Old Masters”, Auden comments on the general indifference to suffering in the world. The theme is apathy which shows that there are too many people who care little about events in their lives. He uses allusions in Christian history and Greek mythology to describe the theme and write in a tone of critical irony. The poem asserts that anguish is most accurately represented in art as a commonplace feeling and not as a dramatic emotion of tragic proportions.

Auden wrote, “In so far as poetry, or any of the arts, can be said to have an ulterior purpose, it is, by telling the truth, to disenchant and disintoxicate.” The poem juxtaposes ordinary events and extraordinary ones, although the later seems deflate to everyday events with his descriptions. Life goes on not only while a “miraculous birth occurs”, but also while “the disaster” of Icarus’ death happens.

The poem consists of two unequal stanzas, the first of 13 lines and the second of 8. The meter is irregular, the lines are of varying length, rarely end-stopped; and the style is conversational—consistent with the poem’s theme of nonchalance towards the spectacular. Written during the early stage of a devastating world war, the poem uses colloquialisms such as “anyhow” and “behind” (as an anatomical noun) to reinforce the widespread ignorance of and indifference to the cunning forces of history.

Questions

1. How will "Musée des Beaux Arts" be different if the speaker addresses more intimately and let the readers know more about his own thoughts and feelings?

2. What is the intention of the poet to mention Brueghel in the poem?

3. With whom do you sympathize most in this poem, Icarus, the kids, or the animals? And why?

4. In what way is "Musée des Beaux Arts" a reflective verse or reflective in nature? Why do the other people in the poem react indifferently to Icarus' death?

Chinese Translation

美术馆

关于痛苦他们总是很清楚的，
这些古典画家：他们深知它在
人心中的地位；深知痛苦会产生，
当别人在吃，在开窗，或正作着
　　无聊的散步的时候；
甚至当老年人热烈地、虔敬地等候
神异的降生时，总会有些孩子
并不特别想要它出现，而却在
树林边沿的池塘上溜着冰。
他们从不忘记：
即使悲惨的殉道也终归会完结
在一个角落，乱糟糟的地方，
在那里狗继续着狗的生涯，
　　而迫害者的马
把无知的臀部在树上摩擦。

在勃鲁盖尔的《伊卡鲁斯》里，比如说；
一切是多么安闲地从那桩灾难转过脸：
农夫或许听到了堕水的声音
　　和那绝望的呼喊，
但对于他，那不是了不得的失败；
太阳依旧照着白腿落进绿波里；
那华贵而精巧的船必曾看见
一件怪事，从天上掉下一个男童，
但它有某地要去，仍静静地航行。

（查良铮　译）

Unit 18 Seamus Heaney

Introduction to the Author

Seamus Heaney (1939-2013) is a poet, playwright, translator and recipient of Nobel Prize in Literature in 1995. Born in Derry, Northern Ireland, he was educated at St. Columb's College and Queen's University, Belfast. In 1972, he moved from Belfast to Glanmore, Wicklow, working for a time as a freelance writer, and then taught at Carysfort College in Dublin.

Heaney first came to the public attention in the mid-1960s. His first collection, *Death of a Naturalist* (1966), is rooted in childhood experiences of life in rural Derry. *Door in the Dark* (1969) shows a willingness to go beyond the familiar into the unknown. *Wintering Out* (1972) deals with exposure and endurance in poems that are circumspect about the re-emergent civil and sectarian conflicts of the Northern Ireland Troubles. From then on, Heaney tried his hands in other fields, such as translation and play adaptation. During the following 50 years, he published more than 10 poetic collections and 2 plays, translated many classic Irish and British poems, which brought him numerous honors and literary awards. His major works are such poetic collections as *North* (1975), *The Haw Lantern* (1987), *The Spirit Level* (1996), translated works as *Beowulf* (2001) and *Sweeney Astray* (1984), and two plays *The Cure at Troy* (1990) and *The Burial at Thebes* (2004).

Being a son from a peasant family and starting writing in the time of Northern Irish Troubles, Heaney's poetry is characterized by his rural and parochial life, allusions to sectarian difference, and interweaving contemporary Irish Troubles with a historical context and wider human experience. Heaney uses his works to reflect upon the Troubles, the often-violent political struggles that plagued the country during Heaney's adulthood. For his strong sense of nationhood and responsibility of role as a poet, he is celebrated as the most important Irish poet since W. B. Yeats. Before winning the Nobel Prize in 1995, Heaney had already won international recognition. From the 1980s to 2006, Heaney was both the Harvard and Oxford professor of poetry. On 6 June 2012, he was awarded the Lifetime Recognition Award from the Griffin Trust for Excellence in Poetry.

Clearances[1]
In Memoriam M. K. H., 1911-1984

When all the others were away at Mass
I was all hers as we peeled potatoes.
They broke the silence, let fall one by one
Like solder weeping off the soldering iron[2]:
Cold comforts set between us, things to share
Gleaming in a bucket of clean water
And again let fall. Little pleasant splashes
From each other's work would bring us to our senses.

So while the parish priest at her bedside
Went hammer and tongs at the prayers for the dying
And some were responding and some crying
I remembered her head bent towards my head,
Her breath in mine, our fluent dipping knives—
Never closer the whole rest of our lives.

1. 本诗出自希尼 1987 年的诗集《山楂灯笼》(*The Haw Lantern*)，是 10 首十四行组诗的第 3 首。
2. solder, soldering iron：电焊加热焊接金属时发出的嘶嘶声。

Text Analysis

The poem was written in memory of the poet's late mother, Margaret Kathleen McCann. In content, it depicts two unforgettable scenes between the mother and son. In the first stanza, the poet recalls peeling potatoes with his mother some day. Peeling potatoes—an ordinary rural work—becomes an effective means of communication, which brings both cold comforts during their silent working. The alliterated phrase "cold comforts" utters a kind of unique and amazing way of communication in both diction and sound effect. Then the second stanza recalls the scene of the mother's deathbed. The farewell between the mother and son means a second-time face to face silent "talk". However, this time turns out to be the last. Great grieve and sadness at the death of the mother brings to the poet a sense of emptiness, as totally cleared.

In poetic form, the poem is written in Italian sonnet, consisting of an octave and a sestet, in accordance with the two-part division in content. In addition, the last but one line "Her breath in mine, our fluent dipping knives—" is made up of two phrases. The juxtaposed two words "breath" and "knife" skillfully join the two memorable scenes together, and the leaping from breath to knife, from the present to the past indicates the quick shifting of the poet's memory flow in his brain.

Questions

1. Why is the poem entitled as "Clearances"? What's the relationship between the persona and "she" in the poem? How do you interpret the "cold comforts" to describe the relationship?

2. Please define the term "elegy". Can you please mention other English elegies you have learned and state the main features of this kind of poetic form?

3. What are the differences between the English sonnet and the Italian sonnet? Please scan the rhyme scheme of this sonnet.

Chinese Translation

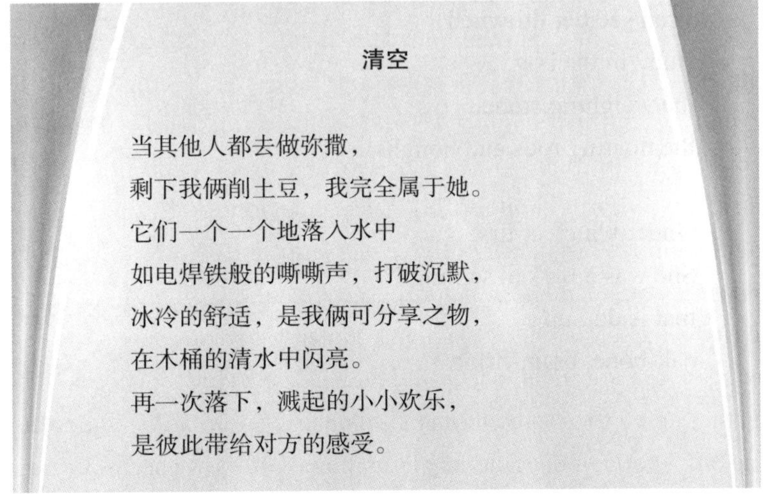

清空

当其他人都去做弥撒，
剩下我俩削土豆，我完全属于她。
它们一个一个地落入水中
如电焊铁般的嘶嘶声，打破沉默，
冰冷的舒适，是我俩可分享之物，
在木桶的清水中闪亮。
再一次落下，溅起的小小欢乐，
是彼此带给对方的感受。

当教区牧师来到她的床前，
为临死的人祈祷敲钟，
一些人回应，一些人哭泣
我记得她的头转向我，
她的呼吸融进我的呼吸，我们流利快削的刀——
一生中从未有过的亲近。

（李成坚　译）

Punishment[1]

I can feel the tug
Of the halter at the nape
Of her neck, the wind
On her naked front.

It blows her nipples
To amber beads
It shakes the frail rigging
Of her ribs.

I can see her drowned
Body in the bog,
the weighing stone,
the floating rods and boughs.

Under which at first
She was a barked sapling
that is dug up
oak-bone, brain-firkin[2]:

her shaved head
like a stubble of black corn,
her blindfold a soiled bandage,
her noose a ring

to store
the memories of love.
Little adultress,
before they punished you

you were flaxen-haired,
undernourished, and your
tar-black face was beautiful,
My poor scapegoat,

I almost love you
but would have cast, I know,
the stones of silence.
I am the artful voyeur

of your brain's exposed
and darkened combs[3],
your muscles' webbing
and all your numbered bones:

I who have stood dumb
When your betraying sisters,
cauled[4] in tar,
wept by the railings,

who would connive
in civilized outrage
yet understand the exact
and tribal, intimate revenge.

1. 这是希尼20世纪70年代创作的系列“沼潭诗”（bog poems）之一。其沼潭诗和地名诗（place-name poems）代表性地反映出诗人对于北爱尔兰政治危机和文化困境的诗性回顾和反思。
2. firkin: small cask，小桶。
3. comb: cellular structure, as in honeycomb，蜂窝。
4. caul：作名词时，指胎膜。在此，该词作动词用，意为像胎膜一样完全包裹或涂抹。

Text Analysis

In the poem, the girl's body (bog body) is hanged with heavy stones and dumped into the bog for adultery two thousand years ago. From the girl's nipples blown by wind "to amber beads", and "her shaved head like a stubble of black corn", the poet may imagine the punishments the girl had. Confronted with the violence towards "my poor scapegoat", "I" can do nothing except expressing my personal and secret love to the girl, for a timeless pattern of ever-recurring and inescapable conflicts happen again: nowadays, your betraying Catholic sisters are still cauled in tar and weeping by the railing for fraternizing with British soldiers.

Before such violence, Heaney does not intent to rebuke anyone or anything; he is trying to discover and restore the sources of life beneath his country's divided powers. As he focuses on the coldness caused by sectarian divisions in contemporary society, he aims at presentation.

Questions

1. For what crime has the female to bare the punishment during her life time? Why does the poet call this kind of punishment as tribal and intimate revenge?

2. Why does the poet mention "your betraying sisters" in the last but one stanza? In what way does the poet put contemporary troubles in a larger historical frame?

3. What's the poet's attitude towards the violent punishment? How do you interpret the title "Punishment" ?

Chinese Translation

惩罚

我能感觉到
她的脖子上
绞索的拖扯，风
在她裸露的前胸。

将她的乳头
吹成琥珀珠，
摇荡她的肋骨
那脆弱的缆索。

我能看到她在沼泽中
溺死的身体，
那使她沉陷的石头，
漂浮着的粗枝细杈。

她曾是那下面
一棵被剥了皮的小树
被人挖出来
骨头如橡木，脑子似小桶：

她被剃过的头
像黑谷地收割后的残茬，
她的蒙眼布是条脏绷带，
她的绞索是枚戒指

珍藏着
爱情的记忆。
小淫妇，
在人们惩罚你之前

你有亚麻色的头发，
缺乏营养，你
焦黑的面庞曾经漂亮，
我可怜的替罪羔羊。

我几乎爱上了你
但那时我也只会，我知道，
将沉默的石块投向你。
我是狡黠的窥淫人

窥看你大脑暴露的
变暗的沟回，
你网状的肌肉
和所有你那些编着号的骨头：

我沉默地伫立
当你背叛了的姐妹们，
涂着柏油，
在栏杆边哭泣，

我默默地纵许
这文明的暴行
更领悟了这严酷的
族群的、私密的复仇。

（吴德安　译）

下篇

美国诗歌

TRANSCENDENTALISM AND AMERICAN POETRY OF THE 19TH CENTURY

Unit 19　Ralph Waldo Emerson

Introduction to the Author

Ralph Waldo Emerson (1803-1882) is an American essayist, lecturer, and poet; he was also a Fellow of the American Academy of Arts and Sciences. Emerson was born in Boston, Massachusetts on May 25, 1803, as the son of a Unitarian minister. He was educated at the Boston Latin School and Harvard. After graduating from Harvard Divinity School, he took positions in the church but when he began to disagree with the church's methods, he eventually resigned the religious positions. He then toured Europe and met people like John Stuart Mill and Thomas Carlyle, William Wordsworth, Samuel Taylor Coleridge. Emerson corresponded with Carlyle for half a century; he later served as an unofficial literary agent in the U.S. for Carlyle. Emerson returned to the U.S. and later moved to Concord, Massachusetts. For the rest of his life he made a living as a popular lecturer in New England and much of the country. Nicknamed the Concord Sage, Emerson as a lecturer and orator became the leading voice of intellectual culture in the United States. James Russell Lowell remarked that Emerson was not only the "most steadily attractive lecturer in America", but also "one of the pioneers of the lecturing system".

Emerson's thoughts were provocative and far-reaching in their influence. "Nature" emphasizes individualism and rejects traditional authority. His speech "The American Scholar" (1837) is considered America's "Intellectual Declaration of Independence": by declaring literary independence in the United States it actually urges Americans to free from Europe. "The Divinity School Address" discounts Biblical miracles: for this, he was denounced as an atheist and a poisoner of young men's minds. Owing to these speeches he was not welcomed by Harvard for many years, but his message attracted young disciples, who joined the informal Transcendental Club. He was the center of the Transcendental Club which included Margaret Fuller, Ellery Channing and Henry David Thoreau. Emerson translates Carlyle's notion of "great men" into "representative men", poets or prophets who "transcend" the particular through intense self-absorption. Emerson encourages people to trust instinct, to use their potential talents for authentic self-discovery as the great men have done, and to perceive Nature as a source of inspiration and great truths. In his writings Emerson never espouses fixed philosophical tenets, but develops certain ideas such as individuality, freedom, the ability for humankind to realize almost anything, and the relationship between the soul and the surrounding world.

Emerson grew up in America, so he had a strong sense of nationhood. Yet he was never an isolationist; instead, he developed his thinking mainly from European traditions, while he was also introduced to Indian philosophy and much of his writing has strong shades of nondualism. He also came to know classical Chinese thinking via various means. Emerson remains in the center of American thinking, and his central idea "the infinitude of the private man" is highly influential in the American cultural tradition.

Emerson's works not only influenced his contemporaries, such as Walt Whitman and Henry David Thoreau, but continue to influence thinkers and writers in the United States and around the world down to the present. Notable thinkers under Emerson's influence include Nietzsche, William James, Herman Melville, Nathaniel Hawthorne and Henry James, et al., among whom some were Emersonians in denial—they could not escape his influence despite seeing themselves in opposition to the sage. While Whitman might cast influences on some later poets, their genuine influences could be traced back to Emerson who served as an initiator of the American tradition in many ways.

Days[1]

Daughters of Time, the hypocritic Days,
Muffled and dumb like barefoot dervishes[2],
And marching single in an endless file,
Bring diadems[3] and fagots[4] in their hands.
To each they offer gifts after his will,
Bread, kingdoms, stars, and the sky that holds them all.
I, in my pleachéd[5] garden, watched the pomp,
Forgot my morning wishes, hastily
Took a few herbs and apples, and the Day
Turned and departed silent. I, too late,
Under her solemn fillet saw the scorn.

Notes

1. 爱默生 1874 年出版诗集 *Parnassus*（《诗坛》或《帕纳塞斯》），其中还收录其他人的作品。爱默生以散文闻名，诗歌成就较为一般。当代著名理论家和文学批评家哈罗德·布鲁姆（Harold Bloom）的《英语最佳诗歌》（*The Best Poems of the English Language*）收入数首爱默生诗歌，但他也表明这些诗和作者最好的散文不可比。此诗创作于 1851 年，爱默生时年 48 岁。批评界和读者一般认为，这是他写得最好的一首诗，他自己对此表示认可。此诗共 11 行，每行为五步抑扬格，但尾韵不规整。
2. dervishes：dervish 的复数形式。dervish 指（伊斯兰教的）托钵僧，（伊斯兰教的）苦修僧人。另外，也可指印度教的禁欲主义者，尤指具有非凡的技艺和忍耐力的人。
3. diadems：diadem 的复数，指王冠，皇冕（王权的象征）。
4. fagot：也可拼为 faggot，指枝条捆，柴捆；或任何成捆的东西。
5. pleached：指（树枝、藤蔓等的）交错盘结、编结，如篱笆或拱形藤架、凉亭、走廊。

Text Analysis

The poem provides us with a sharp contrast between material and spiritual things: diadems, kingdoms and stars versus fagots and pleached garden. The relationship between the material and the spiritual is Emerson's major concern as the leader of the Transcendental Club. In "Nature", he maintains that nature is the symbol of spirit, yet man should try to reach the spiritual realm beyond the material things. The speaker in the poem chooses herbs and apples, i.e. the material things instead of the spiritual and the more significant things, and thus makes a wrong choice. According to the original sin of Puritan notion, man's wrong choice in the poem is doomed owing to man's evil nature.

Choice is an obvious topic of this poem, and it is actually an everlasting motif for mankind. The poem reenacts the Blakean myth of the fall into individuality, and thus the frames that begin to emerge in Emerson as a central conflict in American poetry: the self versus abyss, a dialectic later characterized explicitly by E. A. Robinson in his poem "Man Against the Sky" and by W. Stevens in his "Notes Towards a Supreme Fiction", and probably Robert Frost's most famous rendering of the theme in "A Road Not Taken".

Emerson's poetry is foreshadowed by his essays which stand among the best in American literature. He puts too much stress on expressing ideas as if poetry is the artistic form to echo his philosophy. His poetry therefore risks dogmatism instead of lyricism which is generally considered poetry's foremost aim. This reminds us of the poetry of China's Song Dynasty, characterized by its orientation to ration, as compared especially with Tang poetry's fine art of lyricism. However, Emerson still brought forward some good poems, including "Days".

In writing technique, he believes that line lengths, rhythms, and phrases are determined by breath; this is followed and developed in Whitman's free verse. Besides, this understanding of poetic rhythm foreshadow the theories of the modern poet Charles Olsen.

Questions

1. Why does the author say that the days are "hypocritic"? Do you agree with this judgment? Give your reasons.
2. What attitudes of religion, nature and man are shown in this poem?
3. Emerson's poem "The Day's Ration" addresses similar issues as "Days". What similarities and differences do you find in these two poems?

Chinese Translation

日子

时间老人的女儿，伪善的日子，一个个
裹着衣巾，暗哑如同赤足的托钵僧，
单行排列，无穷无尽地进行着，
手里拿着皇冕与一捆捆的柴。
她们向每一个人奉献礼物，要什么有什么，
面包、王国、星与包罗一切星辰的天空。
我在我矮树交织的园中观看那壮丽的行列，
我忘记了我早晨的愿望，匆忙地
拿了一点药草与苹果，日子转过身，
沉默地离去。我在她严肃的面容里
看出她的轻藐——已经太晚了。

（张爱玲　译）

Unit 20 Edgar Allan Poe

Edgar Allan Poe (1809-1849) is the father of detective story and a master of horror tale. He is also one of the greatest American poets and a controversial literary figure in the history of American literature. His position in the history of American literature is unique for his writing represents a category difficult to generalize.

On January 19, 1809, Edgar Allan Poe was born in Boston, Massachusetts, to parents who were itinerant actors. Poe's childhood was miserable. His parents died before he was three. He was later raised by John Allan, a prosperous tobacco exporter in Richmond, Virginia. At 17 Poe entered the University of Virginia. However, after less than one year of school, he was forced to leave due to the lack of money. In 1827, Poe enlisted in the United States Army. That year he published his first collection of poems *Tamerlane, and Other Poems*. After two years, his second collection *Al Aaraaf, Tamerlane and Minor Poems* was published. His early verses reflected the influence of English Romantics such as Lord Byron, John Keats, and Percy Bysshe Shelley. Unfortunately, neither of these two collections received public attention.

Following his military service, Poe accepted an appoint- ment to West Point, but he was again forced to leave for reasons not completely clear. He then moved to Baltimore and lived with his father's sister, Mrs. Maria Clemm, and her daughter Virginia. Poe began to show his true talent in writing short stories around this time. In 1835, he became the editor of *The Southern Literary Messenger* in Richmond. He then married his 13-year-old cousin, Virginia Clemm in 1836. In the next ten years Poe edited many literary journals and established himself as an editor, a short-story writer, and a poet. He published some of his best-known stories and poems including "The Fall of the House of Usher", "The Tell-Tale Heart", "The Murders in the Rue Morgue" and "The Raven". He also gained stature as a well-known literary critic.

Poverty haunted Poe in his entire life. After Virginia's death from tuberculosis in 1847, Poe's life-long struggle with depression worsened. On October 3, 1849, he was found in a state of semi-consciousness and died four days later. His death remained a mystery.

For a long time after his death American literary criticism did not do justice to Poe's talent and genius. However, it is quite ironical that Poe enjoyed welcome and praise in Europe. Now

Poe's status as a great writer of fiction, a preeminent poet, and a first-rank critic is unquestionable. He remains a dominant influence in the world of letters. His writings are highly praised in America as well as in the whole world, leaving visible imprint on writers from different countries.

For Poe, a successful poem should be short and readable at one sitting. Most importantly, it should not be didactic but must be pure. Poe also lays stress on rhythm. He defines true poetry as "the rhythmical creation of beauty" (qtd. in Quinn 334) and underlines that "music is the perfection of the soul, or idea, of poetry" (429). His ideas on poetry have made him a principle forerunner to the "art for art's sake" movement in the 19th-century European literature.

To Helen[1]

Helen[2], thy beauty is to me
  Like those Nicéan barks of yore[3],
That gently, o'er a pérfumed sea,
  The weary, way-worn wanderer bore
  To his own native shore.

On desperate seas long wont to[4] roam,
  Thy hyacinth[5] hair, thy classic face,
Thy Naiad[6] airs have brought me home
  To the glory that was Greece
And the grandeur that was Rome[7].

Lo! In yon brilliant window-niche
  How statue-like I see thee stand,
  The agate lamp within thy hand!
Ah, Psyche[8], from the regions which
  Are Holy-land!

1. 爱伦·坡曾写过两首《致海伦》，本诗为两首中的前一首，该诗最初发表于1931年，诗中的海伦是为了纪念坡的同学罗伯特·斯坦纳德（Robert Stanard）的母亲简·斯坦纳德（Mrs. Jane Stith Stanard）。斯坦纳德夫人端庄美丽，是坡少年时期心中美的化身。1824年4月，31岁的斯坦纳德夫人病故，坡伤心欲绝，对斯坦纳德夫人的思念使他写出了第一首《致海伦》。该诗于1945年由坡做了一些修改，其中最显著的修改是将1931年版本中的"the beauty of fair Greece, / And the grandeur of old Rome"改为本文中的"the glory that was Greece, / And the grandeur that was Rome"。第二首《致海伦》发表于1948年，该诗中的海伦指的是女诗人莎拉·海伦·惠特曼（Sarah Helen Whitman），坡曾在当年向这位比他大五岁的女诗人求过婚。
2. 海伦是希腊神话中的绝世美人。16岁时嫁给斯巴达王墨涅拉奥斯（Menelaus）成为斯巴达王后。后来特洛伊王子赫克托耳（Hector）和二王子帕里斯（Paris）到访斯巴达，帕里斯把她拐去，带回特洛伊。斯巴达王大怒，他向哥哥迈锡尼国王阿加门农（Agamemnon）求助，希腊联军组织一千艘船舰出征，而引起著名的特洛伊战争（The Trojan War）。
3. Nicean barks of yore：古代尼西亚人的航船。尼西亚是小亚细亚西北部古卑斯尼亚的一座古城（今属土耳其）。在该句诗中，坡可能受到柯勒律治的诗歌"Youth and Age"的启发，柯勒律治在该诗中曾写道："Like those trim skiffs, unknown of yore"。
4. wont to：accustomed to.
5. hyacinth：风信子花。在古希腊神话中，太阳神阿波罗钟爱的少年海辛瑟斯（Hyacinthus）有一头美丽的长发，在他被误杀后，他的血泊中长出了纤细修长、迎风招展的美丽的风信子花。
6. Naiad：古希腊罗马神话中的水泉女神。
7. To the glory that was Greece, / And the grandeur that was Rome 在世界文学中常常被引用，展现了古希腊和古罗马的辉煌宏伟。
8. Psyche：普赛克，古希腊罗马神话中嫁给爱神厄洛斯（Eros，又名丘比特）的绝世美女。厄洛斯禁止她看见自己的形象，但普赛克未能克制住好奇心，在夜晚举灯看见了丈夫的模样，险被丈夫抛弃。此外，psyche一词还有心灵、灵魂的意思。

"To Helen" is a three stanza lyric that has been called one of the most beautiful love poems in the English language. The theme of this poem is to eulogize the beauty of a woman, Mrs. Jane Stith Stanard. Beauty, as Poe underlines in this poem, appears to refer to the woman's soul as well as her body. At the beginning of the poem, Poe compares her to Helen of Troy, who is supposed to be the quintessence of physical beauty. Then at the end of the poem, Poe represents the woman as Psyche, the quintessence of soulful beauty.

As is typical with many of Poe's poems, the rhythm and rhyme scheme of "To Helen" is irregular but musical in sound. The rhyme scheme is ababb, cdcec, fggfg. It is to be observed that the poem is a melody with skilful artistry of alliteration such as "weary, way-worn wanderer", assonance such as "wont to roam", and masculine end rhyme such as "me" rhyming with "sea" in the first stanza. Vowels and diphthongs are also used to bring about the slow rhythm which demonstrates the speaker's admiration and implies that the woman's beauty is soothing yet inaccessible.

Poe opens the poem with a simile—"Helen, thy beauty is to me / Like those Nicean barks of yore" — that compares the beauty of Helen to small sailing boats that carry home travelers in ancient times. In this stanza, Helen's beauty is soothing, providing security and safety. Her beauty is as hypnotic for the speaker as the barks that transport wanderers home from Troy. Poe extends this boat imagery into the second stanza, declaring that Helen brings him home to the shores of the greatest civilizations of antiquity, classical Greece and Rome, and making connections between the beauty of the woman with the classical beauty of ancient Greece and Rome. In the last stanza, Poe imagines that the woman stands in a recess in front of a window, holding an agate lamp, as Psyche does when she discovers the identity of Eros.

Throughout the poem, Poe uses allusions to mythology and the classical age to invoke the readers' impression of an idealized woman near to perfection, like a Greek statue.

Questions

1. In the first stanza, what likeness does Poe draw between Helen and the "Nicean barks"? Why does Poe choose to refer to those ships as "Nicean barks" instead of other ships?

2. Briefly explain why Poe uses the word "glory" in reference to ancient Greece and "grandeur" in reference to ancient Rome.

3. Do archaic or quaint words such as "thy", "thee", "lo", and "yon" enhance the effect of the poem?

4. Poe is adept at describing beauty. His poems usually write about the beauty of women, flowers, landscapes, sunsets and so on. Please write a short essay that attempts to define beauty.

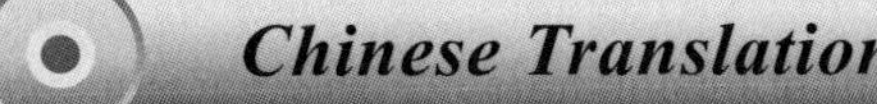

Chinese Translation

致海伦

海伦，
你的美对于我犹如尼萨的船舸，
在往昔，
它们滑过芬芳的海波，
把漂泊者从倦人的旅羁载回故国的陆地。

经历了海风多次的吹拂——
你那风信子般的美发，
你典雅的脸庞，
水仙女的风姿，
带我回到希腊的熠熠光华和古罗马的气魄。

看！
在一个华美的窗龛你犹如雕像那样伫立，
玛瑙明灯擎在手里！
啊，赛琪，你来自彼岸那不可及的圣地！
（李文俊　译）

Annabel Lee[1]

It was many and many a year ago[2],
　　In a kingdom by the sea
That a maiden[3] there lived whom you may know
　　By the name of ANNABEL LEE;
And this maiden she lived with no other thought
　　Than to love and be loved by me.

She was a child and *I* was a child,

In this kingdom by the sea,
But we loved with a love that was more than love—
I and my ANNABEL LEE—
With a love that the wingéd seraphs of Heaven
Coveted[4] her and me.

And this was the reason[5] that, long ago[6],
In this kingdom by the sea,
A wind blew out of a cloud[7] by night
chilling my ANNABEL LEE;
So that her highborn kinsmen came
And bore her away from me,
To shut her up in a sepulchre[8]
In this kingdom by the sea.

The angels, not half so happy in Heaven,
Went envying her and me:
Yes! that was the reason (as all men know,
In this kingdom by the sea)
That the wind came out of the cloud chilling,
And killing[9] my ANNABEL LEE.

But our love it was stronger by far than the love
Of those who were older than we—
Of many far wiser than we—
And neither the angels in Heaven above,
Nor the demons down under the sea[10],
Can ever dissever[11] my soul from the soul
Of the beautiful ANNABEL LEE:

For the moon never beams, without bringing me dreams
Of the beautiful ANNABEL LEE;
And the stars never rise, but I see the bright eyes
Of the beautiful ANNABEL LEE[12];
And so, all the night-tide, I lie down by the side
Of my darling, my darling, my life and my bride[13],
In her sepulchre there by the sea—
In her tomb by the side of the sea.

Notes

1.《安娜贝尔·李》是诗人爱伦·坡1849年去世后才发表的一篇诗作，代表诗人唯美主义风格的顶峰。在其著名的文学评论《创作原理》(*The Philosophy of Composition*)中，爱伦·坡曾说人世间最伤感的莫过于死亡，而美丽的年轻女子的死亡更让人痛彻心骨。诗中美丽的安娜贝尔·李正是坡一生挚爱——年轻的亡妻弗吉尼亚(Virginia)的化身。全诗用过去式讲述了一段凄美哀怨的爱情故事，该诗音韵优美、节奏感强，充满着浓浓的忧伤，体现了坡的诗歌创作原则，即音乐美和忧郁美。
2. 该句中，两个many点出时间之久远及二人爱意之悠长。此外，该诗节中反复出现m及n，头韵的用法也值得注意。
3. 坡在此将安娜贝尔·李称为maiden，意为未婚女子、处女。这种称呼暗示诗歌的叙述者与安娜贝尔·李的关系尚未到达婚嫁阶段。
4. coveted: envied, resented.
5. this was the reason: the seraphs' envy.
6. 该句中的long ago呼应了文中第一节第一行的many and many a year ago。
7. a cloud：在此采用a cloud而不用the sky，意在预示灾难及黑暗的降临，指涉的是天使的嫉妒。
8. sepulchre：为sepulcher的英式表达。相比较美式英语，英式英语显得更为正统权威。
9. Chilling and killing：中间韵(internal rhyme)的一例。
10. 在该诗节中，诗人主要聚焦于：(1)地球，人类聚集的领域；(2)天堂：天使之地；(3)地狱：魔鬼之域。他与安娜贝尔·李的爱比任何尘世的爱都要强烈，终将逃离天使和恶魔的掌控。
11. dissever：separate into parts or portions. ever dissever采用中间韵(internal rhyme)。
12. 坡在此强调光的意象，将月光与他做的有关安娜贝尔·李的梦，星光和安娜贝尔·李的双眸联系在了一起。
13. 在该诗行中，诗人采用了回指修辞(anaphora，又名首语重复)。

Text Analysis

"Annabel Lee" was written in May 1849, a few months before Poe's death. Although the poem may refer to many women in Poe's life, most critics acknowledge it to be in memory of Virginia Clemm, Poe's young wife who married him at 13 and died in 1847 when she was less than 25.

The theme of this poem is eternal love. The love between the narrator and Annabel Lee is so strong and pure that even the seraphs, the highest order of angels in heaven, envy it. They attempt to destroy their love by sending a chilling wind which eventually kills Annabel Lee. However, their love remains because the lovers' souls are still united.

The poem describes Annabel Lee as a "maiden" and declares that "I was a child and She was a child /… / But we loved with a love that was more than love". This way of expression is consistent with the ideals of the Romantic era. Many Romantics from the 18th and 19th centuries regard adulthood as a corruption of pure childhood. Poe views the narrator's childhood love for Annabel Lee as more eternal and purer than the love of adults.

The poem has a peaceful and musical rhythm. It makes good use of repetition of many words and refrain phrases such as "in this kingdom by the sea", "my ANNABEL LEE" and "of the beautiful ANNABEL LEE", etc. In addition, although the poem's stanzas have an irregular length and structure, its rhyme scheme continually emphasizes "me", "Lee", and "sea", reflecting the overall musicality of the poem.

The tone of this poem is melancholy and grievous. It sets a romantic and loving mood in the beginning. Then with the death of Annabel Lee, the mood changes to a certain dark, wilful melancholy, a cold mood that frequently appears in Poe's poems. Word choice and sentence arrangement also help to create the tragic feeling of Annabel Lee's death, which can be revealed from the last part of this poem: "And so, all the night-tide, I lie down by the side / Of my darling—my darling—my life and my bride, / In her sepulchre there by the sea— / In her tomb by the sounding sea".

Questions

1. The love story between the narrator and Annabel Lee is moving and tragic. Can you find similar motif in other writings?
2. What does the name "Annabel Lee" indicate? Can it be replaced by other female names?
3. What is the speaker's attitude towards those who are older than he and Annabel Lee?
4. What does Annabel Lee die of ?

Chinese Translation

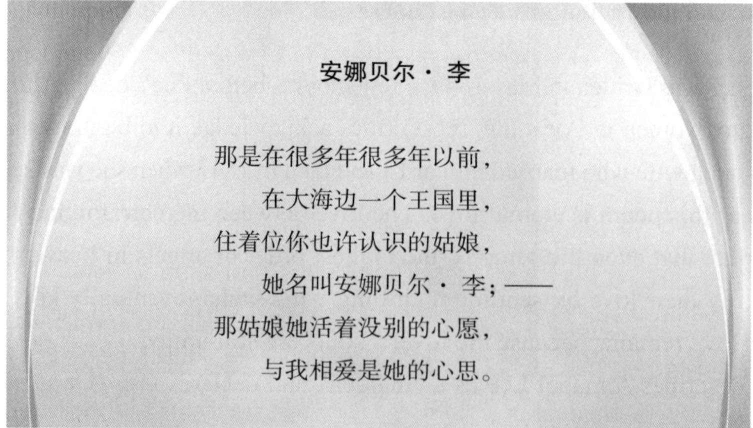

安娜贝尔·李

那是在很多年很多年以前，
　　在大海边一个王国里，
住着位你也许认识的姑娘，
　　她名叫安娜贝尔·李；——
那姑娘她活着没别的心愿，
　　与我相爱是她的心思。

她是个孩子，我也是孩子，
　　在大海边的那个王国里，
但我俩以超越爱的爱相爱——
　　我和我的安娜贝尔·李——
以一种爱连天上的六翼天使
　　对她和我也心生妒意。

而这就是原因，在很久以前，
　　在大海边那个王国里，
趁黑夜从云间吹来一阵冷风
　　寒彻我的安娜贝尔·李；
于是她出身高贵的亲属前来
　　从我的身边把她带去，
把她关进了一座石凿的墓穴，
　　在大海边的那个王国里。

在天堂一点也不快活的天使
　　对她和我一直心存妒意；
对！那就是原因（众所周知，
　　在大海边那个王国里）
趁黑夜从云间吹来一阵冷风，
　　冻煞我的安娜贝尔·李。

但我俩的爱远比其他爱强烈
　　与那些更年长的人相比——
　　与许多更聪明的人相比——
无论是那些住在天堂的天使
　　还是那些在海底的鬼蜮
都永远不能将我俩的灵魂分开，
我和我的安娜贝尔·李：——

因为当月放光华我总会梦见
　　我美丽的安娜贝尔·李；
而每当星斗升空我总会看见
　　她那明亮而美丽的眸子；
所以我整夜都躺在我爱人身旁，
我的爱，我的生命，我的新娘，
　　在大海边她的石墓里——
　　在海边她的墓地。

（曹明伦　译）

Unit 21 Walt Whitman

Introduction to the Author

Walt Whitman (1819-1892) is a poet, essayist and journalist. Often called the father of free verse and of American modern poetry, he is among the most influential poets in American literature history.

He was born on May 31, 1819 in Brooklyn, New York, the second son of Walter Whitman and Louisa Van Velsor. He received only six years of formal school education (1825-1830). At the age of twelve, he then sought employment for further income for his family; he was an office boy for two lawyers and later was an apprentice and printer's devil for the weekly Long Island newspaper *The Patriot*. From 1836 to 1841, he taught at various schools in Long Island. Later he turned to journalism as a full-time career. He founded a weekly newspaper, *Long-Islander*, and later edited a number of Brooklyn and New York papers. During the Civil War (1861-1865), overcome by the suffering of the many wounded in Washington, Whitman decided to stay and work in the hospitals and stayed in the city for eleven years. He took a job as a clerk for the Department of the Interior, but he was fired when the Secretary of the Interior, James Harlan, discovered that Whitman was the author of *Leaves of Grass*, which Harlan found offensive.

Whitman lived a poor life most of his life. From time to time, he had to receive financial support to get by from his friends and writers both in the United States and England. If he had excess money, he would buy supplies for the patients he took care of, his widowed mother and one invalid brother. In 1873, he suffered a paralytic stroke, so he was induced to move from Washington to the home of his brother—George Washington Whitman. His mother, having fallen ill, was also there and died that same year in May. Both events were difficult for Whitman and left him depressed. He died of bronchial pneumonia on March 26, 1892.

Whitman contributed more than five books of poetry. The most important is *Leaves of Grass*, which he edited and revised almost the rest of his life since the first edition in 1855. He stressed that a poet must be closely concerned with the society and his own country. He wrote in the preface to the 1855 edition of *Leaves of Grass*, "The proof of a poet is that his country absorbs him as affectionately as he has absorbed it." Whitman's poetry breaks the boundaries of poetic form and is prose-like. He openly wrote about death and sexuality, including prostitution, which at the very beginning of its publication caused wide criticism and even insulting comments. He is labeled as the father of free verse, though he did not invent it. A British critic Mary Whitall Smith Costelloe once wrote, "You cannot really understand America without Walt Whitman, without *Leaves of Grass*." The modernist poet Ezra Pound called Whitman "America's poet, ... He is America." The literary critic, Harold Bloom wrote, as introduction to the 150th anniversary of *Leaves of Grass*, "If you are American, then Walt Whitman is your imaginative father and mother, even if, like myself, you have never composed a line of verse. You can nominate a fair number of literary works as candidates for the secular Scripture of the United States. They might include Melville's *Moby-Dick*, Twain's *Adventures of Huckleberry Finn*, and Emerson's two series of *Essays* and *The Conduct of Life*. None of those, not even Emerson's, are as central as the first edition of *Leaves of Grass*."

Song of Myself [1](Excerpt)

I celebrate[2] myself, and sing myself,
And what I assume[3] you shall assume,
For every atom belonging to me as good belongs to you.

I loafe[4] and invite my soul,
I lean and loafe at my ease[5] observing a spear[6] of summer grass.

My tongue, every atom of my blood, form'd from this soil, this air,
Born here of parents born here from parents the same,
and their parents the same,[7]
I, now thirty-seven years old in perfect health begin,
Hoping to cease[8] not till death.

Creeds[9] and schools in abeyance[10],
Retiring back a while sufficed[11] at what they are, but never forgotten,
I harbor for good or bad, I permit to speak at every hazard[12],
Nature without check with original energy.

Notes

1. free verse：自由诗。自由诗是诗体的一种，19 世纪中叶源于欧美。其结构自由，段数、行数、字数等没有一定规定，它在章节、音步、押韵等方面都比较自由、灵活，没有格律诗那样严格，在西方以美国诗人惠特曼为创始人。法国诗人古斯塔夫·卡恩（Gustave Kahn）于 19 世纪 80 年代末第一个使用自由诗“vers libre”这一术语，它对应英语中的 free verse。所选诗歌为《自己之歌》（“Song of Myself”）的第一部分，全诗共 52 部分，1336 行。该诗是惠特曼出版的第一本诗集《草叶集》的代表作，诗人终生对其不断地修改与完善。本诗也是美国文学史上富有里程碑意义的巨作。
2. celebrate：praise, honor，赞扬，赞美。
3. assume：该词在本诗中可以作复义词理解，既可理解为“假定、想象”，又可理解为“承担义务”。
4. loafe：loaf, spend time idly，虚度光阴。
5. at one's ease：completely relaxed，（感到）完全放松。
6. spear：long pointed leaf，长而尖的叶。
7. 此句中，诗人运用了重复修辞格来增强语言的力量和节奏感，意思是：父母在这里把我生下来，同样，父母的父母在这里把他们生下来，依此类推。
8. cease：come to an end，stop，停止，终止。
9. creed：system of beliefs or opinions, especially religious beliefs，信条，教义（尤指宗教信仰）。
10. abeyance：be suspended temporarily，not be in force or use for a time，（指权利、规则等）暂时中止，（指问题等）缓议，暂时无效或停用。
11. suffice：be enough，be adequate，能满足，足够的。
12. hazard：(thing that can cause) danger, risk，危险，有危险的事物，风险。

Text Analysis

"Song of Myself" is among the most important pieces by Walt Whitman. The poem in all contains 1336 lines of 52 sections, untitled in the beginning when first collected in *Leaves of Grass*, which contained only twelve poems. What is selected above is the opening part of the long poem.

The poem made its first appearance in 1855, which received few complimentary comments but derogatory and even humiliating remarks. One reason is that Whitman's works broke the American poetic tradition in its form. Historically, American poetry followed the metrical patterns characterized with rhymes, iambic or trochaic cadence with accentuated syllables, paralleled lines, and formal versification. But Whitman's poem seems to be liberated from the fetter-like principles. It is more like a prose than a poem except for the poetic lines. However, one thing which has to be stressed is that free verse is not absolutely free. For example, the poem "Song of Myself " has its own peculiar cadence based upon the figurative use of repetition as well as syntax structure, like "I celebrate **myself**, and sing **myself**", "And what I **assume** you shall **assume**", "For every atom **belonging to me** as good **belongs to you**", "**Born here of parents born here from parents the same, and their parents the same**".

Thematically, the poet sings high praise of the freedom of humanities. The poem is romantic, confessional, democratic, and symbolic. In the 1850s, although America had got its political independence, its cultural position was still very weak and dependent. Besides, the nation's political democracy was poor. Whitman wrote in the preface to the 1855 edition of *Leaves of Grass*, "The proof of a poet is that his country absorbs him as affectionately as he has absorbed it." He believed there was a vital, symbiotic relationship between the poet and his society. The speaker "I" is dominating in not only the poem "Song of Myself " but also in the book *Leaves of Grass*. We can understand it as either the poet's personal self, or American "I", or an "I" of universality, or a poetic "I". The speaker's confidence in the beauty of humanity, his strong expression of man's personality, and powerful tone all bring readers unprecedented freshness and impact.

Questions

1. T. S. Eliot once said, "No poet, no artist of any art, has his complete meaning alone. His significance, his appreciation is the appreciation of his relation to the dead poets and artists. You cannot value him alone; you must set him, for contrast and comparison, among the dead." In this sense, when we set Walt Whitman and his *Leaves of Grass* in the historic background, how can we value his achievements and appreciate his literary works?
2. Does the speaker "I" in the poem refer to the poet? Who do you think "I" refer to?
3. What does the speaker sing for? For "my" living, health, liberty, nature or something else?

Chinese Translation

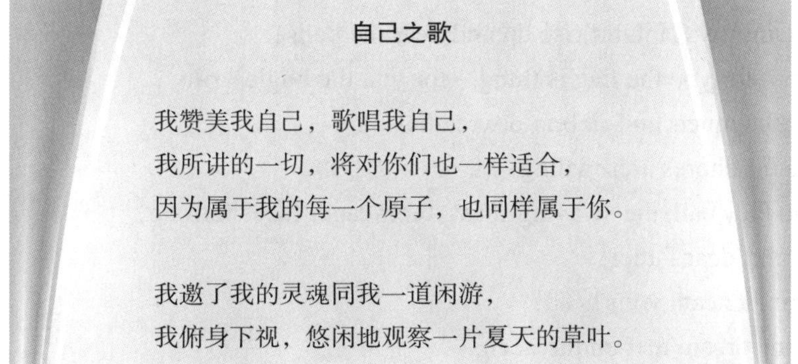

自己之歌

我赞美我自己，歌唱我自己，
我所讲的一切，将对你们也一样适合，
因为属于我的每一个原子，也同样属于你。

我邀了我的灵魂同我一道闲游，
我俯身下视，悠闲地观察一片夏天的草叶。

我的舌，我的血液中的每个原子，
　　都是由这泥土这空气构成，
我在这里生长，我的父母在这里生长，
　　他们的父母也同样在这里生长，
我现在是三十七岁了，身体完全健康，
希望继续不停地唱下去直到死亡。

教条和学派暂时搁开，
退后一步，满足于现在它们所已给我的一切，
　　但绝不能把它们全遗忘，
不论是善是恶，我将随意之所及，
毫无顾忌，以一种原始的活力述说自然。
（楚图南、李野光　译）

O Captain! My Captain![1]

O Captain! My Captain! our fearful trip is done[2];
The ship has weather'd every rack[3], the prize we sought is won;
The port is near, the bells I hear, the people all exulting[4],
While follow eyes the steady keel[5], the vessel[6] grim and daring[7]:
But O heart! heart! heart!
O the bleeding drops of red,
Where on the deck my Captain lies,
Fallen cold and dead.
O Captain! my Captain! rise up and hear the bells;
Rise up—for you the flag is flung—for you the bugle[8] trills[9];
For you bouquets and ribbon'd wreaths—
for you the shores a-crowding;
For you they call, the swaying mass, their eager faces turning;
O Captain! dear father!
This arm beneath your head;
It is some dream that on the deck,

You've fallen cold and dead.
My Captain does not answer, his lips are pale and still;
My father does not feel my arm, he has no pulse nor will;
The ship is anchor'd safe and sound[10], its voyage closed and done;
From fearful trip, the victor ship, comes in with object won[11];
Exult, O shores, and ring, O bells!
But I, with mournful tread,
Walk the deck my captain lies,
Fallen cold and dead.

Notes

1. 该诗为一首挽歌（elegy）。挽歌定义如下：a mournful, melancholic or plaintive short poem，especially a funeral song or a lament for the dead, usually formal or ceremonious in tone and diction, caused by the death of a person。惠特曼此诗为纪念美国第 16 任总统林肯而作，这是美国内战期间最著名的诗篇之一。
2. done：结束，完成。
3. weather every rack：渡过各种难关。
4. exult：狂喜，欢呼。
5. 此句为倒装句，正常语序为：While eyes follow the steady keel, keel 意思为"（船的）龙骨"。
6. vessel：船。
7. grim and daring：此处指船的外在气质——威严而勇敢。
8. bugle：号角，喇叭。
9. trill：鸣响。
10. safe and sound：安然无恙。anchor'd safe and sound：安全停靠。
11. 该句正常语序为：The victor ship comes in with won object from fearful trip，意思是"胜利的船只从可怕的航行中归来，目标已经达到"。

Text Analysis

The poem was written in 1865. The main political and social problem during Whitman's time was slavery and the rights of African Americans. Whitman called himself the poet of America and was concerned most with the end of slavery. He felt quite depressed when he saw the Civil War break out. He immensely admired Abraham Lincoln because of his political standpoint of universal equality as stated in the Constitution. "The captain" in the poem refers to Abraham Lincoln, the captain of the ship. And the ship refers to the United States of America.

The first line shows a happy and exciting mood in addressing the captain. The phrase "our fearful trip is done" implies the end of the Civil War. The second line suggests that "the ship" of the country has gone through a difficult time of the Civil War, and "the prize we sought is won" tells that the battle was won to end the slavery. The following two lines express American people's happy mood to "exult" in the return of the ship. But the coming four lines express the poet's strong sense of grief and heartache when he employs the repetition of his call "heart! heart! heart!" The captain bled, lay still, cold and died (in lines 6 to 8). This is no doubt referring to the assassination of Abraham Lincoln and Whitman's sorrow for the death of his idol. The next stanza (from lines 9 to 12) shows how the captain is welcomed and admired by the people nationwide and how the poet wishes the captain would "rise up" and join the "mass" to enjoy the "exulting scene". The last stanza tells that the speaker finally accepted the fact that the captain had died. In lines 13 and 18, the speaker calls the captain "father", which is referring to Lincoln as the father of the United States. Lines 19 and 20 are concluding statements that summarize the entire poem. The United States is "anchor'd safe and sound". It is safe now from the war with "its voyage closed and done, from fearful trip, the victor ship, comes in with object won". The country has accomplished its goal of the abolishment of slavery and the unification of people after a fearful war. This poem has employed an obvious rhyme scheme, which is unusual for Whitman. The rhyme scheme is aabb, cded, fghh, idjd, kkaa, fded. Two examples of alliteration are in line 10 "flag is flung", as well as in line 19 "safe and sound". Repetition occurs many times in this poem, for example "O Captain! My Captain" and "fallen cold and dead".

Questions

1. Who is the captain? Why does the poet call him captain instead of president or leader?

2. Compared with most of other works by the poet, this poem is more metrical. The poet has employed some poetic techniques like rhymes, images and symbols. Can you tell what special effects they have made?

Chinese Translation

啊，船长，我的船长哟！

啊，船长，我的船长哟！我们可怕的航程已终了，
我们的船渡过了每一个难关，我们追求的锦标已经得到，
港口就在前面，我已经听见钟声，听见了人们的欢呼，
千万只眼睛在望着我们的船，它坚定、威严而且勇敢；
　　只是，啊，心哟！心哟！心哟！
　　　啊，鲜红的血滴，
　　　　就在那甲板上，我的船长躺下了，
　　　　　他已浑身冰凉，停止了呼吸。

啊，船长，我的船长哟！起来听听这钟声，
起来吧，——旌旗正为你招展，——号角为你长鸣，
为你，人们准备了无数的花束和花环，——为你，
　　人群挤满了海岸，
为你，这晃动着的群众在欢呼，转动着他们殷切的面孔；
　　这里，船长，亲爱的父亲哟！
　　　让你的头枕着我的手臂吧！
　　　　在甲板上，这真是一场梦——
　　　　　你已经浑身冰凉，停止了呼吸。

我的船长不回答我的话，他的嘴唇惨白而僵硬，
我的父亲，感觉不到我的手臂，他已没有脉搏，
　　也没有了生命，
我们的船已经安全地下锚了，它的航程已经终了，
从可怕的旅程归来，这胜利的船，目的已经达到；
　　啊，欢呼吧，海岸，鸣响吧，钟声！
　　　只是我以悲痛的步履，
　　　　漫步在甲板上，那里，我的船长躺着，
　　　　　他已浑身冰凉，停止了呼吸。

（楚图南　译）

Unit 22 Emily Dickinson

Introduction to the Author

Emily Dickinson (1830-1886) was born in Amherst, Massachusetts. Her grandfather was the founder of Amherst College, and her father the chief lawyer of the town. Dickinson had no formal education but read widely in her father's study. She was active and social as a teenager but grew to be increasingly introspective with the failed experience of love in her early twenties, and was called "Amherst Recluse" in literary history.

Dickinson began to write poetry when she was 20; after her death, her collected poems reached 1775; with 25 poems scattering in her diary made public in the later half of the 20th century, she had an opus of 2000 poems. But in her life she had only 7 poems published, and mostly "operated" (in her words) by the editors in their punctuation and wording. 115 of Emily's poems were published in 1890, with more to come in the following years. The poems were well received by critics and the reading public, however, it was not until 1955 that the first variorum edition of her *Complete Poems* was published by Thomas Johnson, which "officially" announced Dickinson's full entrance into American poetry.

Emily Dickinson's poetry is generally divided into three periods. The first period is before 1861: her poems are rather conventional with natural feelings. The second spans between 1861 and 1865, marking the poet's most creative time, with passion and energy. The third period is after 1866. As a moderate woman in the Victorian time, and also owing to her personal reasons, Dickinson seldom took travels; this explains her limited images and thematic concerns. Yet she employed the images in a delicate manner, with a variety of shades of implications. Nature, love, death and immortality are the usual subjects of her poetry.

Dickinson is good at using conceits, and employs images and metaphors in various fields. Her poems usually take the form of hymnal stanza. In each four-line stanza, eight feet appear in the first and third lines, and six in the second and fourth; iambic foot is used in each line; the second and fourth lines form end rimes. Poetic licenses are frequent, such as half rhyme; dashes are often used to replace traditional punctuation marks (actually not regular dashes, but signs, going upward or downward); nouns denoting abstract qualities are often capitalized; ellipses are commonplace, etc.

With the rise of modern poetry, Emily Dickinson becomes highly popular, and is regarded as precursor of some poetic schools and literary theories like the Imagist poetry and feminist theory. She is now one of the favorite poets among the literary critics.

712[1]

Because I could not stop for Death—
He kindly stopped for me—
The Carriage held but[2] just Ourselves—
And Immortality[3].

We slowly drove—He knew no haste
And I had put away
My labor and my leisure too,
For His Civility[4]—

We passed the School, where Children strove
At Recess—in the Ring[5]—
We passed the Fields of Gazing Grain[6]—
We passed the Setting Sun—

Or rather—He[7] passed Us—
The Dews drew quivering and Chill—
For only Gossamer[8], my Gown[9]—
My Tippet[10]—only Tulle[11]—

We paused before a House that seemed
A Swelling of the Ground—
The Roof was scarcely visible—
The Cornice[12]—in the Ground—

Since then—'tis Centuries—and yet
Feels shorter than the Day
I first surmised the Horses' Heads

Were toward Eternity—

Notes

1. 狄金森的诗歌无标题，命名其诗歌的方法有二：学界一般以首行作为标题，或者以编号名之。这和莎士比亚的诗歌的命名方式是一样的。我们在提供中译文时采取了灵活的处理。
2. but：only，只有。
3. Immortality 和 Death 一样，被拟人化。狄金森认为死亡并不恐怖，而是具有亲和力的，宛若朋友一般。诗人 1866 年 6 月 9 日给 T. W. Higginson 的信显示出她对 Immortality 的态度："You mention Immortality. That is the Flood subject. I was told that the Bank was the safest place for a Finless Mind. I explore but little since my mute Confederate, yet the ' infinite Beauty' —of which you speak comes too near to seek. To escape enchantment, one must always flee. Paradise is of the option. Whosoever will Own in Eden notwithstanding Adam, and Repeal."
4. Civility：死神（Death）在诗中是以彬彬有礼的绅士形象出现的。死神停步等待女性诗人，反映了"宫廷式爱情"（courtly love）的传统。
5. Recess：休息；Ring：环状物，这里指操场。
6. Fields of Gazing Grain：庄稼成熟时节，稻谷因为颗粒饱满而低垂。
7. He：指太阳。
8. Gossamer：轻而软的精细材料，在此指薄纱织就的衣服。
9. Gown：长袍。
10. Tippet：披肩。
11. Tulle：薄纱，绢网。
12. Cornice：此处指屋檐。

Text Analysis

Emily Dickinson's attitude towards death is typical in this poem. Death is personified as a gentleman who takes his casual journey with the speaker. His cordiality and consideration have nothing to do with intimidation; on the contrary, he is inviting, so the speaker is not alert at all but is willing to accompany Death the driver of the carriage. This reflects the author's viewpoint of death, characteristic in Christian understanding, which holds that death is merely destruction of flesh, while spirit could achieve immortality only through the stage of death. The poet thinks that death is calm and even happy, and is a privilege to another world.

The poem symbolizes the three stages of life figuratively: "School, where Children strove" represents childhood; "Fields of Gazing Grain" refers to maturity; and "Setting Sun" denotes old age. The progression of these life stages to death and to eternity itself is so natural that the speaker seems unconscious of the progression to death, and she in the poem serves as a representative of human being. Casual, commonplace images and remembered images of the past are employed to clarify infinite conceptions through the establishment of a dialectical relationship between reality and imagination, the known and the unknown. By viewing this relationship holistically and hierarchically ordering the stages of life to include death and eternity, Dickinson suggests the interconnected and mutually determined nature of the finite and infinite.

The poem is a recollection of the journey that was taken "Centuries" ago. The speaker attempts to identify the eternal world by its relationship to temporal standards, as she states that "Centuries" in eternity are "shorter than the [earthly] day". By calling on the earthly experiences, the speaker not only settles her temporal past but also views these happenings from a higher awareness. The poem therefore starts from the sensual and "lower" world and reaches figurative world of immortality; in this way, the poet dialectically shapes meaning from the limitations of life, allowing the readers momentarily to glimpse a universe in which the seemingly distinct and discontinuous stages of existence are holistically implicated and purposed.

Questions

1. What attitude of the speaker towards death can you infer from the poem?

2. Emily Dickinson is taken by the Imagist as their forerunner. Do you think this poem can be understood as an Imagist poem?

3. What is the tone of the poem? How does it work for the arguments?

Chinese Translation

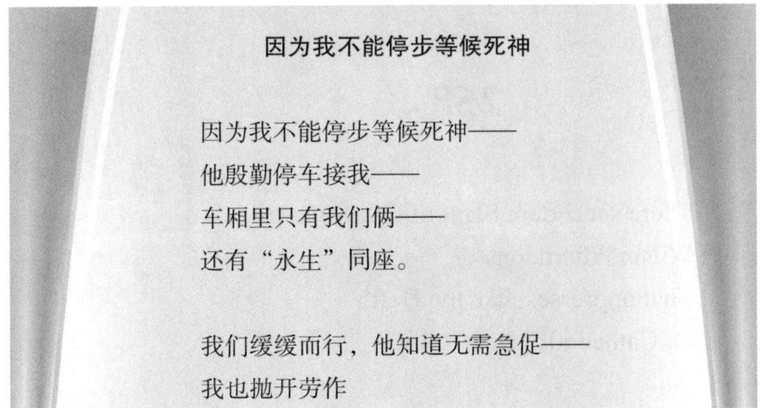

因为我不能停步等候死神

因为我不能停步等候死神——
他殷勤停车接我——
车厢里只有我们俩——
还有"永生"同座。

我们缓缓而行，他知道无需急促——
我也抛开劳作

和闲暇，以回报
他的礼貌——

我们经过学校，恰逢课间休息
孩子们正喧闹，在操场上——
我们经过注目凝视的稻谷的田地——
我们经过沉落的太阳——

也许该说，是他经过我们而去——
露水使我颤抖而且发凉——
因为我的衣裳，只是薄纱——
我的披肩，只是绢网——

我们停在一幢屋前，这屋子
仿佛是隆起的地面——
屋顶，勉强可见——
屋檐，低于地面——

从那时算起，已有几个世纪
却似乎短过那一天的光阴
那一天，我初次猜出
马头，朝向永恒——

（江枫　译）

258

There's a certain Slant of light[1],
Winter Afternoons[2]—
That oppresses, like the Heft[3]
Of Cathedral Tunes—

Heavenly Hurt, it gives us—
We can find no scar[4],
But internal difference,
Where the Meanings, are—

None may teach it—Any—
'Tis the Seal Despair[5]—
An imperial affliction[6]
Sent us of the Air[7]—

When it comes, the Landscape[8] listens—
Shadows—hold their breath—
When it goes, 'tis like the Distance
On the look of Death—

1. 过了正午，太阳斜照，故有此说。
2. 第 2 行如果前面加上 On，成为 On Winter Afternoons，则可实现韵律的规整，但这样恐有违诗人的原意。
3. Heft 兼有“重量”与“体积”之义，二者在诗行中似乎都能成立，虽然翻译只能取其一。二义并立，则说明了 heft 一词的张力，大教堂中琴声呈现立体化的效果；如此理解，heft 具有英国诗歌理论家和批评家燕卜荪（William Empson）所谓的复义（ambiguity）。
4. 第 5 行和第 6 行中的 Hurt 和 scar 相呼应，指教堂中的冬日斜阳给人带来的“创伤”。虽然查无踪迹（no scar），却造成了内在的伤害。
5. Seal Despair：正常的顺序是 Despair Seal，这样的安排是根据尾韵的需要。
6. imperial affliction：affliction 系承前面的 Hurt 和 scar 而来，它们共同营造了一种虚无缥缈但似乎又切实存在的感觉，无所在但仿佛又无所不在。imperial 的使用，是对这种“伤害”的质地的刻画。
7. Sent us of the Air 中的 of 如果改为 through，理解起来会容易些。of 则显示出这种伤害不仅是借由空气来传递，而且就存在于空气之中，真的是无所不在。
8. Landscape 和下一行中的 Shadows 都是拟人化的用法。

Text Analysis

This poem reflects Emily Dickinson's ability of addressing abstract ideas to the full. It begins with something concrete—one winter afternoon, the sunshine in a church—but after this the poem engages itself in the abstract quality. The "Heft / Of Cathedral Tunes", the "Heavenly Hurt" and "no scar" it leaves on the man；the "Seal Despair", the "imperial affliction", and finally, the "Distance / On the look of Death"：all these are puzzling us；we are confused and even astonished how these are associated with each other, and how they all work together to do whatever mission. Further, the "Heavenly Hurt" makes internal differences：yes, the above-mentioned things do make differences；they are the internal differences because these abstract qualities are significant and essential, so the differences they make are internal and central. The "imperial affliction / Sent us of the Air"：the hurt is welcome (it is "imperial"), though invisible (no scar)；it comes by air, so invisible；it is of air, so inevitable and fundamental.

The poet impresses us with her ability of employing the conceits which, however irrelevant they seem to appear, would weave into an organic unity and bring astonishing artistic effect. The peculiar images could only come from someone indulged in the metaphysical thinking of issues like death, religion and immortality, etc. Yet the poet's concern is evident in her addressing the spiritual realm beyond the real and physical world.

Questions

1. Imagine if the poet had presented the unnamed hurt in a direct manner instead of in the highly symbolic manner, could she still achieve the artistic effect? Why or why not?

2. The poem starts with something physical and specific only to arouse her speculation on the metaphysical thinking. It reminds us of "Xing", one way that initiates the classical Chinese poetry. How do you understand this?

3. Have you found some other poems also by Emily Dickinson that have similar way of addressing abstract qualities? Give some examples.

Chinese Translation

冬日的下午

冬日的下午往往有一种
斜落下来的幽光，
压迫着我们，那重量如同
大教堂中的琴响。

它给我们以神圣的创伤；
我们找不到斑痕。
只有内心所引起的变化，
将它的意义蕴存。

没有人能够使它感悟；
它是绝望的烙印，
一种无比美妙的痛苦，
借大气传给我们。

当它来时，四野都倾听，
阴影全屏住呼吸；
当去时，远得像我们
遥望死亡的距离。

（余光中　译）

MODERN AMERICAN POETRY

Unit 23 Robert Frost

Robert Lee Frost (1874-1963) is unparalleled to any other American poets of his time. He is the only poet in American literary history who won the Pulitzer Prize for four times.

Robert Frost was born in San Francisco, California, where he spent most of his childhood years. At the age of eleven, the family moved across the country to Massachusetts upon the death of Robert Frost's father. During his high school years in Lawrence, Massachusetts, Frost became interested in reading poetry and wrote his first poems. He was enrolled at Dartmouth College in 1892 and later at Harvard in 1897, though he never earned a formal degree. Frost drifted through many occupations after abandoning studies. However, he never abandoned writing poetry. In 1894, his first professional poem "My Butterfly: An Elegy" was sold and published in a New York magazine *The Independent*, which signified a landmark in his writing career.

In 1895, Frost married Elinor Miriam White who was the major inspiration in his poetry. In 1900, the couple lived on a farm just over the Massachusetts line in New Hampshire farm purchased by his grandfather. It was on that farm that Frost wrote many of the poems that would make up his first published volume. However, Frost was never a successful poultry farmer. In 1912, he sold his farm and sailed with his family from Boston to England. There Frost experienced English country living, published his first volume of poems, and made acquaintance with a lot of influential British poets such as Edward Thomas, Robert Graves. He also established a friendship with Ezra Pound, who recognized the worth of his work and helped to promote his *A Boy*'s *Will* and *North of Boston* (1914). At this stage of writing in England, Frost boldly employed ordinary language and cadences in his poems. In 1915, he returned to the U.S. and was then favored by editors and critics in the literary arena of both New York and Boston.

During the 1930s, as he became more honored and revered, Frost endured a series of family disasters which became the direct cause of the dark tone in his later poetry. By the end of his life, Frost had become the most celebrated poet in America for his extraordinary virtues in poetic writing. He became the only poet in American literary history who was invited by the U.S. Government to read his poem at the presidential inauguration. In 1963, the 88-year-old poet died of complications from prostate surgery in Boston and was buried at the Old Bennington Cemetery in Vermont with his epitaph quoting the last line from his poem "The Lesson for Today" (1942): "I had a lover's quarrel with the world".

Frost's works are commonly considered to be associated with the landscape of rural New England. However, this does not mean that the poet is a regional or minor poet. The poet's mastery of traditional verse forms and metrics, his adherence to common colloquial language and traditional forms, the great charm of ambiguity revealed in his poetry, and his great endeavor in pursuing and meditating on universal themes make him a quintessentially modern poet.

The Road Not Taken[1]

Two roads diverged[2] in a yellow wood,
And sorry I could not travel both
And be one traveler, long I stood
And looked down one as far as I could
To where it bent in the undergrowth;

Then took the other, as just as fair[3],
And having perhaps the better claim,
Because it was grassy and wanted wear[4];
Though as for that the passing there
Had worn them really about the same,

And both that morning equally lay
In leaves[5] no step had trodden black.
Oh, I kept the first for another day!
Yet knowing how way leads on to way,
I doubted if I should ever come back.

I shall be telling this with a sigh[6]
Somewhere ages and ages[7] hence:
Two roads diverged in a wood, and I—

I took the one less traveled by,
And that has made all the difference[8].

Notes

1.《未选择的路》是弗罗斯特于1915年创作的一首名诗，最初收录在诗人的第三本诗集《山间》(1916)中。该诗描述了诗人在穿行森林时遇到岔道，一番思虑后选择了人迹稀少的那条路。诗人在诗中也感叹道：既然选择了现在的路，那么想要回到另一条路已近乎不可能。将来再次谈起这事时，只会一声叹息：全因当时的选择，才有了日后的种种差别。据称该诗的写作背景与弗罗斯特在1912年做出的重要决定有关。他当时放弃了教书的职业，将自己的农场变卖，举家来到英国，从此选择了诗歌创作之路。因此，如果说教书象征着平坦、安稳的生活，那么选择写诗则是一条少有人走的路，诗人最终选择了这条人迹罕至的荒凉之道，因此在回首往事时，他也许正会发出诗歌中所发出的一声感慨。这首诗行文简单，但哲理丰富、思想细腻，且诗歌内涵多元开放，是弗罗斯特最著名的诗歌之一。
2. diverge: split, extend in different directions.
3. fair: visually appealing.
4. wanted wear：此处采用了头韵及拟人的修辞手法。
5. 落叶满地（In leaves）与前文的 a yellow wood 呼应，暗示此时正逢金秋，也有成熟、丰实、广博的寓意。
6. sigh：叹气、叹息。该词是一个颇有悬念的词汇，诗歌中的“我”因何叹息，读者无从知晓，也使该诗具备了更广阔的阐释空间。
7. ages and ages 给读者以时间绵长之感，它与前行 I shall be telling this with a sigh 共同呼应，将时间定格在遥远的未来的一天。
8. 在该诗的语境中，difference 一词可做截然不同的解读，它可以是积极的（positive），也可以是消极负面的（negative）。这两种不同的解读直接关系到叙述者曾经做出的选择正确与否。此外，也有人认为弗罗斯特在该句中使用了反讽（irony）修辞，诗人真正的意图与字面含义相反，即：当初的选择如今并未带来任何不同。

Text Analysis

“The Road Not Taken” was written in 1915 and published in 1916 in the collection *Mountain Interval*. It is the first poem in the volume and is printed in italics. It is one of the most important poems written by Frost, an expression of Frost’s emotions, life experience and thought.

The famous poem, written in plain language, a fixed stanza structure and rhyme scheme, is quite constructive for the readers to start their consideration of their life journey. Its great charm lies in its metaphor of the road as a symbol of life and the crossroads as a symbol of important decision man is supposed to make.

At the beginning of the poem, the narrator encountered two nearly identical paths in a yellow wood. He wished to travel both, yet there was only one that he could choose. The first road "bent in the undergrowth" and the other one was "grassy and wanted wear". The narrator took the other one and kept "the first for another day". Meanwhile, he was quite sure that he could not come back to make another decision. In the last stanza of this poem, the narrator sighed with emotion: "I took the one less traveled by, / And that has made all the difference". The last stanza has caused considerable controversy. The readers are left to ponder the question: what difference the choice has made to us, to nature, and to the universe? The narrator predicted that in the future he would speak of his decision and how this decision have had a great impact on his life. There has been much critical discussion about the word "sigh". The sigh may refer to our regret that we can only choose but one path. We always sigh that we cannot take both roads, but the fact that we make the choice is of ultimate importance. This sigh may also be that of contentment that the persona luckily took the right one. The ending is ironic, suggesting that any choice makes a difference—there is nothing special about this decision. However, this interpretation is not the only one. The poem is also read as advocating choosing the "less traveled road" in life and suggesting that we should not always follow the general trend and should instead maintain our individuality.

The poem is celebrated partly because it is apparently a gnomic utterance, written in plain language and easy to understand. However, it is one of Frost's best as well as most riveting and complicated poems. It is a profound work in its apparent simplicity and real ambiguity. It is more than a poem about nature, not about the season or the road. Frost refused the tag of "nature poet" since he had written only two poems without a human being in them, which signifies that the poem is mainly about human condition and nature is taken as the background.

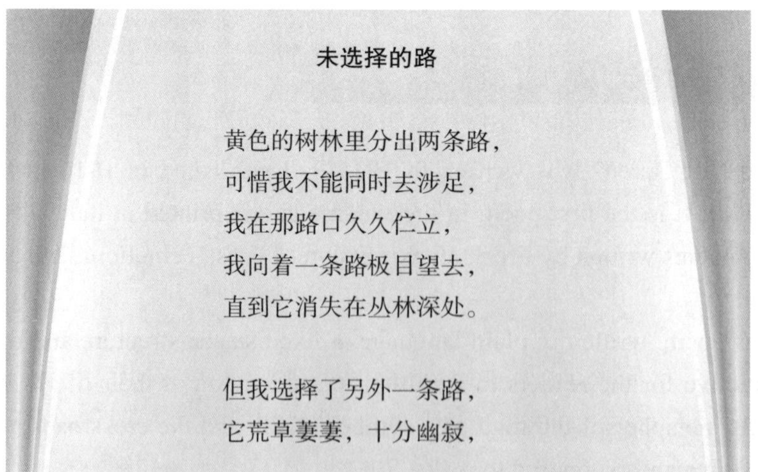

未选择的路

黄色的树林里分出两条路，
可惜我不能同时去涉足，
我在那路口久久伫立，
我向着一条路极目望去，
直到它消失在丛林深处。

但我选择了另外一条路，
它荒草萋萋，十分幽寂，

显得更诱人、更美丽；
虽然在这两条小路上，
很少留下旅人的足迹。

那天清晨落叶满地，
两条路都未经脚印污染。
呵，留下一条路改日再见！
但我知道路径绵延无尽头，
恐怕我难以再返回。

也许多少年后在某个地方，
我将轻声叹息把往事回顾：
一片树林里分出两条路——
而我选择了人迹更少的一条，
从此决定了我一生的道路。
（顾子欣　译）

Nothing Gold Can Stay[1]

Nature's first green[2] is gold[3],
Her hardest hue[4] to hold.
Her early leaf's a flower[5];
But only so an hour.
Then leaf subsides to leaf[6].
So Eden[7] sank to grief[8],
So dawn goes down to day[9].
Nothing gold can stay.

1.《金色从来不常驻》是弗罗斯特的一首抒情哲理短诗，也是弗罗斯特的名篇之一。该诗写于 1923 年，当年十月发表在《耶鲁评论》(*The Yale Review*) 上，后被收录

到弗罗斯特诗集《新罕布什尔州》(*New Hampshire*)中，该诗集还收录了弗罗斯特的其他名篇如《雪夜林边驻》("Stopping by Woods on a Snowy Evening")。《金色从来不常驻》运用叶、花、黄金等隐喻来表达时光易逝的主题。

2. first green 在此意指刚刚显露生命迹象且破土而出的幼芽，指涉的是自然界中的新生事物。这种幼芽的颜色介于黄色与绿色之间。
3. gold 在此一语双关，既可表示幼芽的颜色，又体现其如黄金般珍贵。
4. hue: the property of a color as determined by its dominant wavelength.
5. 采用暗喻的修辞手法，将初绽的新芽比作一朵娇花。
6. subside 一词表现了从嫩叶到绿叶的转变过程，而该词也暗示了作者认为嫩叶更为难得娇贵。
7. "伊甸园"是《圣经》中上帝在东方为亚当和夏娃所造的栖息地，是被金色笼罩的纯洁、祥和、极乐的圣地。但亚当和夏娃受到撒旦诱惑而偷食禁果，最终被逐出伊甸园。人类也从此离开乐园，开始了他们苦难的历程。该典故在此同样影射了好景不常在的主题。
8. 初绽的嫩叶未过几时便长成树叶，金子般珍贵的嫩叶随即消失，这使得伊甸园陷入一片悲哀中。
9. So dawn goes down to day：日出时阳光给大地铺撒上一层金黄的色彩，而不久白日降临，金色不再。

Text Analysis

"Nothing Gold Can Stay" was written in 1923 and collected in Frost's *New Hampshire*, Frost's first collection to win a Pulitzer Prize. In this eight-line poem, there are only forty words, most of which are monosyllabic, simple and of Anglo-Saxon origin. It is one of the shortest poems by Frost and the only one which was not written in pentameter or tetrameter, but in trimeter, consisting of six-syllable lines, with three stressed or accented syllables in each line. However, under the simple appearance, there exists much philosophy in it.

The poem begins by describing a natural scene: the first green. The first green is actually gold, making the readers think of the leaves first budding in spring and manifesting a golden hue. However, this hue is difficult to stay long because the early leaves with golden hue will soon grow to maturity and turn darker green. Accordingly, the natural landscape will also change from golden dawn to bright day. Through his description of this natural phenomenon, Frost intends to convey the motif of this poem: nothing gold can stay; the most beautiful and valuable things in life often have the least longevity.

The rhyme scheme of this poem is strict, and the end-rhymes yield the following：aabbccdd. Besides that, Frost applies a lot of poetic devices in this poem. In "Nature's first green is gold", "Her hardest hue to hold", and "So dawn goes down to day", alliteration is applied to draw the readers' attention. It also refers to nature as a female, which may remind the readers of "Mother Nature" who provides sustenance for human beings. The poem contains a biblical allusion as well. "Eden" refers to the Garden of Eden, which is described most notably in the Book of Genesis. It is the paradisiacal place where Adam and Eve once lived. However, the couple disobeyed God and ate the forbidden fruit. As the result of it, they were banished from the Garden of Eden and from then on brought death into the world. This biblical allusion shows that good times don't last long, echoing the motif of this poem.

"Nothing Gold Can Stay" is meaningful and far-reaching. It explores the idea that happiness, perfection and bliss can never endure. However, different readers would get different enlightenment from reading this poem. Some may see the poem as pessimistic and sentimental while some may find optimism. Robert Frost successfully captures a clear and concise truth in this poem, hence making the poem one of the most popular and powerful.

Chinese Translation

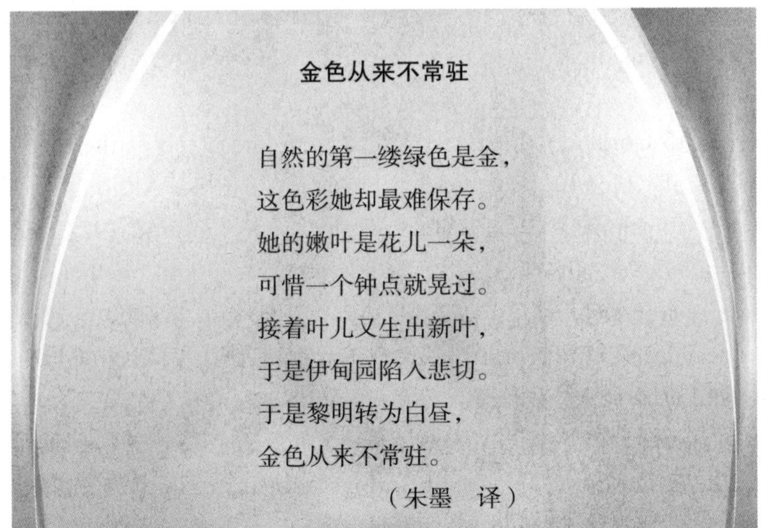

金色从来不常驻

自然的第一缕绿色是金，
这色彩她却最难保存。
她的嫩叶是花儿一朵，
可惜一个钟点就晃过。
接着叶儿又生出新叶，
于是伊甸园陷入悲切。
于是黎明转为白昼，
金色从来不常驻。

（朱墨　译）

Unit 24 Wallace Stevens

Introduction to the Author

Wallace Stevens (1879-1955) was born in Reading, Pennsylvania into a prosperous attorney's family. He attended Harvard University as an undergraduate from 1897 to 1900. During his Harvard years he began to write poems. He entered New York Law School on his father's advice and graduated with a degree in 1903. He was admitted to the U.S. Bar in 1904 and practiced law in New York City until 1916.

During his years in New York, Stevens became acquainted with a number of writers and painters in Greenwich Village, including the poets William Carlos Williams, Marianne Moore, and E. E. Cummings. In 1914, under the pseudonym "Peter Parasol", he sent a group of poems under the title "Phases" to Harriet Monroe for a war poem competition for *Poetry* magazine. Stevens did not win the prize, but his peoms were published by Monroe in November of that year.

Stevens moved to Connecticut in 1916, having found a job at the Hartford Accident and Indemnity Co., of which he became vice president in 1934. Although he had begun to establish an identity for himself in the literary world, it was not until 1923 that his first book of poems, *Harmonium*, was published. The book's poor reception together with the author's growing business responsibilities greatly discouraged him so that he published very little for more than a decade. Yet the reprinting of *Harmonium* in 1931 resulted in an increase in critical attention and ushered in his years of steady publication.

Stevens wrote poems during the difficult time of the Great Depression and the two World Wars. Yet he seemed uninterested in the sufferings and frustrations of the time. Instead, he saw beauty, pleasure, excitement, and meaning in the wretchedness of life. Like the English poet Samuel Tylor Coleridge, he placed great emphasis on imagination, which, in his opinion, had such transformative power that it could change the sordid reality and retrieve the lost order and faith.

Stevens experimented with a variety of styles. His poems display exotic imagery, odd sounds, curious analogies, and inscrutable titles. A constant theme in his later poetry is the interrelation between the ideal and the real. This is conveyed in the dealing with a series of oppositions between the inner and outer worlds, for instance, between subject and object, and between fiction and fact.

Stevens won the Bollingen Prize in 1950 and received the National Book Award and Pulitzer Prize in 1955. Besides *Harmonium*, his major works include *Ideas of Order* (1935), *The Man with the Blue Guitar* (1937), *Notes towards a Supreme Fiction* (1942), *The Auroras of Autumn* (1951), *The Necessary Angel* (1951), and *The Collected Poems* (1954).

Anecdote of the Jar

I placed a jar in Tennessee[1],
And round it was[2], upon a hill.
It[3] made the slovenly wilderness[4]
Surround that hill.[5]

The wilderness rose up to it,[6]
And sprawled[7] around, no longer wild.
The jar was round upon the ground[8]
And tall and of a port in air[9].

It took dominion everywhere.[10]
The jar was gray and bare[11].
It did not give of bird or bush[12],
Like nothing else in Tennessee[13].

1. Tennessee：田纳西州，在美国南部。
2. round it was：倒装，正常语序为 it was round。
3. It 指代的是 jar。
4. slovenly wilderness：杂乱的荒野。
5. 第三、四行描写了坛子带来的变化。杂乱无序的荒野在坛子的影响下环绕着山坡，变得井然有序起来。这两句使用了拟人的修辞格。使役动词 made 赋予坛子人的品性。
6. 该行进一步说明坛子如何影响了荒野。没有坛子时，山顶可能只有稀疏的草皮；有

Notes

了坛子后，荒野的一切，包括动植物，都朝着山顶生长或活动。行末的it既可指山顶，也可指坛子。

7. sprawled：蔓延。
8. 该行进一步对坛子进行了描述，补充了它位于地表之上的细节。
9. of a port in air：port，举止，姿态；air，风度，气度，意为气度非凡。
10. took dominion：控制，统领。
11. 该行说明，虽然坛子在小山上仿佛君临天下，但它仅仅是个普通的坛子。
12. give of：相当于produce, grow, raise，滋生，哺育。
13. 11～12行似乎说明，虽然坛子获得了某种意义上的统治地位，但它本身并没有生命，也不能滋养或哺育荒野中的生命。

Text Analysis

This poem consists of three four-line stanzas. Its sounds are mostly round and silky, floating around our tongue just like a smooth jar would feel in our hands. The word "round" appears twice, and the same sound is repeated in the words "surround", "around", and "ground". Another sound "air" is also repeated in "everywhere" and "bare". So the dominant sounds in this poem are soft, smooth, and easy to deal with. But just like the jar, alone in the wilderness on the Tennessee hill, there are some parts of the sounds of this that don't quite fit. First of all, the sound of "jar" itself. It is almost a clunky, forced, and strange noise, in contrast with the smooth and easy sounds. These tiny bumps in the rhythm of the poem produce a jarring effect, suggesting there is conflict in the world of this poem.

Just like the contrasting sounds, there are contrasting images throughout the poem. In the opening stanza, the speaker puts an empty jar upon a hill in "the slovenly wilderness". Then, the jar takes over, and the wilderness is ruled by the jar and seems no longer wild. In the second stanza, the jar is like a dignified king high up on the throne, while the wilderness is like the obedient masses sprawling around to pay tribute to the king. In the last stanza, although the jar controls everything, it does not have real life. What's more, there are things it can't do but the wilderness can, like growing bush and breeding birds.

One interpretation of the poem is that it is about the relationship between nature and man. Without the jar, a symbol of man's invention, the wilderness is slovenly with everything in its developing in its own way. With the appearance of the jar, everything in the wilderness changes dramatically. It now has a center, and then an order. Yet there is conflict in the apparent order. Another interpretation is that the jar stands for imagination while the wilderness stands for reality. Thus, the poem is about the transformative power of imagination, which can tidy up the messy and chaotic reality.

The poem could also take on other different interpretations from different perspectives. From the New Critical perspective, it is about writing poetry and making art generally. A post-structuralist critic might say that it involves temporal and linguistic disjunction, especially in the strange syntax of the last two lines. From a feminist perspective, it reveals a poem concerned with male dominance over a traditionally feminized landscape. A cultural critic might find a sense of industrial imperialism.

Questions

1. Whom do you think the "I" mentioned in the first line of the poem is?

2. When the poem is read aloud, how do the sounds in this poem impact on the readers?

3. What do you think is the significance of "Tennessee" in this poem? What makes this particular state special, or not?

4. Many critics have compared "Anecdote of the Jar" as a reaction to Keats's "Ode on a Grecian Urn". What do you think is the connection between the two poems?

Chinese Translation

坛子轶事

我把一个坛子放在田纳西，
圆的，在山顶上。
它使杂乱的荒野
围拢那山冈。

荒野向它升起，
在它四围蔓延，不再野性。
坛子是圆的，在地上
高高的，气宇轩昂。

它统辖四周，
坛子灰扑扑光秃秃，
它并不哺育鸟儿或树木，
不像田纳西的任何东西。

（刘朝晖　译）

The Snow Man

One must have a mind of winter[1]
To regard the frost and the boughs[2]
Of the pine-trees crusted with snow; [3]

And have been cold a long time[4]
To behold[5] the junipers shagged with ice[6],
The spruces[7] rough in the distant glitter[8]

Of the January sun; [9]and not to think
Of any misery in the sound of the wind, [10]
In the sound of a few leaves,

Which is the sound of the land,
Full of the same wind
That is blowing in the same bare place[11]

For the listener, who listens in the snow,
And, nothing himself [12], beholds
Nothing that is not there and the nothing that is. [13]

1. a mind of winter：冬日的心境。
2. bough：树干，树枝。
3. crusted with snow：覆盖着一层变硬了的雪。
4. have been cold a long time：省略句，承前省略了 one must。
5. behold：与第一节中的 regard 是近义词。
6. the junipers shagged with ice：被冰雪覆盖的杜松。
7. spruces：云杉，松柏科四季常绿树。
8. 这一行的中心词是 spruces，与上一行中的 junipers 同为 behold 的宾语。

9. 从第一行到此处，诗歌主要表达了一种“天人合一”的思想：人必须得有和冬天一样的心境，才能去凝视寒霜和挂雪的松枝；必须经历过风霜，才能去观察垂下冰凌的杜松和一月份阳光下闪着冷光的云杉。

10. and not to think / Of any misery in the sound of the wind：其主句仍然是诗歌开头的 One must have a mind of winter。从这里开始，诗歌表达了融于自然，忘掉自我，享受自然的思想。

11. 这一诗节中 same 一词出现了两次，暗示自然并没有发生质的变化。

12. nothing himself：他自己不存在。这个词组放在谓语动词 beholds 前，可以理解为 beholds 的一个前提，暗示只有用“忘了自己”的态度去看待自然，才能沉浸于自然，融于自然，最终万物皆如旧，体会万物的人却达到了“物我两忘”的化境。

13. Nothing that is not there and the nothing that is：这句 nothing 出现了两次，都是上一行 beholds 的宾语，第二个 nothing 可以理解为特指第一个 nothing，如果这样理解，那该行的意思就是“不在那儿却实际存在的虚无”；第二个 nothing 也可理解为定语从句 that is 的先行词，that is 承前省略了 there，这样一来，该行的意思则是“不在那的虚无和在那的虚无”。

Text Analysis

In this poem, the action of a mind is dramatized as it becomes one with the scene it perceives. At the instant when the mind ceases to bring something of itself to the scene, the scene ceases to exist fully. The poem is addressed to “one”, who can be “we” or “any human being”.

As the speaker says, to perceive the winter scene truly, we must have “a mind of winter”, until correspondence becomes identification. The mind of winter is the mind of the snow man. With such a mind, we see the images of winter: “pine-trees crusted with snow”, “junipers shagged with ice”, “spruces rough in the distant glitter / Of the January sun”. We hear the cold sibilants evoking the sense of barrenness and monotony: “sound of the wind”, “sound of a few leaves”, “sound of the land”, “same wind”, “same bare place”, “For the listener, who listens in the snow”.

The “one” with whom we have identified ourselves has now become “the listener, who listens in the snow”; he has become the snow man, and he knows winter with a mind of winter, knows it in its strictest reality, stripped of all imagination and human feeling. At that point, he sees the winter scene reduced to absolute fact, as the object not of the mind, but of the perfect perceptual eye that sees “nothing that is not there and the nothing that is” there.

One of the themes of the poem is just an approach towards reality, the conflict between the rational consciousness of the existential "void" or "nothingness", between the will to see things as they are, and the innate human tendency to create worlds (even poetic ones), to reinterpret what we see in artistic (or philosophical, or moral) terms.

But of course we learn eventually that if a mind of winter were achieved, the snow man would not in fact look at pine trees, junipers, or spruces, since these designations are the most elementary examples of human abstraction and classification. Neither would he behold objects that are crusted, shagged, or glittering—all metaphors imposed on the scene. He would not see these objects in the light of a January sun, time and its divisions constituting another human ordering. He would not be aware that the spruces are being observed in the "distant glitter", since the concept of distance assumes a point of view. In brief, the qualities of the scene that interest us, which are described in such a way that they constitute the motive for assuming a particular kind of mental state, are precisely what are lost when this state is realized. In this sense, the language of the poem keeps reasserting a man-made world that it attempts to get rid of.

Questions

1. The poem is entitled "The Snow Man", but throughout the poem, the snow man does not appear. How do you understand this?

2. What does it mean that "One must have a mind of winter / To regard the frost and the boughs / Of the pine-trees crusted with snow"? Is it an invitation in philosophical and artistic terms to look at reality without superimposing interpretations on it?

3. Does this poem remind you of any ancient Chinese thinker? In what sense is the thinker's idea similar to that expression in this poem?

Chinese Translation

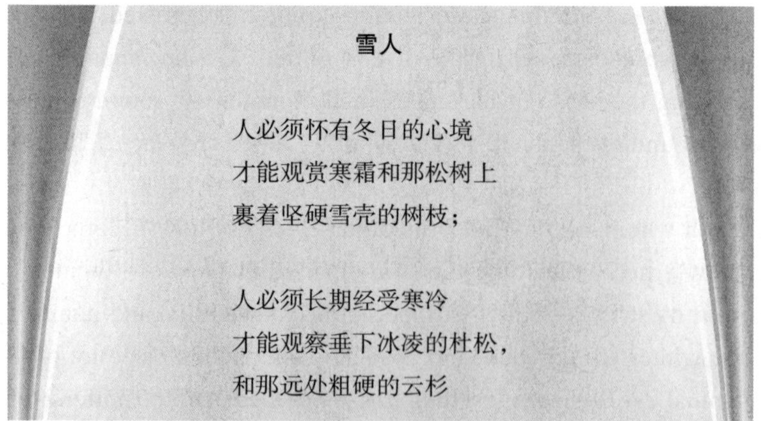

雪人

人必须怀有冬日的心境
才能观赏寒霜和那松树上
裹着坚硬雪壳的树枝；

人必须长期经受寒冷
才能观察垂下冰凌的杜松，
和那远处粗硬的云杉

在一月阳光中的闪烁；才能
不去想蕴含于风之萧萧
叶之瑟瑟中的那份凄凉。

那是大地的声音，
大地刮起同样的风
在同一片荒野上吹拂。

那风为雪中的聆听者所刮，
自身虚无的他，看到了
彼在的虚无，此在的虚无。

（刘朝晖　译）

Unit 25 William Carlos Williams

Introduction to the Author

William Carlos Williams (1883-1963) is a poet, novelist, essayist, playwright and translator. He was born in Rutherford, New Jersey. He majored in medicine in the University of Pennsylvania (where he met and befriended Ezra Pound), and sustained the medical practice as a family doctor all his life. Early in his writing, Williams was a Post-Romanticist and was under the influence of the English Romantic poets like John Keats; later, with his friend Pound's advice, he decided to base his writings on his hometown Rutherford. Yet he was not provincial but rather aimed at the general, as explained in his motto "The local is the universal". He was critical of Pound's and especially of T. S. Eliot's expatriation. As a literary nationalist he committed himself to America's cultural and social heterogeneity, while at the same time clearing of myths and metaphysics and freeing his writing from what he saw as the worn-out language of British and European culture. Following Pound, Williams was one of the principal poets of the Imagist Movement, though like Pound, as time went on, he began to increasingly disagree with the movement when Amy Lowell managed to bring it under her influence. In 1915, Williams began to associate with a group of New York artists and writers known as "The Others". The association linked his poetry writing with the modern tradition of art and literature.

As a full-time physician, Williams practiced medicine in the daytime and wrote at night. He wrote short-scaled poems mainly, and his famous pieces are mostly of this sort, such as "The Red Wheelbarrow", "This is just to say", etc. However, ambitious Williams also experimented with long and complex project; his epic *Paterson* identified the doctor-poet with his city, with the poem's fragmented vignettes following out the city's history and the human lifespan in a self-generating, self-completing open form. Williams sought to renew language through fresh, raw idioms that grew out of the lively social reality. He was serious with and dedicated to the techniques of meter and lineation, and sought to invent an entirely fresh—and singularly American—poetic. He came up with the "variable foot" which referred to the method of determining line breaks, and his aim of experimenting with the "variable foot" was to show the American (opposed to European) rhythm that he claimed to be present in everyday American language.

Williams won the first National Book Award for Poetry, and was posthumously awarded the Pulitzer Prize. In much of his life time he was overshadowed by the immense popularity of Pound and Eliot; however, his work received increasing attention in the 1950s and 1960s as younger poets, including the Beat Movement, the San Francisco Renaissance, the Black Mountain School, and the New York School, were impressed by the accessibility of his language and his openness as a mentor.

Spring and All[1]

By the road to the contagious hospital[2]
under the surge of the blue
mottled clouds[3] driven from the
northeast—a cold wind. Beyond, the
waste[4] of broad, muddy fields
brown with dried weeds[5], standing and fallen

patches of standing water[6]
the scattering of tall trees

All along the road the reddish
purplish, forked, upstanding, twiggy
stuff of bushes and small trees
with dead, brown leaves under them
leafless vines[7]—

Lifeless in appearance, sluggish
dazed spring approaches—

They enter the new world naked[8],
cold, uncertain of all
save that they enter. All about them
the cold, familiar wind[9]—

Now the grass, tomorrow
the stiff curl of wildcarrot leaf
One by one objects are defined[10]—
It quickens: clarity, outline of leaf

But now the stark dignity of
entrance[11]—Still, the profound change

has come upon them: rooted, they
grip down[12] and begin to awaken

1. 该诗选自 *Spring and All* (1923)，这是一部诗歌和散文交织的集子，该诗为其中的第一首诗，其标题沿用集子的标题，或者以第一行 By the road to the contagious hospital 为题。
2. contagious hospital：这是诗的核心意象，全诗乃是记录前往传染病院一路所见的景象。
3. the surge of the blue / mottled clouds：可以理解为（1）blue 和 mottled 连用，blue 和 mottled 两个形容词都是修饰名词中心词 clouds，读作 blue mottled clouds，意为"蔚蓝的斑点星散的天空"；（2）由于是跨行，可不作如上解读，而是将 blue 看成一个名词，意为"蔚蓝的天空"，则该词后省略了标点（和多数其他行一样）。
4. waste：wasteland，指休耕的土地。艾略特的名作《荒原》（*The Waste Land*）的标题也是此义。
5. brown with dried weeds：因枯干的野草而成为棕黄。其前置词为上一行末尾的 fields。
6. standing water：静止不动的水，死水。standing: not flowing, stagnant.
7. 这一节依然描写路边一派冬的气息。leafless 和下一行的 lifeless 分别位于所在行的开始，形成呼应。它们也通过头韵相互关联，暗示 leaf 和 life 之间的联系。
8. They enter the new world naked：they 作为人称代词所指为何，在这里模糊不清。从下文来看（尤其是第 26 行的 upon them 和 they），they 指春天生长的多种植物：草和野胡萝卜。这些植物都被拟人化：naked，cold，uncertain（第 16～17 行）。另外，the new world naked 是威廉斯的一个重要意象，著名的威廉斯研究专家马里亚尼（Paul Mariani）的一本影响深远的著作，或许是最重要的威廉斯传记即以此为题：*William Carlos Williams: A New World Naked*。
9. the cold，familiar wind：寒冷、熟悉的风。这是可以感受到的初春的一种信息。第 4～5 节写在残冬的一片萧瑟之中，春天姗姗而来。

Notes

10. objects are defined：叶子（objects）可以辨认出来（defined：暗示叶子长出了形状）。
11. the stark dignity of / entrance：（叶子）以全然庄严的姿态进入（春天）。
12. grip down：grip down in earth，牢牢地扎入地底。第 6～7 节描绘布满荒原的野草和野胡萝卜正向地底深深扎根，开始了新的生命。荒原野草之中出现了春天的盎然生机。

Text Analysis

Williams has the following remarks on this poem："One of the best images I have ever perpetrated, which even Yvor Winters liked. But just at this point he parted company from me for the classic forms." Yvor Winters, poet and critic, began his career as an admirer and imitator of the Imagist poets and especially of Williams；but by the end of the 1920s he had formulated a neo-classic poet that excluded most of Williams' verse (although he continued to praise the technique of this particular poem). Williams felt that he had lost another "disciple". This remark of Williams has two implications：Winters once liked the image of the poem together with the way the image was presented, i.e. Williams' version of modern American poetry, using lively mundane language to bring forward daily experience；but later he turned to the neo-classic poetics in spite of his love for the techniques of this particular poem.

This in a very condensed manner actually pinpoints two orientations of modern American poetry, with Eliot and Pound leading one and Williams leading the other. T. S. Eliot's *The Waste Land*, for example, begins with the famous description of spring (with April as its specific setting)："April is the cruelest month, breeding / Lilacs out of the dead land, mixing / Memory and desire, stirring / Dull roots with spring rain". Eliot's "April is the cruelest month", because the happenings there are seldom associated with the "normal" April which should be considered among the best months, just as lilacs are bred "out of the dead land". In writing, Eliot again and again appealed to myth, legend and religious allusions, Williams, on the other hand, stuck to the lively experience of locality. The rough and even unpleasant images permeating the poem impress us deeply with their genuine fitting into the environment, together with the sense of low-brow, down-to-earth presence of the seemingly trivial and yet inevitable part of our life. In his "new world naked", energies are prepared for resurrection and for a hopeful future, as made clear at the end of the poem；this forms sharp contrast with Eliot's waste land. In writing, this poem's provisional quality and seemingly unfinished structure match its rough and yet energetic atmosphere, and thus the poem constitutes a coherent totality in its form and content.

Questions

1. What is the tone of this poem? What attitude of the author can you infer from the poem?

2. What images are typical in representing the locality of northeast America in early spring time? Why do you think so?

3. This poem of Williams describes spring scenery, which reminds us of the spring description in T. S. Eliot's famous *The Waste Land* and even in the prologue of Geoffrey Chaucer's *The Canterbury Tales*. Compare these descriptions of spring and try to see the authors' different concerns.

Chinese Translation

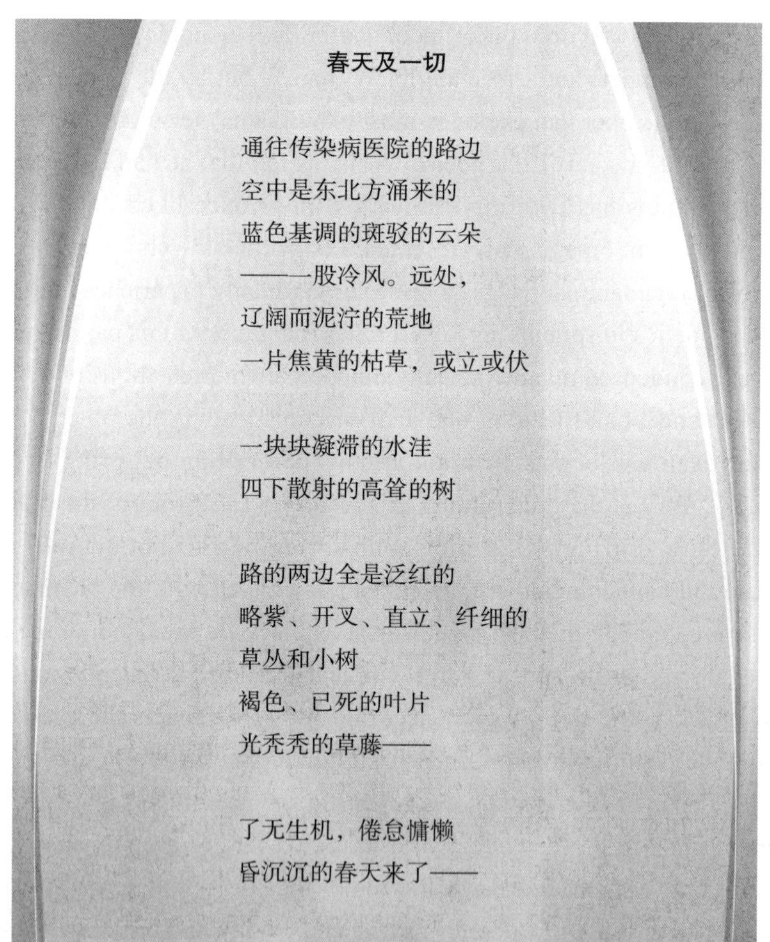

春天及一切

通往传染病医院的路边
空中是东北方涌来的
蓝色基调的斑驳的云朵
——一股冷风。远处，
辽阔而泥泞的荒地
一片焦黄的枯草，或立或伏

一块块凝滞的水洼
四下散射的高耸的树

路的两边全是泛红的
略紫、开叉、直立、纤细的
草丛和小树
褐色、已死的叶片
光秃秃的草藤——

了无生机，倦怠慵懒
昏沉沉的春天来了——

它们进入这片新世界，赤裸着
感到寒冷，除了进入
一切都不确定。四周
寒冷、熟悉的风——

眼下是草，明天
野胡萝卜叶僵硬的卷曲

物体逐一被定义——
进展很快：明晰，叶的轮廓

而眼下入口赤裸的尊严
——依然，深刻的变化
降临于它们：植根地下，它们
抓牢地面，开始觉醒

（张跃军　译）

Unit 26 Ezra Pound

Introduction to the Author

Ezra Pound (1885-1972) is one of the most influential poets in American poetry in the 20th century. Pound was born in Hailey, Idaho in 1885, and spent his formative years in Wyancote, Pennsylvania where his father worked as an assayer. He studied at the University of Pennsylvania for two years and then transferred to Hamilton College, receiving a degree in 1905. After graduation there he taught at Wabash College for two years, then traveled to Spain, Italy and London. In January 1909, Pound met the novelist Olivia Shakespeare, W. B. Yeats' former lover, at a literary salon, and was invited to attend her Tuesday salons where he was introduced to her daughter Dorothy, an artist, who became his wife in 1914. Through Olivia Shakespeare he was introduced to W. B. Yeats, the greatest living poet in Pound's view, and they became close friends. While in London, together with T. E. Hulme, Richard Aldington, F. S. Flint, and H. D., Ezra Pound launched the famous Imagist movement between 1912 and 1917, which opened a new page for the modernist literature in the world. In 1924, Pound moved to Italy. He became involved in Fascist politics, and did not return to the U.S. until 1945, when he was arrested on the charge of treason for broadcasting Fascist propaganda by radio to the U.S. during the WWⅡ. In 1946, he was acquitted, but declared mentally ill and committed to St. Elizabeth's Hospital in Washington, D.C. After continuous appeals from a number of noted writers like Robert Frost for his release from the hospital in 1958, Pound then went back to Italy and settled in Venice, where he died in 1972.

Pound's significant contributions to poetry began with his promulgation of Imagism, a movement in poetry which derived its technique from sources including classical Chinese and Japanese poetry—stressing clarity, precision, and economy of language and giving up traditional rhyme and meter in order to, in Pound's words, "compose in the sequence of the musical phrase, not in the sequence of the metronome". "In a Station of the Metro" was a typical example, the most well-known as not only the Imagist but also Pound's personal representative work. Pound was also famous for the generous support with which he improved the works of such major contemporaries as W. B. Yeats, Robert Frost, William Carlos Williams, Marianne Moore, H. D., James Joyce, Ernest Hemingway, Conrad Aiken, E. E. Cummings,

Charles Olson, and especially T. S. Eliot, whose masterpiece *The Waste Land* was drastically revised and improved by Ezra Pound.

Pound is very fruitful not only in poetry, but also in critical as well as cultural essays. Among all the works of poetry, *The Cantos* is the most outstanding. He spent more than half a century writing the long poem which is made up of 117 chapters. According to the modern American poet Robert Bly, *The Cantos* is like an encyclopedia, concerning almost everything like politics, economy, business, history, and geography. The poet employed different languages including ancient English, modern English, French, Chinese, Japanese, German, Italian and Greek. Pound also translated many books, including some Chinese classical works. The book *Cathay* which he translated from Chinese ancient poetry was said to be very successful. Some of the poems were often collected in some American literature teaching materials.

In a Station[1] of the Metro[2]

The apparition[3] of these faces in the crowd;
Petals[4] on a wet, black[5] bough[6].

1.《在地铁站》一诗被公认为意象主义与庞德本人的经典之作，也是许多文学教材的必选作品。该诗的创作过程及诗歌本身很好地诠释了“意象主义”的美学原则：用简练经济的语言，自由而富有音乐感的语言节奏，更重要的是，用精确的意象来表达诗歌的情感。它创作并发表于 1913 年。具体地说，诗人描述的是其本人在法国巴黎协和（La Concorde）地铁站的一段亲身体验（详见 Text Analysis 部分）。所以，从主题上来说，该诗并不是要表达一个宏大而富有隽永意义的题材，也不是要表现海枯石烂断人心肠式的爱情之歌，它不过是日常生活中的一个平淡插曲。正因为如此，大多数读者最初在不了解它的创作背景而接触它时，往往会觉得它晦涩乏味，有无厘头之惑。事实上，《在地铁站》一诗呈现给读者的不是某种崇高的情感，而是客观而漂亮的画面。而这正是意象主义所致力追求的诗歌创作方式。

2. 关于意象（image / imagery），我们很难给其下一个精确而具体的定义。任何一个物象、场景、事件、动作，甚至气味、声音等，以及语言修辞中的明喻、暗喻甚至典故等都可以被视为意象，对诗歌和诗人来说，意象至关重要，对诗人而言，它是表

达情感和情绪的手段和媒介，对读者来说，它能召唤起读者的联想和情感，引起共鸣。所以，庞德曾不无夸张地表示：诗人若能穷其一生觅得一个好的意象，也比著述等身要强。《在地铁站》一诗由 apparition, faces, crowd, petal, wet, black, bough 等意象词组成，其中 wet 和 black 是形容词，但因表具体的存在状态和颜色也被视为意象。因此，整首诗歌就是由意象并置（juxtaposition）来完成，连一个基本的动词都没有。

3. apparition：幽灵；（特异景象等的）显现。此意象蕴含着一种动态美，诗人把地铁站的人群面孔与幽灵联系在一起。
4. petals：花瓣。诗人将花瓣与面孔联系起来，既富有生活气息，也将诗人美的生活哲学呈现给读者。意象主义很重要的一项创作原则就是通过呈现而不是描述来表现事物。
5. wet 与 black 均富有画面感。
6. bough：树枝。

Text Analysis

According to Ezra Pound's own recollection, in 1913, when out of a metro train at La Concorde in Paris, he came upon a beautiful face, and then another and another, and then a beautiful child's face, and then another beautiful woman, which aroused a strong impulse in him to write this down. "I tried all that day to find words for what this had meant to me, and I could not find any words that seemed to me worthy, or as lovely as that sudden emotion. And that evening, as I went home along the Rue Raynouard, I was still trying and I found, suddenly, the expression." He suggested that he had wished to put down what he had seen in color painting rather than in word writing. "I do not mean that I found words, but there came an equation... not in speech, but in little splotches of colour. It was just that—a 'pattern', or hardly a pattern, if by 'pattern' you mean something with a 'repeat' in it. But it was a word, the beginning, for me, of a language in colour. I do not mean that I was unfamiliar with the kindergarten stories about colours being like tones in music. I think that sort of thing is nonsense. If you try to make notes permanently correspond with particular colours, it is like tying narrow meanings to symbols." Originally, Pound finished the poem with more than thirty lines, which failed to reach his poetics expectation. He said, "[A] Chinaman said long ago that if a man can't say what he has to say in twelve lines he had better keep quiet." He obtained the inspiration from Japanese poetic form hokku, which he turned to for the image to solve the problem which had troubled him that long. He thinks the prestige of the image is "clarity", clarifying the author's intention. And he also criticized the earlier tradition of the employment of the image, "All poetic language is the language of exploration. Since the beginning of bad writing, writers have used images as ornaments. The point of Imagism is that it does not use images as ornaments. The image is itself the speech. The image is the word beyond formulated language." Over more than one year's revision, Pound eventually brought about the two-line, fourteen-word poem.

Artistically, the poem can be regarded as the outcome of Pound's as well as Imagist experiment. From this experiment, it can be summed up that the process of Imagist writing is a process of looking for the "image".

1. What does the poet intend to tell his readers in the poem?
2. What is your understanding about the functions of imagery in poetry?
3. Compare this poem with William Carlos Williams's short poem "The Red Wheel-barrow". Can you tell the similarities as well as the differences between the two poems?

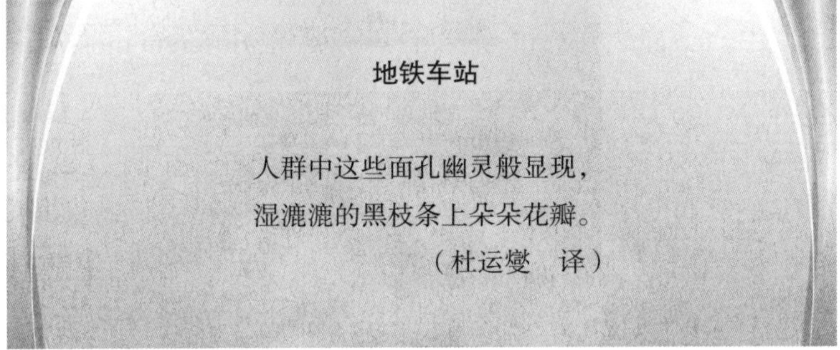

地铁车站

人群中这些面孔幽灵般显现，
湿漉漉的黑枝条上朵朵花瓣。
（杜运燮　译）

The River-Merchant's Wife[1]: A Letter[2]

While my hair was still cut straight across my forehead
I played about the front gate, pulling flowers.
You came by on bamboo stilts, playing horse[3],

You walked about my seat, playing with blue plums[4].
And we went on living in the village of Chokan[5]:
Two small people, without dislike or suspicion.
At fourteen I married My Lord you.
I never laughed, being bashful[6].
Lowering my head, I looked at the wall.
Called to, a thousand times, I never looked back[7].

At fifteen I stopped scowling[8],
I desired my dust to be mingled with yours
Forever and forever and forever[9].
Why should I climb the look-out[10]?

At sixteen you departed[11],
You went into far Ku-to-yen[12], by the river of swirling eddies[13],
And you have been gone five months.
The monkeys make sorrowful noise overhead.[14]

You dragged your feet[15] when you went out.
By the gate now, the moss is grown, the different mosses,
Too deep to clear them away!
The leaves fall early this autumn, in wind.
The paired butterflies are already yellow with August
Over the grass in the West garden;
They hurt me. I grow older.
If you are coming down through the narrows[16] of the river Kiang,
Please let me know beforehand,
And I will come out to meet you
As far as Cho-fu-Sa[17].

Notes

1. "The River-Merchant's Wife: A Letter"是庞德对李白诗《长干行》的翻译，也有人说是诠释与再创造，曾入选《美国名诗105首》，进入美国大学课堂"美国现代诗歌选读"课程，被誉为20世纪美国"最美的诗"。关于庞德翻译中国古诗，这里有必要简单交代：西班牙裔美国学者厄内斯特·费诺罗萨（Earnest Fenollesa）在19世

纪20年代对东亚的艺术有着浓厚兴趣，尤其对中国诗歌和日本诗歌有独到的研究。他毕业于哈佛大学，曾于1878年在日本东京大学任哲学教授，后任日本帝国政府的艺术研究员。他回美国后，创作两卷本《中日艺术时代》(*The Epochs of Chinese and Japanese Art*)。1908年他和妻子玛丽·费诺罗萨（Mary Fenollesa）访问伦敦，以便与英国博物馆的专家们探讨自己的著作。不料突发心脏病，于1908年9月去世。由于费诺罗萨有关中国诗的笔记仍需整理，其中每首诗只有原文、日文读音，以及每个字的释义与理解，因此他的妻子极需一位诗人将她丈夫的遗稿变成优美的英文诗。1913年秋，玛丽·费诺罗萨与庞德见了面，并答应将她丈夫的遗稿寄给庞德。费诺罗萨的笔记记录了大约150首中文诗，其中有屈原、宋玉、班婕妤、白居易、李白、陶潜、王维等人的作品，庞德最后仅选译了19首。它们是《诗经·小雅》中的《采薇》，汉古诗《青青河畔草》，李白诗12首，其中包括《长干行》《江上吟》《侍从宜春苑奉诏赋龙池柳色初青听新莺百啭歌》《天津三月时》《玉阶怨》《胡关饶风沙》《忆旧游谯郡元参军》《黄鹤楼送孟浩然之广陵》《送友人》《送友人入蜀》《登金陵凤凰台》《代马不思越》，郭璞的《游仙诗》，汉乐府《陌上桑》，卢照邻的《长安古意》，陶渊明的《停云》，王维的《送元二使安西》。庞德的译诗取名为《华夏集》(*Cathay*)，1915年出版后立刻引起轰动，艾略特的评价是："庞德是中国诗歌之发明者，通过他的文字我们终于能真正地了解原文了。"

2. 李白的原诗题为"长干行"。《长干行》又作《长干曲》，乐府旧题，原是长江下游一带民歌，源于《清商西曲》，内容多写船家妇女的生活。而庞德对标题进行改动显然出于他对原作的个人解读。如果抛开原作而直接理解庞德的英诗，该标题也具有很强的暗示效果。
3. 李白的原诗句为"郎骑竹马来"。竹马：儿童以竹竿当马骑。庞德将"竹马"译为bamboo stilts，意思是"竹高跷"，而playing horse属于庞德的"创新"。
4. 李白的原诗句为"绕床弄青梅"。床：指坐具。
5. Chokan：指地名，李白原作中为"长干里"。长干里是南京古代著名的地名，遗址在今秦淮河以南至雨花台以北。早在春秋战国时代，长干里一带已经是南京人口最密集地区，也是本地区经济命脉之所在。
6. bashful：羞怯的，忸怩的。
7. 第7～10行描绘初婚后的羞涩，再现新婚的甜蜜之状。
8. scowl：皱眉，怒视。
9. 李白原作此处为"常存抱柱信"，李白借用典故来表示女子坚守信约，对爱情的忠贞不渝。抱柱信：《庄子·盗跖》中"尾生与女子期于梁下，女子不来，水至不去，抱梁柱而死"。显然庞德没有直译，而是重复forever（永远）一词，以求达到相似的效果。

10. 李白原作此处为“岂上望夫台?”“望夫台”位于湖北省石首市内楚望山与绣林山交界处，“绣林十景”之一。赤壁大战后，刘备娶了孙权的妹妹孙尚香，两人相亲相爱，如漆如胶。这时，益州刘璋请刘备入川相助，谋士庞统也力主入川，夺取益州，以图大业，刘备忍痛割爱，告别新婚夫人，率兵入川。离别时，两人依依不舍，约定归期，洒泪相别。刘备入川后，孙尚香无时不想念自己的丈夫，常派人打听丈夫的行踪和消息。每当天高气爽或是喜鹊登枝时，她就登上宫后的东岳山，踮脚向夫君远去的方向瞭望。望郎心切，尚嫌山低，她就派人垫石为台，以期看见丈夫的身影。天长日久，石台被踏出一道深深的脚印。这对女人的脚印，经过1000多年的风吹雨打，至今仍然依稀可辨，此石台便为望夫台。look-out 此处意为“瞭望台”。11～14 行描写女子回忆婚后夫妻的恩爱，山盟海誓，如胶似漆。
11. depart：启程，离开。
12. Ku-to-yen：地名。李白原诗句为“瞿塘滟滪堆”，显然庞德没有直译。
13. swirling eddies：漩涡。swirl：旋转；eddy：涡流。
14. 第 15～18 行描述女子对丈夫远行经商的遥思之情，并为之担惊受怕，无限深情。
15. drag one's feet：故意拖沓。此处说明商人远行时恋恋不舍之情。
16. narrow：狭窄的水道。
17. Cho-fu-Sa：地名。李白原作为“长风沙”，位于今安庆市迎江区长风乡元桥村，是一处自古与瞿塘、滟滪并称的险段。根据该女子的描述，长风沙距离遥远，但即便如此，她也将不顾险途，为解相思之情而前往迎接自己的心爱之人。

Text Analysis

The poem expresses a wife's strong lovesickness towards her husband, a merchant who went a long journey for business. The first stanza of 6 lines is organized around a central image of the river-merchant and his wife when they were still children. The clear picture that the woman brought to mind suggests that the ties between her and her husband were quite close. The repetition in three separate lines of the verb “playing” to describe the little girl's activity at the front gate, as well as the little boy's presence on stilts and his circling around where she sits, emphasizes the natural, contented activity of children — almost as a part of the natural world referred to here by “flowers” and “blue plums”. This stanza establishes the presence of the “I” and the “you” in the poem. The second stanza depicts the woman's and man's adulthood—they got married although “I” was just fourteen years old. In ancient cultures, early marriages are customary, and it is the custom for the wife to refer to her husband with a respectful title. In the case of this poem the formality of the title is softened by the direct address of "you" added right after it. Lines 8-9 establish the child-wife's shyness in this formal adult situation by offering a picture of her bent head and averted eyes, a shyness so extreme that she could not respond to her husband, no matter how many efforts he made. The third stanza expresses the speaker's strong love for her husband. "I desired my dust to be mingled with yours / Forever and forever and forever." She says that she wishes to stay together even after they two died. It is clear that there is nothing she wishes for after the death of her husband, so deep is her love for him now. From line 15 to 18, an image of separation is developed in these lines as the husband takes on his role as a river-merchant and travels the waters, conducting his work in a distant world. The wife's statement of the length of his absence is expressed in one line, giving it full and emphatic force. The last stanza consists of 11 lines, the first of which tells what she recollects the moment when her husband departed. Line 19 shows that the husband hates to be away from his wife. The next two stanzas stress the feeling of the woman's lovesickness, especially when she came to the very gate where her husband left, and it was covered with deep mosses. The closing lines of the poem and the "letter" the river-merchant's wife reaches out from her lonely world of sorrow to her husband in a direct request: please let me know when and by what route you are returning, so that I may go to meet "you". Her village is a suburb of Nanking and she is willing to walk to a beach several hundred miles upstream from there to meet her husband, so deeply does she yearn to close the distance between them.

Questions

1. Pick out the images employed in the poem and explain the functions they play.

2. Compare this English version with its original Chinese one. Which one do you prefer? Why?

3. T. S. Eliot once said that for their age, Ezra Pound was the inventor or creator of Chinese ancient poetry in the west. What is your understanding about Eliot's comment when you read this poem? What did Pound invent in his translation?

Chinese Translation

（附：李白原诗）

长干行

妾发初覆额，折花门前剧。
郎骑竹马来，绕床弄青梅。
同居长干里，两小无嫌猜。
十四为君妇，羞颜未尝开。
低头向暗壁，千唤不一回。
十五始展眉，愿同尘与灰。
常存抱柱信，岂上望夫台。
十六君远行，瞿塘滟滪堆。
五月不可触，猿声天上哀。
门前迟行迹，一一生绿苔。
苔深不能扫，落叶秋风早。
八月蝴蝶来，双飞西园草。
感此伤妾心，坐愁红颜老。
早晚下三巴，预将书报家。
相迎不道远，直至长风沙。

Unit 27 T. S. Eliot

Introduction to the Author

T. S. Eliot (Thomas Stearns Eliot), a poet, critic, and editor, is America's most influential literary expatriate since Henry James. He is also regarded as one of the two most important poets in the 20th century (the other is W. B. Yeats). He was born in St. Louis, Missouri. His father, Henry Ware Eliot, president of the Hydraulic-Press Brick Company, was a businessman and his mother, Charlotte Champe Stearns, a former teacher, was an energetic social work volunteer at the Humanity Club of St. Louis, and an amateur poet with a taste for Ralph Waldo Emerson. He received his school education at private schools in his birthplace and in Milton, Massachusetts, before he entered Harvard, where he studied philosophy. He graduated from Harvard in 1909 and spent most of the next five years in England working towards a PhD in philosophy. He actually finished his doctoral dissertation, but never returned to take his oral defence. In 1915, he married Vivien Haigh-Wood, a beautiful and intelligent woman whose emotional changes and demands, and nervous instability made his family life a misery. He eventually left her in 1933, and they lived apart until her death 14 years later. After his marriage, Eliot settled down in London. In 1927, he became a British citizen and converted to Roman Catholicism to prove what he once claimed himself as "a classicist in art, a royalist in politics, and an Anglo-Catholic in religion".

The time Eliot started to write poetry dated from 1910 to 1911 when he was in France. There he met with the French symbolists, in particular, Jules Laforgue, helped him to find his own voice and style. His first poetic work, *Prufrock and Other Observations*, was a great contribution to the modernist movement in poetry, characterized by the combination of hard clear image, mysterious symbols, and a restrained subjective feeling. His *The Waste Land*, published in 1922, was a milestone not only to his own literary career but also to the development of modernist poetry. His later poems included "Journey of the Magi" (1927), "Ash Wednesday" (1930), and "Four Quartets" (1943). In 1948, Eliot was honored with the Nobel Prize for Literature for the progressive refinement and illustration of the aesthetic theory through his works. He was also a successful playwright. His most well-known play, *The Cocktail Party* (1950), made him a lot of money. His another famous play *Murder in the*

Cathedral (1935) seemed to be the most durable and interesting of all his plays.

Eliot is also a very important literary theorist and critic. His theoretical pieces like "Tradition and the Individual Talent" are manifestos of literary modernists. His famous definition of "objective correlative" becomes very important for the development of the New Criticism, which holds dominating influences on both poetic criticism and poetic writing for almost half a century in Anglo-American literature history. His important critical essays were collected into books. The most famous is *The Sacred Wood*, published in 1920.

The Love Song of J. Alfred Prufrock[1]

S'io credesse che mia risposta fosse
A persona che mai tornasse al mondo,
Questa fiamma staria senza piu scosse.
Ma perciocche giammai di questo fondo
Non torno vivo alcun, s'i'odo il vero,
Senza tema d'infamia ti rispondo[2].

Let us go then, you[3] and I,
When the evening is spread out against the sky
Like a patient etherised upon a table[4];
Let us go, through certain half-deserted streets[5],
The muttering retreats
Of restless nights in one-night cheap hotels
And sawdust restaurants with oyster-shells[6]:
Streets that follow like a tedious[7] argument
Of insidious[8] intent
To lead you to an overwhelming question[9] ...
Oh, do not ask, "What is it?"
Let us go and make our visit.

In the room the women come and go
Talking of Michelangelo[10].

The yellow fog that rubs its back upon the window-panes,
The yellow smoke that rubs its muzzle[11] on the window-panes
Licked its tongue into the corners of the evening,
Lingered upon the pools that stand in drains[12],
Let fall upon its back the soot[13] that falls from chimneys[14],
Slipped by the terrace[15], made a sudden leap,
And seeing that it was a soft October night,
Curled once about the house, and fell asleep[16].

And indeed there will be time[17]
For the yellow smoke that slides along the street,
Rubbing its back upon the window-panes;
There will be time, there will be time
To prepare a face[18] to meet the faces that you meet;
There will be time to murder and create,
And time for all the works and days[19] of hands
That lift and drop a question on your plate;
Time for you and time for me,
And time yet for a hundred indecisions,
And for a hundred visions and revisions[20],
Before the taking of a toast and tea.

In the room the women come and go
Talking of Michelangelo.
And indeed there will be time
To wonder, "Do I dare?" and, "Do I dare?" [21]
Time to turn back and descend the stair[22],
With a bald spot in the middle of my hair—
(They[23] will say: "How his hair is growing thin!")
My morning coat, my collar mounting firmly to the chin[24],
My necktie rich and modest, but asserted by a simple pin[25]—
(They will say: "But how his arms and legs are thin!")
Do I dare
Disturb the universe?
In a minute there is time
For decisions and revisions which a minute will reverse.[26]

For I have known them all already, known them all—
Have known the evenings, mornings, afternoons,
I have measured out my life with coffee spoons;[27]
I know the voices dying with a dying fall
Beneath the music from a farther room[28].
So how should I presume?[29]

And I have known the eyes already, known them all—
The eyes that fix you in a formulated phrase[30],
And when I am formulated, sprawling on a pin[31],
When I am pinned and wriggling[32] on the wall,
Then how should I begin
To spit out all the butt-ends of my days and ways[33]?
And how should I presume?

And I have known the arms already, known them all—
Arms that are braceleted[34] and white and bare
(But in the lamplight, downed with light brown hair[35]!)
Is it perfume from a dress
That makes me so digress[36]?
Arms that lie along a table, or wrap about a shawl[37].
And should I then presume?
And how should I begin?[38]

……

Shall I say, I have gone at dusk through narrow streets
And watched the smoke that rises from the pipes
Of lonely men in shirt-sleeves, leaning out of windows?…

I should have been a pair of ragged claws
Scuttling across the floors of silent seas[39].

……

And the afternoon, the evening, sleeps so peacefully!
Smoothed by long fingers,
Asleep … tired … or it malingers[40],

Stretched on the floor, here beside you and me.
Should I, after tea and cakes and ices[41],
Have the strength to force the moment to its crisis[42]?
But though I have wept and fasted, wept and prayed[43],
Though I have seen my head (grown slightly bald) brought in upon a platter[44],
I am no prophet—and here's no great matter[45];
I have seen the moment of my greatness flicker[46],
And I have seen the eternal Footman hold my coat, and snicker,
And in short, I was afraid.[47]

And would it have been worth it[48], after all,
After the cups, the marmalade, the tea[49],
Among the porcelain, among some talk of you and me,
Would it have been worth while,
To have bitten off the matter with a smile[50],
To have squeezed the universe into a ball[51]
To roll it toward some overwhelming question,
To say: "I am Lazarus, come from the dead,
Come back to tell you all, I shall tell you all" [52]—
If one, settling a pillow by her head,
Should say: "That is not what I meant at all;
That is not it, at all." [53]

And would it have been worth it, after all,
Would it have been worth while,
After the sunsets and the dooryards and the sprinkled streets,
After the novels, after the teacups, after the skirts that trail along the floor[54]—
And this, and so much more?—
It is impossible to say just what I mean!
But as if a magic lantern threw the nerves in patterns on a screen[55]:
Would it have been worth while
If one, settling a pillow or throwing off a shawl,
And turning toward the window, should say:
"That is not it at all,
That is not what I meant, at all." [56]

……

No! I am not Prince Hamlet[57], nor was meant to be;
Am an attendant lord[58], one that will do
To swell a progress, start a scene or two[59],
Advise the prince[60]; no doubt, an easy tool[61],
Deferential[62], glad to be of use,
Politic[63], cautious, and meticulous[64];
Full of high sentence[65], but a bit obtuse[66];
At times, indeed, almost ridiculous—
Almost, at times, the Fool[67].

I grow old … I grow old …
I shall wear the bottoms of my trousers rolled[68].

Shall I part my hair behind? Do I dare to eat a peach[69]?
I shall wear white flannel trousers[70], and walk upon the beach.
I have heard the mermaids singing, each to each[71].

I do not think that they will sing to me.

I have seen them[72] riding seaward on the waves
Combing the white hair of the waves blown back
When the wind blows the water white and black.

We have lingered in the chambers of the sea[73]
By sea-girls wreathed with seaweed red and brown
Till human voices wake us, and we drown.[74]

1. J. Alfred Prufrock 是诗人虚构的人名，是本诗的主人公、叙述者。Prufrock 这一人名可以设想为是由 prude 和 frock 合成的。Prude 是“过分拘谨的人、装作正经的人”的意思；frock 意为“外衣”，所以 prufrock 这个名字就暗含此人是一个过分拘谨的人，我们就此不难看出艾略特的良苦用心。本诗诗人采用了戏剧独白（dramatic monologue）的方式。
2. 这段引文出自但丁《神曲》第 27 章，为意大利语，是但丁在地狱里询问受罪的吉德（Guido）时他的回答：“假如我的回话是向着一个可以回到阳间的人，那么我的火光就不再闪烁了；但是，没有一个人可以从这里再走出去（假如我听到的这句话是真实的），那么我就是回答了你也不怕什么”。

3. 关于 you 的身份问题，并无定论，诗人解释为“未名男性同伴”，而一些批评家将他视为 Prufrock 的精神化身，也有人将他作为读者。
4. etherize：麻醉。table 这里指“手术台”。
5. half-deserted streets：半荒废的街道。这里借用一种破败的景象来描述叙述者悲观颓丧的精神面貌。
6. 为了押韵，5～7 行的语序倒装，正常的语序为：The muttering of restless night in one-night cheap hotels and sawdust restaurants with oyster-shells retreats。muttering 意为“低语声”；retreat 意为“撤退、消退”；sawdust 为“锯屑”之意；oyster-shells 意思是“牡蛎壳”。
7. tedious：冗长乏味的。
8. insidious：潜在的，阴险的。
9. 第 8～10 行中的街道象征着叙述者的意识状态，诗人在诗歌的开篇部分采用意识流手法。出现在街道上的那些无序的意象正是叙述者心里不安与躁动的反映。overwhelming question：重要的问题，难以抵抗的问题，压倒性的问题。
10. 第 13～14 行在本诗中出现多次，第一次出现时与街道了无生气的情形形成共鸣，Michelangelo（米开朗琪罗）是意大利文艺复兴时期成就卓著的科学家、雕刻家、画家与诗人。诗人用嘲讽的口吻来讽刺这些走来走去的女士们，她们谈论着米开朗琪罗并不是因为她们热爱艺术、欣赏他，而是在人群中相互炫耀而已。
11. muzzle：（动物的）鼻嘴部。
12. drain：下水道，阴沟。
13. soot：烟灰。
14. 第 19 行的正常语序为：Let the soot that falls from chimneys fall upon its back。its 指代前面出现的 yellow fog / smoke。
15. terrace：台阶。
16. 第 15～20 这一诗节中有一非常重要的意象 yellow fog / smoke，常被理解为“黄色的猫”，它慵懒、倦怠，显然，具有一定的象征意义。
17. there will be time 在本诗中多次出现，喻旨明显，尤其是用来凸显主人公优柔寡断的性格。
18. prepare a face：准备化妆的意思。
19. works and days：诗人借用典故，公元 8 世纪希腊诗人海希奥德（Hesiod）创作了一首农事诗《工作与时日》（*Works and Days*），诗人的目的是将农夫繁忙而有意义的劳动与诗中主人公无聊空虚的生活形成鲜明的对比。
20. visions and revisions：指不断地想象与幻想，虚构心目中的画面。
21. Do I dare: Do I dare to propose to the lady?
22. Time to turn back and descend the stair: There will be time to turn back and go down the stairs.
23. They：这里指那些女性。
24. my collar mounting firmly to the chin：我的衣领紧贴着我的下巴。mount：上升、攀爬。

25. My necktie rich and modest，but asserted by a simple pin：此处说明 Prufrock 并不是一个十分富有的上等阶层，modest：此处为“得体不夸张”的意思，assert 意为“系住与维持”。
26. 第 37～48 行这一诗节充分表明叙述者矛盾、犹豫、缺乏自信的自然心态。他向往爱情，对女性保持一种本能的冲动，但对自己的穿着和外在形象都不断地怀疑，因而无法采取果敢而必要的行动。
27. 第 52 行，measure out 度量，量出，在此处表“打发、消磨时光”。全句的本意是“我一咖啡勺一咖啡勺地量好我的时间”，暗指自己虚度光阴，生活消极。
28. 第 52～53 行中，a dying fall 通常是指音乐中起于高音后缓缓结束的曲调，此处指房内女人们的谈话也是以这样一种方式结束，需要特别说明的是，这是西方上层人群社交时所常采用的方式，所以，诗人以此来讥讽西方上层人士虚无糜烂的生活。
29. presume 有双重含义：猜测；放肆或胆敢做某事。第 54 行在诗中多次出现，进一步阐释了叙述者的懦弱、不自信的性格。
30. formulate：用规范的语言表达；formulated phrase：陈词滥调，套话，无聊的话语。
31. sprawl on a pin：趴伏在针上。诗人借用“小针”（pin）来表达叙述者的尴尬状态：当听到有人在窃窃议论他时，他仿佛趴伏在针上，意思是如同身上有小虫叮咬，浑身不自在。
32. wriggle：蠕动，扭动。
33. spit out：吐出；butt-ends：烟蒂。Prufrock 把自己的余生比作烟蒂，说明他没有规划过自己的人生，并对自己的生活缺乏必要的信心。
34. Arms that are braceleted：arms wearing bracelets，戴镯子的手臂。
35. downed with light brown hair：指那些露出来的胳膊在灯光下映射出浅棕色的毛发。
36. digress：走神，注意力不集中。
37. shawl：（女性用的）披巾，围巾。
38. 第 62～69 行描述 Prufrock 一次无聊的幻想：与那些女士们发生性关系，但因自己性无能而倍感失败与挫折。
39. 第 73～74 行，Prufrock 将自己比作一种非常原始的生物——蟹类，在静寂的海底乱走乱窜，他一方面厌倦了喧嚣而无趣的人间，另一方面他倍感自己的无能与软弱。ragged claws：海蟹；scuttle：疾走。
40. malinger：装病。装病的目的是躲避责任与义务。
41. after tea and cakes and ices：指下午晚些时候。ices：指冰激凌一类的食品。这里不是单纯描述叙述者的生活方式，更重要的是体现他作决定时的犹疑与担心。
42. force the moment to its crisis：to consider the moment as the crisis time，把此刻当作最关键的时候。这里表明，Prufrock 已决定抛下犹豫，鼓起勇气向对方示爱。对他来说，这样的时刻似乎生死攸关。
43. I have wept and fasted，wept and prayed：诗人借用《旧约全书》中的典故。原文：“And they mourned，and wept and fasted until evening for Saul and for Jonathan his son

and for the people of the LORD and for the house of Israel，because they had fallen by the sword.”(2 Samuel 1:12) Prufrock 的意思是为了获得女士的爱，他已尽了最大的努力。fast：戒斋。

44. 第 82 行出自《新约全书》中施洗者约翰的故事，约翰的头被希律王（Heroid）呈送给女王希罗底（Herodias）：“Give me here on a platter the head of John the Baptist.”很明显，诗人借此典故来表明 Prufrock 求爱的决心：不惜用自己的生命来换取。
45. I am no prophet：我不是个预言家，Prufrock 缺乏信心，因而无法预计自己的追求将是什么样的结果。and here's no great matter：（我的死）不是件大不了的事情。Prufrock 不断地重复以表自己的决心，而这正是他犹豫缺乏勇气的另一种表现。
46. flicker：飘摇、摆动。I have seen the moment of my greatness flicker，意思是 Prufrock 已意识到自己的了不起，有突如其来的伟大感。
47. And I have seen the eternal Footman hold my coat, and snicker，这一诗节的最后两行，叙述者又原态毕现：犹疑不断，缺乏信心。所以才说，“in short, I was afraid”。And 表转折，意思是“但是，可是”；eternal：永恒的；Footman：男仆；snicker：窃笑，暗笑。
48. have been worth it：it 指的是“向女士示爱”一事。但这里运用虚拟语气，很显然，Prufrock 并没打算真正采取行动。该诗行接下来重复多次，再次表明叙述者的胆小、优柔寡断的性格。
49. the cups, the marmalade, the tea：包括下一行的 porcelain 都是上层社会日常生活的象征。marmalade：果酱；porcelain：瓷器。
50. To have bitten off the matter with a smile：to solve the problem in an easy and peaceful way，这里的 matter 就是指向女士示爱的问题。
51. squeezed the universe into a ball：艾略特借用英国玄学派诗人马维尔（Andrew Marvell）的《致羞涩的情人》（“To His Coy Mistress”）中的诗行：“Let us roll all our strength and all / Our Sweetness up into one ball”来表明 Prufrock 正一门心思鼓足勇气向女士示爱。
52. 第 94～95 这两行出自《新约全书》，拉撒路（Lazarus）是耶稣的学生、朋友，他穷困潦倒，靠乞讨过日，他浑身生疮，常常被带到财主家的门口，希望捡些财主桌子上掉下来的东西充饥，连狗也来舔他的疮。他死后，财主在地狱的火里受煎熬，而拉撒路死后第四天就得以复生，并过着非常幸福的生活。事实上，就在他死后的那四天里，他被带到阴间，目睹那些富人们在地狱里遭受折磨，所以，当他复生离开之时，富人们一再要他带口信给自己的家人，要家人善待穷人，以免死后遭受磨难。此处 Prufrock 把自己当作拉撒路，一方面，他不欣赏上层社会的生活方式，另一方面，他自知无力改变现状，只是表达自己的失望之情而已。“拉撒路”一词在英语中就是贫穷的代名词。
53. 第 96～98 行中，one 指代女士，这里说明 Prufrock 担心自己示爱后被女士拒绝。
54. 第 101～102 行中，the sunsets, the dooryards, the sprinkled streets，the novels, the teacups 等都是上层社会人群日常生活的一部分。sprinkled streets：洒过水的街道。

Notes

55. 第 104～105 这两行表明 Prufrock 似乎无法表达自己的内心思想，正如同“一盏魔灯把神经在屏幕上组成一种模式”一样难以实现。
56. 第 106～110 这五行中，Prufrock 再次表示对自己示爱后被拒的担心。
57. 众所周知，莎士比亚剧中的哈姆雷特是个忧郁、优柔寡断的典型代表。Prufrock 知道自己并没有哈姆雷特那样高贵的身份，同时，他也不希望自己像哈姆雷特那样优柔寡断，但事实上，他有过之而无不及。
58. an attendant lord：侍臣，小人物。
59. progress：原指英国伊丽莎白时期帝王外出时跟随巡行的队伍，当时的舞台演出中也有那些跟随帝王跑龙套的队伍。swell a progress：壮大队伍的意思；start a scene or two：捧一两次场。这里 Prufrock 把自己比作舞台演出中的小角色，跑龙套的角色。
60. Advise the prince：此处 Prufrock 认为自己应扮演《哈姆雷特》戏剧中波洛尼厄斯（Polonius）的角色，该角色足智多谋，有很好的口才。
61. an easy tool：Prufrock 知道自己不是一个决定性的人物，无非是替主子效劳而已，因而将自己说成是“简单而供使用的工具”。
62. deferential：毕恭毕敬的。
63. Politic：Prufrock 认为自己有智谋，做事讲究策略。
64. meticulous：谨小慎微的。
65. Full of high sentence：满口高调。sentence 用的是古义，即“意见”或“警句”。出自乔叟《坎特贝雷故事》一书，乔叟形容克拉克（Clerk）的语言简洁，并且“full of high sentence”。
66. obtuse：迟钝的。
67. Fool：丑角。Prufrock 认为自己就像戏剧中的一个丑角，遭人愚弄调侃，没什么太大的存在价值。
68. wear the bottoms of my trousers rolled：老年人通常生活节俭，当人老了后，身材变得矮小，旧衣旧裤他们不会扔掉，而是卷起裤脚照穿。
69. eat a peach：这里借用亚当与夏娃偷吃禁果的故事，暗示 Prufrock 想做出某种改变。
70. flannel trousers：法兰绒裤。
71. mermaids：美人鱼。美人鱼是“美”的象征。这里出自典故，艾略特引用英国玄学派诗人约翰·多恩（John Donne）的诗作《去抓住一颗流星》(“Go and Catch a Falling Star”)，原文是“Teach me to hear mermaids singing，/ Or to keep off envy's stinging”，“教我听美人鱼唱歌”意思是做不可能的事情。古希腊神话中共有 8 条美人鱼，所以艾略特才说，“each to each”。
72. them：这里指美人鱼。
73. the chambers of the sea：指海底皇宫。显然这是虚构的场所。
74. 全诗的最后两行中 sea-girls wreathed with seaweed red and brown：意思是“海仙头戴着红棕色水草编织的花环”。这里的 sea-girls 暗指希腊神话中的塞壬，这是一种半鸟半女人的怪物，常用美妙的歌声引诱男性，当她们的歌声停止，男人们也将溺

水而亡。所以最后诗人说：Till human voices wake us, and we drown。Prufrock 知道自己无力面对并改变现实，最终的结局是"溺水而亡"。值得注意的是：全诗叙述者一直使用"I"，但最后一节变成了"we"，显然有一定的指代意义。

Text Analysis

Generally, when a man falls in love, he tends to be in a sweet, pleasant, relaxing and enjoyable state of living. But J. Alfred Prufrock is a totally different case. He falls in an endless situation of worries, hesitation, indecisiveness, tension, and lack of confidence. He needs to love and to be loved. And sometimes he has a strong impulse to make a proposal to a lady. But one problem is that he has no clear idea who he should turn to make the proposal. According to the poem, any woman who appears in front of him will be what he seeks after. And this is what T. S. Eliot intends to criticize: love affairs have become a vanity fair. True love does not take place in modern times. Modern people are more involved in their daily trifle and vulgar things like coffee, tea, marmalade, porcelain, and meaningless chattering, as are mentioned in the poem. Therefore, thematically, the poem is quite symbolic and satirical for the modern society where everyone seems to be lingering and absent-minded. The poem is more like a song of bitterness and elegy than a song of love.

Most common readers will find it a little challenging to go deep into the understanding of this poem. The poet has employed a number of allusions from the Holy Bible, and from the works of Dante, Chaucer, John Donne, Andrew Marvell and many others, which makes the poem more difficult. But according to the poet himself, he once expressed his poetics in his well-known essay "Tradition and the Individual Talent" that a poet must have a historical sense. By historical sense, he says, "No poet, no artist, has his complete meaning alone. His significance, his appreciation is the appreciation of his relation to the dead poets and artists." In simple words, Eliot stresses that a poet must base his writing upon a tradition. Eliot opposes the Romanticist poetics expressing one's feelings in a direct and spontaneous way. He puts forward his theory of "objective correlative", which tells that a poet should express his feelings in an objective way. "The only way of expressing emotion in the form of art is by finding a set of objects, a situation, a chain of events which shall be the formula of that particular emotion; ..." We can take the beginning of the love song as an example to interpret his idea of "objective correlative". The seven lines (from the second line to the eighth) are made up of clusters of images like "the evening is spread out against the sky", "Like a patient etherized upon a table", "half-deserted streets", "The muttering", "restless nights in one-night cheap hotels", "sawdust restaurants with oyster-shells", and "Streets that follow like a tedious arguments". These objective images are likely to arouse readers' strong emotion of dullness, inactiveness and lifelessness. The technique of juxtaposition of images is frequently used in Eliot's works like *The Waste Land*, "Preludes", "The Hollow Men" and "Four Quartets". This is the way to express a poet's feelings. Eliot adds that a great poet must know how to sacrifice his personal feelings into the things.

Questions

1. After reading the poem, can you guess who is Prufrock? And can you describe Prufrock's characters?

2. T. S. Eliot employed figures of speech in his writing, for example, repetition is frequently found in this poem. Can you tell how it functions?

3. People often say that poetry is a mirror of the society. How does this poem reflect the social situation?

4. Most often, love songs tend to be pleasant and romantic, but this love song seems quite different. What is your feeling when you read this poem?

Chinese Translation

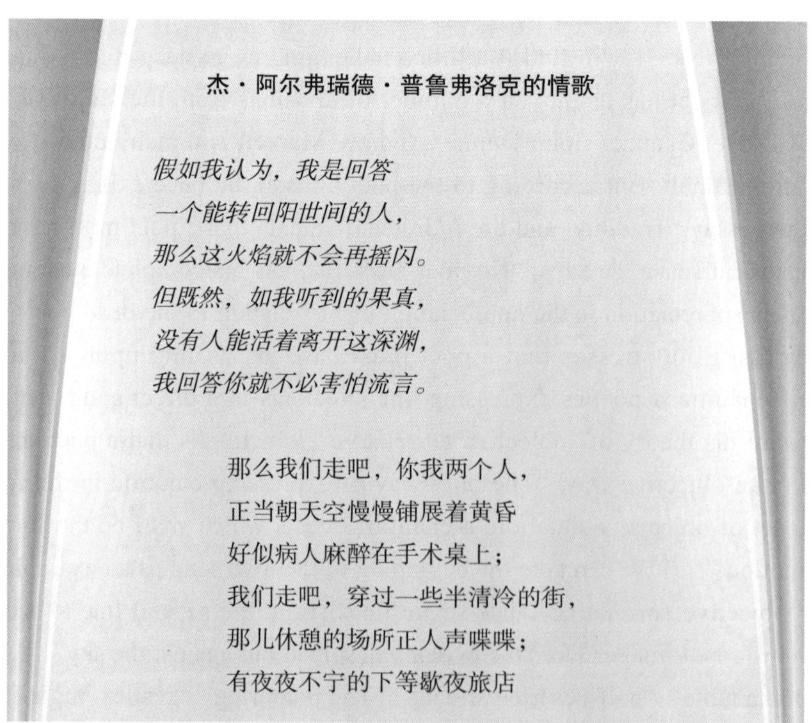

杰·阿尔弗瑞德·普鲁弗洛克的情歌

假如我认为，我是回答
一个能转回阳世间的人，
那么这火焰就不会再摇闪。
但既然，如我听到的果真，
没有人能活着离开这深渊，
我回答你就不必害怕流言。

那么我们走吧，你我两个人，
正当朝天空慢慢铺展着黄昏
好似病人麻醉在手术桌上；
我们走吧，穿过一些半清冷的街，
那儿休憩的场所正人声喋喋；
有夜夜不宁的下等歇夜旅店

和满地蚌壳的铺锯末的饭馆；
街连着街，好像一场讨厌的争议
带着阴险的意图
要把你引向一个重大的问题……
唉，不要问，“那是什么？”
让我们快点去作客。

在客厅里女士们来回地走，
谈着画家米开朗基罗。

黄色的雾在窗玻璃上擦着它的背，
黄色的烟在窗玻璃上擦着它的嘴，
把它的舌头舐进黄昏的角落，
徘徊在快要干涸的水坑上；
让跌下烟囱的烟灰落上它的背，
它溜下台阶，忽地纵身跳跃，
看到这是一个温柔的十月的夜，
于是便在房子附近蜷伏起来安睡。

呵，确实地，总会有时间
看黄色的烟沿着街滑行，
在窗玻璃上擦着它的背；
总会有时间，总会有时间
装一副面容去会见你去见的脸；

总会有时间去暗杀和创新，
总会有时间让举起问题又丢进你盘里
双手完成劳作与度过时日；
有的是时间，无论你，无论我，
还有的是时间犹豫一百遍，
或看到一百种幻景再完全改过，
在吃一片烤面包和饮茶以前。

在客厅里女士们来回地走，
谈着画家米开朗基罗。

呵，确实地，总还有时间

来疑问，“我可有勇气？”“我可有勇气？”
总还有时间来转身走下楼梯，
把一块秃顶暴露给人去注意——
（她们会说：“他的头发变得多么稀！”）
我的晨礼服，我的硬领在腭下笔挺，
我的领带雅致而多彩，用一个简朴的别针固定——
（她们会说：“可是他的胳膊腿多么细！”）
我可有勇气
搅乱这个宇宙？
在一分钟里总还有时间
决定和变卦，过一分钟再变回头。

因为我已经熟悉了她们，熟悉了她们所有的人——
熟悉了那些黄昏，和上下午的情景，
我是用咖啡匙子量走了我的生命；
我熟悉每当隔壁响起了音乐
话声就逐渐低微而至停歇。
　　所以我怎么敢开口？

而且我已熟悉那些眼睛，熟悉了她们所有的眼睛——
那些眼睛能用一句成语的公式把你盯住，
当我被公式化了，在别针下趴伏，
那我怎么能开始吐出
我的生活和习惯的全部剩烟头？
我又怎么敢开口？

而且我已经熟悉了那些胳膊，熟悉了她们所有的胳膊——
那些胳膊戴着镯子，又袒露又白净
（可是在灯光下，显得淡褐色毛茸茸！）
是否由于衣裙的香气
使得我这样话离本题？

那些胳膊或围着肩巾，或横在案头。
　　那时候我该开口吗？
　　可是我怎么开始？

是否我说，我在黄昏时走过窄小的街，
看到孤独的男子只穿着衬衫
倚在窗口，烟斗里冒着袅袅的烟？……

那我就会成为一对蟹螯
急急爬过沉默的海底。

啊，那下午，那黄昏，睡得多平静！
被纤长的手指轻轻抚爱，
睡了……倦慵的……或者它装病。
躺在地板上，就在你我脚边伸开。
是否我，在用过茶、糕点和冰食以后，
有魄力把这一刻推到紧要的关头？
然而，尽管我曾哭泣和斋戒，哭泣和祈祷，
尽管我看见我的头（有一点秃了）用盘子端了进来，
我不是先知——这也不值得大惊小怪；
我曾看到我伟大的时刻闪烁，
我曾看到那永恒的“侍者”拿着我的外衣暗笑，
一句话，我有点害怕。

而且，归根到底，是不是值得
当小吃、果子酱和红茶已用过，
在杯盘中间，当人们谈着你和我，
是不是值得以一个微笑
把这件事情一口啃掉，
把整个宇宙压缩成一个球，
使它滚向某个重大的问题，
说道：“我是拉撒路，从冥界
来报一个信，我要告诉你们一切。”——
万一她把枕垫放在头下一倚，
　　说道：“唉，我意思不是要谈这些；
　　不，我不是要谈这些。”

那么，归根到底，是不是值得，
是否值得在那许多次夕阳以后，
在庭院的散步和水淋过街道以后，
在读小说以后，在饮茶以后，在长裙拖过地板以后，——

说这些，和许多许多事情？——
要说出我想说的话绝不可能！
仿佛有幻灯把神经的图样投到幕上：
是否还值得如此难为情，
假如她放一个枕垫或掷下披肩，
把脸转向窗户，甩出一句：
　　“那可不是我的本意，
　　那可绝不是我的本意。”

不！我并非哈姆雷特王子，当也当不成；
我只是个侍从爵士，能为王家出行，
铺排显赫的场面，或为王子出主意，
就够好的了；无非是顺手的工具，
服服帖帖，巴不得有点用途，
细致，周详，处处小心翼翼；
满口高谈阔论，但有点愚鲁；
有时候，老实说，显得近乎可笑，
有时候，几乎是个丑角。

呵，我变老了……我变老了……
我将要卷起我的长裤的裤脚。

我将把头发往后分吗？我可敢吃桃子？
我将穿上白法兰绒裤在海滩上散步。
我听见了女水妖彼此对唱着歌。

我不认为她们会为我而唱歌。

我看过她们凌驾波浪驶向大海，
梳着打回来的波浪的白发，
当狂风把海水吹得又黑又白。

我们留连于大海的宫室，
被海妖以红的和棕的海草装饰，
一旦被人声唤醒，我们就淹死。

（查良铮　译）

Unit 28 Langston Hughes

Introduction to the Author

James Mercer Langston Hughes (1902-1967) is an American poet, social activist, novelist, playwright, and columnist.

Hughes was born in Joplin, Missouri, and was the second child of the family. His father left the family and divorced his mother, going to Cuba and later to Mexico when Hughes was still a little child. Hughes spent most of his childhood with his maternal grandmother in Lawrence, Kansas. She told him stories about their family and their fight to end slavery. Her storytelling had deep effect on his growth, filling him with pride in himself and his race. He first began to write poetry during this period of time. Hughes struggled with a feeling of loneliness caused by his parents' divorce. He took up reading books as a way to deal with the lack of time his parents spent with him. Among the early influences on his writing were poets Walt Whitman, Carl Sandburg and Paul Lawrence Dunbar. After graduating from high school in 1920, Hughes moved to Mexico City to live with his father for one year. His father had moved there to escape racism in America. His father did not offer much warmth to his son. Yet, Hughes turned the pain caused by his family problems into one of his most famous poems, "The Negro Speaks of Rivers". In 1922, Hughes took a job on a ship and sailed to Africa. He later sailed to France, Russia, Spain and Italy. He wrote poems and short stories during his travels. His experiences while traveling greatly influenced his works. He sent a few of his writings back home. The publishment of his works helped establish him as a professional writer.

Hughes is a fruitful writer. He finished 17 books of poetry, including *The Weary Blues* (1926), *Fine Clothes to the Jew* (1927), *Shakespeare in Harlem* (1942), and *Montage of a Dream Deferred* (1951). Besides, he brought out more than 10 novels and short story books, 12 major plays, some non-fiction books and books for children. Hughes is considered one of the leading voices of the Harlem Renaissance. He is the first poet to use the rhythms of black music. And he helps bring the movement of jazz and the sound of black speech into poetry. Hughes is identified as unashamedly black at a time when blackness was out of fashion. He stresses the theme of "black is beautiful" as he explores the black human condition in a variety of depths.

His main concern is the uplift of his people, whose strengths, courage, and humor he wanted to record as part of the general American experience. In 2002, the scholar Molefi Kete Asante listed Langston Hughes on his list of 100 Greatest African Americans. Postal Service added the image of Langston Hughes to its Black Heritage series of postage stamps.

The Negro Speaks of Rivers[1]

I've known rivers:
I've known rivers ancient as the world and older than the
flow of human blood in human veins.
My soul has grown deep like the rivers.

I bathed in the Euphrates[2] when dawns were young[3].
I built my hut near the Congo[4] and it lulled[5] me to sleep.
I looked upon the Nile[6] and raised the pyramids above it.
I heard the singing of the Mississippi[7] when Abe Lincoln[8]
went down to New Orleans[9], and I've seen its muddy
bosom[10] turn all golden in the sunset.

I've known rivers:
Ancient, dusky[11] rivers.

My soul has grown deep like the rivers.

1. Harlem Renaissance：黑人文艺复兴，又称“新黑人运动”，指的是20世纪20年代到经济危机爆发这10年间美国纽约黑人聚居区哈莱姆的黑人作家所发动的一场文学运动。领导者为兰斯顿·休斯。长期以来，黑人处于一个黑暗的种族歧视时代，他们既享受不到政治权利又无法获得与白人同等的教育机会。这样的历史与社会境遇促使一些黑人知识分子进行思考，该如何利用文艺活动来提高黑人的自我意识，激发民族热情，维护民族尊严。20世纪20年代，当时纽约的哈莱姆区是全国最大的黑人聚居区，几乎集中了全美国最优秀的黑人艺术家和文学家，他们以黑人生活

为自己创作的主要题材，大力推崇黑人民族的优秀文化。因此，以哈莱姆为中心发展起来的黑人文艺运动被称作“哈莱姆文艺复兴”或“新黑人运动”（The New Negro Movement）。它提高了黑人的文艺水平，从中涌现出一批优秀的诗人和小说家，对促进黑人文化事业的发展，提高黑人民族的自尊心产生了深远的影响。

2. the Euphrates：幼发拉底河。

3. when dawns were young：此处诗人采用了拟人修辞手法，可以理解为：（1）黎明刚开始的时候；（2）比喻意义——人类社会早期。很显然，第二种更有深意。

4. the Congo：刚果河。刚果河又称扎伊尔河，非洲第二长河，位于非洲中西部。

5. lull：使入睡；使安静。

6. the Nile：尼罗河。尼罗河是一条流经非洲东部与北部的河流，长 6670 km，是世界上最长的河流。

7. the Mississippi：密西西比河。世界第四长河，也是北美洲流程最长、流域面积最广、水量最大的河流。位于北美洲中南部，注入墨西哥湾。

8. Abe Lincoln：亚伯拉罕·林肯，美国第 16 任总统（1861—1865）。Abe 是 Abraham 的简称。在其总统任内，美国爆发了内战，史称“南北战争”。林肯击败了南方分裂势力，废除了奴隶制度，维护了国家的统一。但就在内战结束后不久，林肯不幸遇刺身亡。

9. when Abe Lincoln went down to New Orleans：此处诗人借林肯途经新奥尔良州来描述黑人的生存和发展状况。早在 1831 年，林肯曾在新奥尔良旅行，对当时黑人被奴役的状况感到非常震撼，并暗下决心一定要废除黑人奴役制度。

10. bosom：胸部，乳房。

11. dusky：黑暗的，昏暗的。

Text Analysis

The poem was first published in *The Crisis* in June 1921, the first of his poems printed in that journal. Langston Hughes wrote it on an envelope while traveling by train to Mexico as he crossed the Mississippi River to St. Louis. In America, the Mississippi River is considered as the “Mother River”, which, when Hughes was crossing it, brought Hughes to a sudden association. It reminded him of the miserable living conditions of the black, who had created a civilization as ancient as the four rivers mentioned in the poem: the Mississippi, the Euphrates, the Nile and the Congo. This brought the poet a strong sense of dignity and pride as of the African origin. It also reminded the poet of Abraham Lincoln who “went down to New Orleans” by raft. When Lincoln crossed the river, he witnessed the poverty-stricken and badly-treated black people, and he promised himself to abolish the slavery system and give the black equal rights.

Evidently, the poet intended to stress the existence, dignity and equality of the black race. In the poem, the rivers are more symbolic, metaphoric, and romantic than realistic. In the first stanza, the analogy between "rivers" and "human veins" is very suggestive and quite expressive: both of them run and flow. In this way, rivers and humans especially the black are closely interrelated, which makes the stand-alone line stanza "My soul has grown deep like the rivers" become natural and understandable. Rivers are similar to human souls in that they run and never end. In this poem, "my soul" refers to the "negro's soul". In this sense, the poem is not purely lyrical but more racially and culturally-loaded, which makes the poem "grow deep".

Questions

1. How do you understand "the rivers" in the poem? If we change "the rivers" into "the mountains" or something else, what effects will it produce?
2. What does the poet mean by saying "I've known rivers: /Ancient, dusky rivers"?
3. What impressions does the title of the poem bring to you?

Chinese Translation

黑人谈河

我知道河流：
我知道河流与世界一样古老，比人类血管
流动着的血液还要古老。

我的灵魂已变得如河流一样深沉。

当黎明还很年轻，我就在幼发拉底河沐浴。
我将小屋建在刚果河畔，河水伴我入眠。
我看着尼罗河，将金字塔建在河上。
当亚伯・林肯去新奥尔良时，我就听到密西西比河
在歌唱，看到它那泥褐色的胸膛在
夕阳下变成了一片金光。

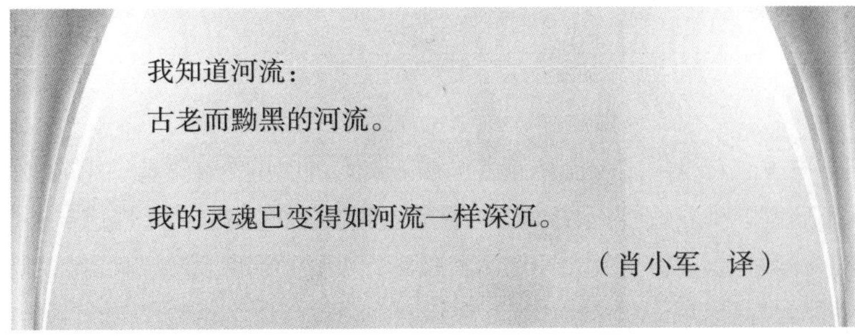
我知道河流：
古老而黝黑的河流。

我的灵魂已变得如河流一样深沉。

（肖小军　译）

A Dream Deferred[1]

What happens to a dream deferred?

Does it dry up
Like a raisin in the sun[2]?
Or fester like a sore—
And then run[3]?
Does it stink[4] like rotten meat?
Or crust and sugar over—
Like a syrupy[5] sweet?

Maybe it just sags[6]
Like a heavy load.

Or does it explode?

1. defer：延缓，耽搁。此诗最初标题为“Harlem”（哈莱姆），后来才改为“A Dream Defered”（延缓的梦），有些选集干脆将二者结合起来：Harlem：A Dream Deferred。
2. raisin：葡萄干。a raisin in the sun 后来被美国著名黑人女作家劳伦·汉斯贝里（Lorraine Hansberry）借用，创作名为《日光下的葡萄干》的戏剧。该剧讲述 20 世纪 50 年代美国芝加哥的一个黑人家庭梦想延缓的故事，曾风靡一时，后来被拍成电影，也很受欢迎。

Notes

3. run：此处与前一行的伤口 sore 联系在一起，当梦想如化脓的伤口一样，血流不止，而人们对它视而不见，那么它将导致死亡。另外，run 也可理解为“奔跑、逃亡、逃跑”。
4. stink：恶臭。
5. syrupy：糖浆似的。
6. sag：下垂。

Text Analysis

The poem is made up of six rhetorical questions which seem to need no reply. In fact, the last five questions are the answers to the first one. The second stanza contains four questions with four similes. The similes are different images like “a raisin in the sun”, “a sore”, “rotten meat”, and “a syrupy sweet” mixed together, which express the speaker’s mixed feelings about a dream deferred.

As we know, Hughes’ poems are mostly concerned with Harlem, which is an emblem of black culture. He hopes to arouse his people a strong racial consciousness of the black. As is mentioned in the Note 1, the poem’s original title was “Harlem”, only later changed into “A Dream Deferred”. If we interpret the title as “Harlem: A Dream Deferred”, it will bring us a much clearer idea about the theme of the poem. The black are like all the images mentioned above, which undoubtedly have their physical existence. No matter how it exists, like “a raisin in the sun”, “a sore”, “rotten meat”, and “a syrupy sweet”, its existence does have some influence. Accordingly, the existence of the black culture should not be ignored. It is a dream. If the dream is deferred, no one is sure what will exactly happen. The poet gives us his answer, although appears prudent and interrogative. “Or does it explode?” This one-line stanza brings us to a sudden and affirmative feeling about the poet’s powerful reply to the first general question “What happens to a dream deferred”. In this sense, the author aims to challenge the conventional prejudice against the black culture.

To add up, the arrangement of the imagery in the poem shows the poet’s great artistic technique. It progresses from the visual (“dry up” and “fester”), to the olfactory (“stink”) and gustatory (“syrupy sweet”), to the kinesthetic (“sag”) and organic (“explode”). This outward-to-inward progression of imagery subtly draws the readers into the poem. The progression symbolizes the progression of the black culture: from energy formation, accumulation, strengthening, and explosion.

Questions

1. According to the poem, what dream has been deferred?

2. If the poem did not end with a rhetorical question but an affirmative sentence "Or it explodes", what difference would it make? Would it make any different effect?

3. If we do not relate the poem with Harlem and we just consider it as a lyrical one, then what dream will it be?

Chinese Translation

延缓的梦

延缓的梦会如何？
它会干瘪
像日光下的葡萄干？
或像伤口溃烂——
然后脓血直流？
它会像腐肉发臭？
或表面结上一层糖壳——
像糖浆一样的甜心？
也许它只会垂落
像沉重的负担。
或者它会爆炸？

（肖小军 译）

POSTMODERN AND CONTEMPORARY AMERICAN POETRY

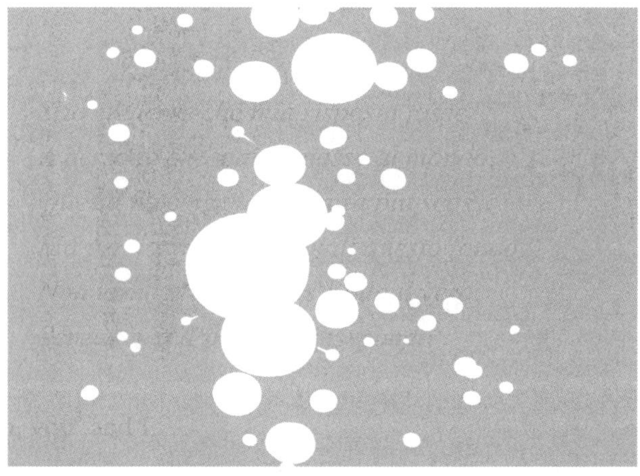

Unit 29　Elizabeth Bishop

Introduction to the Author

Elizabeth Bishop (1911-1979) was born in 1911 in Worcester, Massachusetts. When she was very young her father, a successful builder, died; her mother was committed to a mental asylum, and she was sent to live with her grandparents in Nova Scotia, Canada. Later in childhood, despite of living with her father's wealthier family, Bishop was unhappy owing to the loneliness. Her time in Worcester is briefly chronicled in her poem "In the Waiting Room". She read the Victorian poets heavily, including Alfred, Lord Tennyson, Thomas Carlyle, and the Brownings. She graduated from Vassar College in 1934, majoring in English. And then she gradually earned her literary reputation in New York. Elizabeth Bishop was awarded numerous prizes and titles, in and after her life: she was offered the Fellowship of the Academy of American Poets in 1964 and served as a chancellor from 1966 to 1979; from 1949 to 1950, she became the Poet Laureate of the United States and made Consultant in Poetry for the Library of Congress. Besides, she was a Pulitzer Prize winner for Poetry (1956), a National Book Award winner (1970), and a Neustadt International Prize for Literature (1976).

Bishop was always on the way. In her childhood, she shuttled between her paternal and maternal grandparents' homes across the border line between the U.S. and Canada. When she grew up, with the inheritance left behind by her deceased father, she was able to travel widely without worrying about employment and lived in many cities and countries which she described in her poems. Bishop lived in France for several years in the mid-1930s; in 1938, she purchased a house in the scenic spot of Key West, Florida. From 1950 she settled in Brazil for fifteen years before returning to the U.S. Bishop lectured in higher education for a number of years starting in the 1970s when her inheritance began to run out, in the University of Washington, Harvard University, New York University, and Massachusetts Institute of Technology. Her sudden death happened in Cambridge, Massachusetts, in 1979.

As one of the most influential American poets of the 20th century, Bishop is rooted in American poetic tradition. Her poetry is full of imagination and musical rhythm, and with the help of precise language and exquisite form, it combines moral implication and new thoughts, and expresses a poet's obligation for the society. Unlike her friend Robert Lowell who wrote in the "confessional" style, Bishop's poetry avoids explicit accounts of her personal life, and focuses instead with great subtlety on her impressions of the physical world. Her images are precise and true to life, and they reflect her own sharp wit and moral sense. She wrote slowly and published sparingly, but the technical brilliance and formal variety of her works are astonishing.

The Fish

I caught a tremendous fish
and held him beside the boat
half out of water, with my hook
hast in a corner of his mouth.
He didn't fight.
He hadn't fought at all.
He hung a grunting[1] weight,
battered and venerable[2]
and homely. Here and there
his brown skin hung in strips
like ancient wallpaper,
and its pattern of darker brown
was like wallpaper:
shapes like full-blown roses
stained and lost through age.
He was speckled with barnacles,
fine rosettes of lime[3],
and infested
with tiny white sea-lice,
and underneath two or three
rags of green weed hung down.
while his gills were breathing in
the terrible oxygen
—the frightening gills,
fresh and crisp with blood,

that can cut so badly—
I thought of the coarse white flesh
packed in like feathers,
the big bones and the little bones,
the dramatic reds and blacks
of his shiny entrails[4],
and the pink swim-bladder
like a big peony[5].
I looked into his eyes
which were far larger than mine
but shallower, and yellowed,
the irises backed and packed
with tarnished tinfoil[6]
seen through the lenses
of old scratched isinglass[7].
They shifted a little, but not
to return my stare.
—It was more like the tipping
of an object toward the light.
I admired his sullen face,
the mechanism of his jaw,
and then I saw
that from his lower lip
—if you could call it a lip—
grim, wet, and weaponlike,
hung five old pieces of fish-line,

or four and a wire leader[8]
with the swivel still attached,
with all their five big hooks
grown firmly in his mouth.
A green line, frayed at the end
where he broke it, two heavier lines,
and a fine black thread
still crimped from the strain and snap
when it broke and he got away.
Like medals with their ribbons
frayed and wavering,

a five-haired beard of wisdom
trailing from his aching jaw.
I stared and stared
and victory filled up
the little rented boat,
from the pool of bilge[9]
where oil had spread a rainbow
around the rusted engine
to the bailer[10] rusted orange,
the sun-cracked thwarts[11],
the oarlocks[12] on their strings,
the gunnels[13]—until everything
was rainbow, rainbow, rainbow!
And I let the fish go.

1. grunting：（鱼儿离水时）发出打呼噜般的声音。
2. battered and venerable：鱼儿虽然被打败（被钓上来），受了伤，但依然保持着尊严。
3. rosettes of lime：石灰形成的玫瑰花饰。
4. entrails：内脏。
5. peony：牡丹花。
6. tarnished tinfoil：失去光泽的锡箔。
7. isinglass：云母。
8. leader：接钩绳，其用途是把钓钩连接到鱼线上。
9. bilge：舱底。
10. bailer：水斗，用于从船舱中汲出积水。
11. thwarts：（船的）横坐板。
12. oarlocks：桨架。
13. gunnels：船舷上缘。

This poem is based on actual experience of the author. Its main character is the enormous Caribbean jewfish that Bishop caught at Key West; she once said, "I always try to stick as much as possible to what really happened when I describe something in a poem".

This is a narrative poem and yet its plot is surprisingly rough and simple ("I" caught a fish); what is more, the story is over once it begins. The poem then turns to focus on observation, which records every possible detail of the fish. The accumulation of the details forces its own conclusion, and forcefully brings forward issues like morality. "I" seem to win over the fish by catching it, yet the fish keeps its own dignity and integrity despite of its "loss" to the fisher. In this the fish and the man are equal, and the superficial victory and loss seem meaningless. The fish is beyond itself and turns to symbolize nature: in this understanding, the poem is about man's relation with nature and even with himself. The end of the poem is inspiring in its surprise and "turn". The poem reveals an independent morality carving its own way between the extremes and hypocrisies of convention.

The poem typically shows Bishop's writing themes and concerns. It is about ordinary mundane experience, and the presentation is simple and casual. The vivid images about the fish resort to our senses, and the presentation of all these is well done by employing a full stock of language devices (metaphor, simile, parallelism, etc.). Bishop's writing reminds us of Hemingway, not merely in the use of language, but also in the moral implications (*The Old Man and the Sea* is in our mind, for example).

Questions

1. How does the reservoir of details contribute to the central argument(s) of the poem?

2. As a narrative poem, do you think the poem is successful in its plot development? Why or why not?

3. What ecological implications does the poem possibly have?

Chinese Translation

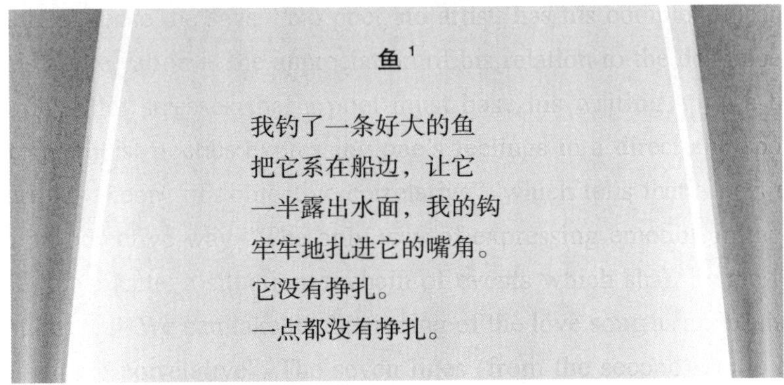

鱼[1]

我钓了一条好大的鱼
把它系在船边，让它
一半露出水面，我的钩
牢牢地扎进它的嘴角。
它没有挣扎。
一点都没有挣扎。

1 这首诗在美国与《老人与海》一样著名，20世纪30年代末毕晓普在佛罗里达和海明威雇佣同一位船长出海钓鱼，她的女友和海明威夫人合开了一家装饰品商店，但海明威的小说要到古巴时期才完成。——译者原注

它沉甸甸地挂着，
受伤而令人起敬，
顶丑的。浑身上下
它那棕色皮肤一条条挂着
好像过时的裱墙纸
褪色的图案暗淡了些
可还是像裱墙纸；
外形犹如盛开的玫瑰
日渐污染、凋零了。
它的身上粘着藤壶，
花纹赏心悦目，
并滋生出
微小的白海虱，
而它的下面，漂浮着
两三根绿色的水草。
它的腮吸进
混浊的氧气
——这吓人的腮，
殷红鲜艳，
尖利刺人——
我想起那些粗糙的白肉
羽毛一样堆砌着，
大大小小的骨刺，
油光光的内脏
红和黑对比鲜明，
还有粉红的鱼鳔
像一朵硕大的牡丹花。
我仔细瞅着它的双眼
远比我的要大许多
可是浅些，泛黄
透过划有伤痕的晶体状的
鱼胶可以看见
虹膜深陷，犹如包裹着
失去光泽的锡箔。
这双眼睛动了一下，可并非
回应我的注视
——倒更像一个物体
朝光亮的方向微移。
我欣赏着那张阴郁的脸
和下颚的结构，接着

我发现它冷酷、湿润，
兵器般的下唇上
（如果算得上是唇的话）
挂着五根旧的鱼线
或者说四根线和一个金属线头
丁环还在上面，
五个大钩子全都
紧紧地含在它嘴里。
绿色的那根，被它拉断后
已经散开，变成两根粗线
和一根细小的黑丝，
当它拉断逃跑时
线绷得太紧，现在卷曲了。
五根头发似的慧须
从它痛苦的下颚上挂下
就像勋章的绶带
散开来飘动一样。
我瞧了又瞧，
喜悦充满了
这租用的小船，
从舱底的积水——
那里油花在生锈的引擎
周围漾开犹如彩虹，
到锈成橘黄色的水斗，
太阳晒裂的坐板和
拴链的浆圈、船舷，
——当一切都成为
彩虹，彩虹，彩虹！
我把鱼放走了。

（蔡天新　译）

Unit 30 Allen Ginsberg

Introduction to the Author

On June 3, 1926, Irwin Allen Ginsberg (1926-1997) was born into a Jewish family in Newark, New Jersey. Under the influence of his parents who were members of the New York literary counter-culture of the 1920s, Ginsberg was raised among different progressive political perspectives. His mother's mental health problems also made him tolerant of madness, neurosis and psychosis.

Walt Whitman had always been Ginsberg's idol. He began reading Whitman when he was in high school and was greatly inspired. In 1943, Ginsberg graduated from Eastside High School and briefly attended Montclair State College before entering Columbia University. In Ginsberg's freshman year at Columbia, he began close friendship with Lucien Carr, who introduced him to a number of future Beat writers such as Jack Kerouac, William S. Burroughs and Neal Cassady. With the group, Ginsberg formulated a philosophical discourse which was called "New Vision", a precursor of the Beat Generation principles he illustrated in his later works. In 1948, Ginsberg graduated from Columbia with a BA degree. Later in that year, he had a vision of the English Romantic poet William Blake speaking to him directly, which he referred to as "Blake vision". Although Ginsberg claimed that no drugs were involved, most people still believed that this vision was partially a product of his extensive experimentation with hallucinogenic drugs.

In 1950, Ginsberg sent a letter and some poems to William Carlos Williams, who provided Ginsberg with much guidance and encouragement and later introduced him to key figures in the San Francisco poetry arena, including Kenneth Rexroth. Under the help of Rexroth, Ginsberg organized the legendary landmark reading at the Six Gallery and read his epic poem "Howl" in public for the first time on October 7, 1955. The event is hailed as the birth of the Beat Generation and from then on Ginsberg as the forerunner of the Beat arouses world-wide attention.

In 1956, *Howl and Other Poems* was published. Shortly after that, the book was banned for obscenity. However, the collection overcame censorship trials and became one of the most widely read poems of the century, which were translated into more than twenty languages. In the 1960s and 1970s, Ginsberg published many collections of poetry, including *Kaddish and Other Poems* (1961), *Planet News* (1968), *Iron House* (1972), *The Fall of America: Poems of These States* (1973), which won him the National Book Award, *First Blues: Rags, Ballads and Harmonium Songs 1971-1974* (1975) and *Mind Breaths* (1978). It was also in this period that Ginsberg converted to Buddhism and studied Eastern religious disciplines extensively under gurus and Zen masters. Ginsberg's political activism was consistent with his religious beliefs. He was involved in many political activities, taking part in decades of non-violent political protest. In the 1980s and 1990s, Ginsberg published collections of poetry such as *Plutonian Ode: Poems 1977-1980* (1982), *White Shroud Poems:1980-1985* (1986), *Cosmopolitan Greetings Poems:1986-1993* (1994), *Illuminated Poems* (1996) and *Death and Fame: Poems 1993-1997* (1999). In his later years, Ginsberg became a distinguished professor at Brooklyn College. On April 5, 1997, Allen Ginsberg died from complications of hepatitis in New York City.

Howl[1] (Excerpt)

I saw the best minds of my generation destroyed by madness, starving hysterical naked[2],
dragging themselves through the negro streets at dawn looking for an angry fix,
angelheaded hipsters[3] burning for the ancient heavenly connection to the starry dynamo[4] in the machinery of night,
who poverty and tatters and hollow-eyed and high sat up smoking in the supernatural darkness of cold-water flats floating across the tops of cities contemplating jazz,
who bared their brains to Heaven under the El[5] and saw Mohammedan angels[6] staggering on tenement roofs illuminated
who passed through universities with radiant cool eyes hallucinating[7] Arkansas and Blake-light[8] tragedy among the scholars of war,
who were expelled from the academies for crazy & publishing obscene odes on the windows of the skull[9],
who cowered in unshaven rooms[10] in underwear, burning their money in wastebaskets and listening to the Terror through the wall,
who got busted in their pubic beards[11] returning through Laredo with a belt of marijuana for New York[12],
who ate fire in paint hotels or drank turpentine in[13] Paradise Alley[14], death, or purgatoried[15]

their torsos night after night
with dreams, with drugs, with waking nightmares, alcohol and cock and endless balls[16],
incomparable blind streets[17] of shuddering cloud and lightning in the mind leaping toward poles of Canada & Paterson[18], illuminating all the motionless world of Time between,
……
who in humorless protest overturned only one symbolic pingpong table, resting briefly in catatonia[19],
returning years later truly bald except for a wig of blood, and tears and fingers, to the visible madman doom of the wards of the madtowns of the East,
Pilgrim State's Rockland's and Greystone's foetid halls[20], bickering with the echoes of the soul, rocking and rolling in the midnight solitude-bench dolmen-realms of love, dream of life a nightmare, bodies turned to stone as heavy as the moon,
with mother finally ******[21], and the last fantastic book flung out of the tenement window, and the last door closed at 4 A.M. and the last telephone slammed at the wall in reply and the last furnished room emptied down to the last piece of mental furniture, a yellow paper rose twisted on a wire hanger in the closet, and even that imaginary, nothing but a hopeful little bit of hallucination[22]—
ah, Carl, while you are not safe I am not safe, and[23]now you're really in the total animal soup of time—
and who therefore ran through the icy streets obsessed with a sudden flash of the alchemy of the use of the ellipse the catalog the meter[24] & the vibrating plane,
who dreamt and made incarnate gaps in Time & Space through images juxtaposed, and trapped the archangel of the soul between 2 visual images and joined the elemental verbs and set the noun and dash of consciousness together jumping with sensation of Pater Omnipotens Aeterna Deus[25]
to recreate the syntax and measure of poor human prose and stand before you speechless and intelligent and shaking with shame, rejected yet confessing out the soul to conform to the rhythm of thought in his naked and endless head,
the madman bum and angel beat in Time, unknown, yet putting down here what might be left to say in time come after death,
and rose reincarnate[26] in the ghostly clothes of jazz in the goldhorn shadow of the band and blew the suffering of America's naked mind for love into an eli eli lamma lamma sabacthani[27] saxophone cry that shivered the cities down to the last radio
with the absolute heart of the poem of life butchered out of their own bodies good to eat a thousand years.[28]

1.《嚎叫》分为三部分，其中第一部分最长也最有力量，充斥着现实和超现实的意象，是一首充满愤怒，充满预言的哀歌。在该部分中，金斯堡对同时代人被社会遗弃，受社会摧残表示愤怒和哀悼。第二部分描写的是莫洛克神（Moloch），关于莫洛克神的幻觉是诗人在吸食毒品的状态下产生的。莫洛克神所代表的是美国军事-工业体制和残酷的社会现实，亦是毁灭这代人的恶魔。第三部分则描写了给予金斯堡写作该诗灵感的艺术家卡尔·所罗门（Carl Solomon），金斯堡将这首诗献给了他。该部分里所罗门是莫洛克神的反对者，也是受害者，诗人将自我形象投射到所罗门这一人物形象之上，肯定了受到莫洛克神侵害的这一代人精神的永恒和形象的光辉。《嚎叫》采用了赤裸裸的语言表达形式，粗鲁且激进，诗歌中充满了对吸毒、酗酒、性放纵和疯狂的描写，是金斯堡狂迷心态的自然表现，诗人宣泄了最直觉的心灵和最真实的情感。本部分节选了第一部分的开头及结尾片段。

2.《嚎叫》是对20世纪四五十年代的美国社会、政治、文化的一种反思，金斯堡认为，当时的美国社会毁灭（destroy）了这一代人，使他们陷入疯狂（madness），令这一代人歇斯底里（hysterical）且脆弱不堪一击（starving，naked）。在金斯堡看来，这一群被社会遗弃的垮掉分子，有最优秀的心灵（the best minds）。他们试图用激进、极端的生活方式来摆脱物质至上的美国社会的精神束缚，从而获得精神上的完满和最终的真实状态。

3. hipsters：or hepcat，as used in the 1940s, referred to aficionados of jazz, in particular bebop, which became popular in the early 1940s. The hipster adopted the lifestyle of the jazz musician，including some or all of the following：dress, slang, use of cannabis and other drugs, relaxed attitude, sarcastic humor, self-imposed poverty and relaxed sexual codes.

4. dynamo：an electric generator。在此，金斯堡将星空比喻成发电厂，与后来的machinery of night相呼应。

5. El：one of the Hebrew names for God. It is also the abbreviation for “Elevated Train”, especially referring to the one in Chicago.

6. Mohammedan angels：angels of Islam. 穆罕默德是伊斯兰教的先知。

7. hallucinating：having illusions after taking drugs.

8. Blake在此指涉的是英国诗人布莱克（William Blake）。布莱克是金斯堡一直崇拜的诗人。他曾在1948年产生幻觉，看到布莱克，听到布莱克朗诵诗歌并与之进行亲密的对话。他本人亦自称在形式和精神上师承惠特曼，而其神秘气质则得自布莱克。

9. 该句诗直接指涉的是金斯堡的生活经历。他曾因在宿舍房间的窗户上涂写淫秽词句引起学监注意，并最终被罚停学。尽管后来金斯堡得以重返校园完成学业，但这段经历令他对学术界颇有微词。

10. unshaven通常用来形容人未刮胡须，在此修饰rooms。

11. 20世纪50年代的嬉皮士大都留着长胡须，到了60年代，嬉皮士运动作为反主流文化中反叛的一翼兴起，它承袭于垮掉的一代，长发、奇装异服、群居、性开放、沉湎毒品、醉心禅宗以及主张非暴力成为他们与众不同的标志。
12. 他们（the best minds）试图从墨西哥越过德克萨斯州拉雷多市，将大麻走私到纽约（墨西哥大麻产量丰富，且价格便宜）。
13. ate fire，drank turpentine 在此应与吸毒行为有关。
14. Paradise Alley：纽约著名的贫民窟。
15. 在但丁的《神曲》中，“Purgatory”名为炼狱山，它介乎地狱和天堂之间。人类的灵魂在这里被洗涤干净，获得升入天堂的资格。
16. 他们沉湎于梦幻、毒品、酒精、性放纵，用这些来经历炼狱的过程。金斯堡是一名同性恋者，该诗中多处有关于同性恋的指涉。
17. blind：dead-end，在此用来形容街道。金斯堡在该行中描写了脑海中的幻象——充满着乌云和闪电的死胡同街道。
18. 新泽西的帕特森是金斯堡自小成长的地方。
19. catatonia：a form of schizophrenia characterized by a tendency to remain in a fixed stuporous state for long periods.
20. foetid：smelly, stinky. Pilgrim State, Rockland, Greystone 应为诗人虚构的精神病机构。
21. 作者在该处使用星号，意在让读者自行想象母亲可能面临的遭遇。值得一提的是，金斯堡本人的母亲由于激进的政治思想而导致严重的幻想症，发作时经常歇斯底里，后被送入精神病院。这使金斯堡从小就从母亲那儿体会到了社会所导致的精神疯狂。
22. 该部分重复使用了“last”一词表明了一切将覆灭的绝望。
23. Carl：指的是 Carl Solomon，在此处，诗人强调了与他同心团结的紧密关系。
24. ellipse, catalog, meter 与诗歌技巧有关，在该部分诗人讲述了他们是怎样倾心于诗歌，侧面解释了他创作该诗的意图。
25. Pater Omnipotens Aeterna Deus：Latin for “All-Powerful Father the Eternal God”.
26. reincarnate：be born anew in another body after death.
27. eli eli lamma lamma sabacthani：My God，My God, why have you forsaken me? 耶稣基督被钉在十字架上的大声呼喊，意为：“我的上帝，我的上帝！为什么离弃我？”
28. 金斯堡认为诗人是世界的拯救者。在最后的诗行中，他将诗歌比喻成他们从身体割下来的各个部分，将诗歌创作看成类似耶稣基督殉道的一种自我牺牲，而他们创作出来的这些诗歌最终在一千年后仍然可以被享用，正如耶稣献上自己的生命为祭物。

Text Analysis

"Howl" is Allen Ginsberg's masterpiece, a visionary, surreal and horrifying epic poem. It is shaped under the influence of many writers such as John Donne, William Blake, T. S. Eliot, Walt Whitman, William Carlos Williams and Herman Melville. In this poem, Ginsberg denounced the destructive forces in America, initiating the readers into the darkness of America in the 1950s.

Consisting of three sections, "Howl" is best-known for its first and second sections, especially the first one. The first section is also the longest. Madness is the main theme of this part. At the beginning of this section, Ginsberg lamented that the best minds of the 1950s were destroyed by madness. Suffering from hysteria, this best generation did not behave normally. The rest of the section is a detailed description of these best minds, illustrating who they were and what they did. Who were those best minds? After reading the section, the readers can get the answer: these best minds of Ginsberg's generation were not those well-fed middle-class people, for example, lawyers, doctors, scientists and those so-called elite from all walks of life. On the contrary, they were jazz musicians, political radicals, poets, artists, drug addicts, world travelers and psychiatric patients—all of those may be associated with the Beat Generation. Ginsberg called these people "the best minds of my generation" and described their experiences in details (his own personal experience was also mentioned in this poem), including openly discussing alcohol abuse, drug use, homosexual activity.

"Howl" does not keep the traditional rhythm of a poem; it is a typical example of free verse. Ginsberg uses a triadic verse form, which can be also detected in the writings of William Carlos Williams. In addition, the poet in this long poem experiments with a breath-length form. He borrows the technique of writing with long lines from Walt Whitman and presents a similar long list of the activities which is called catalog technique.

Questions

1. What does the title "Howl" indicate?

2. Who are "the best minds" mentioned in the first section? Why did Ginsberg consider them to be the best minds?

3. Why did Ginsberg dedicate this poem to Carl Solomon?

4. Does "Howl" celebrate drug use or condemn it?

5. What did you learn the about the Beat culture in general from reading the poem?

Chinese Translation

嚎叫（节选）

我看见这一代最杰出的头脑被疯狂毁坏，饿着肚子歇斯底里赤身裸体，
拂晓时拖着脚步穿过黑人街区找一针够劲儿的毒品，
头脑天使一般的嬉皮士们渴望与这夜的机械那繁星般的发电机发生古老的天堂式的关系，
他们衣衫破烂眼神空虚坐在只有冷水的公寓那超自然的黑暗中，毒品吸得醉意朦胧飘越过城市上空想着爵士乐
他们在高架铁路下对上天披露内心，却看见穆罕默德天使们在被照亮的公寓屋顶上踉跄而行，
他们两眼闪光但冰冷，穿过大学，在幻觉中见到阿肯色见到军事学者们布莱克式的轻佻的悲剧，
他们被赶出学院因为太出格，因为在头头脑脑的窗户上发表猥亵的颂诗，
他们佝偻在没刮脸的房间里，在废纸篓中烧钞票倾听着墙外恐怖之神的声音，
他们一丝不挂地被抓住，猛吸一顿大麻穿过拉雷多返回纽约
他们在色彩鲜丽的旅馆里吞火焰在天堂胡同饮松节油，死去，要不然就夜复一夜
用梦，用毒品，用不眠的噩梦，酒精，阳物和没完没了的舞会把身躯投入炼狱，
而心中无可比拟的死胡同，充满战栗的乌云和闪电，跃向加拿大和斐特森，照亮这两极之间静止的世界，

……

他们毫无幽默感的抗议所推翻的只是一张象征性的乒乓桌，神经紧张时略事休息，
多年后秃光了头，只剩一副血污的假发，几滴眼泪，几根手指，回到东部疯人城病房里疯子们明摆着的末日，
在朝香者之州、罗克兰与格雷斯顿腥臭的大厅里，同灵魂的回声吵架，半夜在爱情的墓地那孤寂的长凳上奏摇滚乐，生活之梦充满梦魇，身体变成石头像月亮一样重，
最后回到母亲身边 ******，最后一本胡思乱想的书扔出公寓窗口，最后一扇门在凌晨四点关上，最后一架电话机摔向墙壁作为答复，最后一间带家具的房间被搬光只剩下最后一只精神柜子，一朵黄色的纸玫瑰挂在柜子的铁丝钩上，甚至这东西也是想象，什么都没了只剩下一丁点儿希望的

错觉——
啊，卡尔，你不安全时我也没有安全，而你现在真的陷进时代的整煮大汤锅——
于是他们奔跑着穿过冰冻的街道，着了迷地幻想炼金术的突然辉光，幻想使用省略法目录册计量表和振动翼，
他们梦想着，把形象并置在时间与空间中制造实体的鸿沟，在两个形象间绊住灵魂的天使长，带着全能的上帝大神的感觉跳起来，联结起基本动词并把名词和意识的破折号合在一起，
用以为人类可怜的散文重新创造句法和格律，站在你面前，无语但睿智只是害羞得颤抖，被拒绝但袒露心灵，以与他光裸但无边际的头脑中思想的节奏保持一致，
疯狂的浪子和天使合着拍子敲打，无人知晓，但却在此写下在死后某个时候要说的话，
穿着爵士乐鬼魂般的衣服，在乐队金色圆号的阴影中升起肉体重现，把美国渴望爱情的赤裸思想吹奏成埃里埃里马拉马萨巴克莎尼萨克管的哭号，震撼城市的每一台收音机，
有这块从他们自己身上割下来的生活之诗的绝对心脏，足够吃一千年。

（赵毅衡　译）

Unit 31 Gary Snyder

Gary Snyder (1930-) is a rarity in the literature arena of the United States. He is well-known not only for his intimate association with the Beat writers, but for his great endeavor of combining various traditions such as Zen Buddhism, Taoism and Native American traditions into his large number of poems celebrating nature.

On the 8th of May, 1930, Gary Snyder was born in San Francisco, California. His family, impoverished by the Great Depression, moved to Lake City, North of Seattle, Washington. The place was significant for Snyder's psychological and environmental ethical development. Snyder grew up in close contact with nature, which enabled him to respect all sentient beings in the universe. Despite moving to the city in 1942, Snyder remained a child of nature and always involved himself in studying Native American ways of life. In his early teens, he became a defender of wildlife. Besides that, in these teenage years, Snyder began to write poetry, fully displaying his talent in poetic writing. In 1947, Gary Snyder received a scholarship to attend Reed College and selected his major in anthropology and literature. After graduation, he took different jobs such as logger and fire lookout in the deep woods. His working experience enlarged the content of his later works and provided him with great opportunities to seek the alternatives to city life and reverence for nature. In the autumn of 1952 Snyder began to study Oriental languages at Berkeley. There he became part of a community of writers, including Allen Ginsberg and Jack Kerouac, who were later considered as the forerunner of the Beat Generation. In 1956, Snyder sailed for Japan to study Zen Buddhism. He was deeply affected by the totally different ideology of Eastern philosophy. Snyder also traveled extensively, visiting India, Indonesia and Turkey. After returning to the United Sates, Snyder built his house in the northern Sierra Nevada Mountains, practicing Zazen and putting his ecological ideas into practice there.

Gary Snyder published numerous books of poetry. His first published work *Riprap* (1959) earned him great reputation, guiding the readers from the western mountains of America to Japan. He then published *Myths and Texts* in the next year and *Regarding Wave* in 1970. His *Turtle Island* (1974) won the Pulitzer Prize for Poetry and *Axe Handles* (1983) won him an American Book Award. He also published *Left Out in the Rain, New Poems 1947-1985* (1986); *The Practice of the Wild* (1990); *No Nature: New and Selected Poems* (1993); *Mountains and Rivers Without End* (1997); *The Gary Snyder Reader (1952-1998)* (1999); and *Danger on Peaks: Poems* (2005).

Gary Snyder's poetry is easily recognizable for its plain oral language, intensively visual images, marvelous landscape of nature, precise and delicate observation of daily life, true insight into the real essence of being, and sparkling cultural and ecological wisdom. He exerted a great influence on his Beat contemporaries. Jack Kerouac modeled his character Japhy Ryder in his *The Dharma Bums* on Snyder. He is esteemed as one of the greatest synthesizing intellects of all ages, possessing a breathtaking ability to reveal clear associations among disparate areas of knowledge.

I Went into the Maverick Bar[1]

I went into the Maverick Bar
In Farmington, New Mexico[2].
And drank double shots of bourbon
Backed with beer.
My long hair was tucked up under a cap
I'd left the earring in the car[3].

Two cowboys did horseplay[4]
By the pool tables,
A waitress asked us
Where are you from?
A country-and-western band began to play
"We don't smoke Marijuana in Muskokie"
And with the next song,
A couple began to dance.

They held each other like in High School dances
In the fifties;
I recalled when I worked in the woods

And the bars of Madras, Oregon.
That short-haired joy and roughness—
America—your stupidity.
I could almost love you again.

We left—onto the freeway shoulders—
Under the tough old stars—
In the shadow of bluffs
I came back to myself,
To the real work, to
"What is to be done." [5]

1. 1955 年 10 月 7 日是"垮掉的一代"诞生之日。在这夜举办的六画廊（Six Gallery）诗歌朗诵会上，加里·斯奈德朗诵了《浆果宴席》("The Berry Feast")，从此人们便将他的名字与菲利普·惠伦、艾伦·金斯堡、杰克·凯鲁亚克等垮掉派领袖联系在了一起。有关斯奈德是否算得上是真正的垮掉派诗人人们至今看法不一，斯奈德本人也曾否认自己属于垮掉派诗人。不过，他与垮掉派诗人关系甚密，且他对垮掉派诗人产生了极大影响，除此之外，他的诗歌有时也有类似垮掉派诗人的创作风格：罗列世俗事件及感官感受，表现嬉皮士放荡不羁的生活态度，对直觉、梦境、神话、吸毒都有所涉及，因此，斯奈德也被称作是垮掉的一代的"冷派"代表。本诗即是一首较典型的垮掉派诗作。斯奈德曾在比尔·莫耶斯的访谈中谈到了该诗的创作背景：20 世纪 70 年代当斯奈德回到美国，在内华达安顿好后应朋友的邀请前往新墨西哥州，该地的黑山委员会（Black Mesa Committee）当时正抗议开采队在纳瓦霍人及霍皮人居住地进行钻井和挖煤的行为。斯奈德一行人途经充满煤尘和石油味的法明顿镇，并停在了一间名叫 Maverick Bar 的酒吧。
2. 斯奈德在莫耶斯访谈中提到，实际上法明顿镇并非位于新墨西哥州，而是在临界的德克萨斯州境内。
3. 将长发塞进帽子，耳环取下来留在车上，是因为考虑到自己的形象与当地牛仔的形象有较大反差。
4. horseplay：rough play in which people push and hit each other，or behave in a silly way.
5. "What is to be done"采用了双引号，援引的应是车尔尼雪夫斯基（Nikolay Gavrilovich Chernyshevsky）的著名小说《怎么办》(*What Shall We Do?*)，列宁对该作品极为推崇，并借此书名写出了在俄国革命中极具影响力的《怎么办》一书。

Text Analysis

"I Went into the Maverick Bar", the fifth poem in Snyder's *Turtle Island*, is quite unusual for Snyder. Compared with other famous poems by Snyder such as "Pine Tree Tops", in which the poetic landscape is not interrupted by human's reason and logical knowledge, "I Went into the Maverick Bar" emphasizes the pronoun "I" from the outset.

In this poem, the poem's first-person narrator enters the Maverick Bar, a working-class bar in Farmington. Tucking his long hair under a cap and leaving his earring in the car in order to lessen his sense of alienation from other people in this bar, the narrator arrives at a scene of "short-haired joy and roughness": American "stupidity" as he calls in the poem. This apostrophe to "stupidity" may remind the readers of the Beat writings such as "Howl" by Allen Ginsberg. The narrator then recalls his good times with the woodsmen in Madras, Oregon. He feels a sense of kinship with these men in the bar. He also recognizes that his own heritage is the same as that of these people. At the end of this poem, Snyder leaves the bar. This time, he feels the difference between him and these people and becomes a countercultural leader. He is conscious of the destructiveness and repressiveness of American cultural heritage. The last three lines are very thought-provoking: "I came back to myself, / To the real work, to / 'What is to be done.'" The last line "What is to be done" is a quotation from Lenin. It aims to convey Snyder's proposal that the contemporary culture should be transformed. Patrick D. Murphy comments on this ending: "The speaker realizes that his responsibility to Turtle Island and to these people requires that he continue to promote his alternative vision. That this vision involves nothing short of complete social transformation is suggested by his defining the 'real work' in terms of 'What is to be done', the title of a major theoretical work by V. I. Lenin on the necessity of a Marxist revolution in Russia at the turn of the century" (*A Placefor Wayfaring*, 105-106).

Questions

1. What is your understanding of "America—your stupidity. / I could almost love you again" ?
2. What does "the real work" refer to?
3. Why does Snyder quote "What is to be done" at the end of this poem?
4. How can you identify the features of the Beat writings in this poem?

Chinese Translation

我走进漂泊者酒吧

我走进新墨西哥州法明顿的
漂泊者酒吧。
喝了两杯掺啤酒的
烈性威士忌。
我的长发塞在帽子下
我的耳环留在汽车里。

两个牛仔在弹子台旁
胡闹，
一个女招待问我们
你们从哪里来

一个西部乡村乐队奏起
《我们在马斯科基不吸大麻》
随着下一支曲子
一对男女跳起舞来。

他们像五十年代的中学生那样
搂抱着跳
我想起在森林工作的时光
和俄勒冈州马德拉斯的酒吧。
那些短头发的欢乐和粗犷——
美国——你的愚蠢。
我几乎又爱上了你。
我们离去——爬上快车道的肩膀——
在倔强的古老的星辰之下——
在峭壁的阴影中
我回到了自我，
回到了真正的工作，回到了
“该怎么办”。

（彭宇　译）

Unit 32 Sylvia Plath

Introduction to the Author

Sylvia Plath (1932-1963) was born in Boston, Massachusetts on October 27, 1932. Her mother, a first-generation American of Austrian descent, was approximately twenty-one years younger than Plath's father, who taught in Boston University both German and biology with a focus on apiology. Shortly after Plath's eighth birthday, her father died, a trauma which emerged frequently in her later poetry.

Throughout her life, Plath suffered from severe depression. Her first serious breakdown occurred in 1953 and led to her first medically documented suicide attempt: she crawled under her house in late August 1953 and took her mother's sleeping pills. After lying unfound there for several days, Plath eventually survived. She then spent six months in psychiatric care and successfully recovered. In 1955, Plath graduated from Smith College.

After graduation, Plath obtained a scholarship to Newnham College, Cambridge. In early 1956, she met the English poet Ted Hughes on a party and married him shortly thereafter. In 1957, Plath returned to Massachusetts and began study with Robert Lowell. She published her first collection of poems *Colossus* in 1960 in England and two years later in America. In 1960 and 1962, Plath gave birth to her two children. Unfortunately, Plath-Hughes' marriage was under tremendous strain. In 1962, the couple separated. That winter, tortured by deep depression, Plath wrote most of the poems which were later collected in her most famous collection *Ariel* (1965). In December 1962, Plath returned to London with her children and rented a flat where William Butler Yeats once lived. She published a semi-autobiographical novel *The Bell Jar* in 1963 under the pseudonym Victoria Lucas. On the cold winter of that year, Plath committed suicide, placing her head in the oven with the gas turned on.

Plath's works are often held within the genre of confessional poetry, which is the poetry of the personal or "I". Her style of writing is often compared to other contemporaries, such as Robert Lowell, Anne Sexton and W. D. Snodgrass. Private experiences with death, trauma, and depression are addressed in her poems, usually in an autobiographical manner.

Sylvia Plath's troubled life and powerful works are up till now a source of controversy. Her poetry, along with her novel *The Bell Jar*, situates her as one of the most talented writers in the 20th-century American literature. Her confessional poems pioneer a type of writing that changes the landscape of American poetry.

Lady Lazarus[1]

I have done it[2] again.
One year in every ten
I manage it—

A sort of walking miracle, my skin
Bright as a Nazi lampshade[3],
My right foot

A paperweight[4],
My face a featureless, fine
Jew linen[5].

Peel off the napkin[6]
O my enemy.
Do I terrify? —

The nose, the eye pits, the full set of teeth?
The sour breath
Will vanish in a day.

Soon, soon the flesh
The grave cave ate will be
At home on me[7]

And I a smiling woman.
I am only thirty.
And like the cat I have nine times to die.

This is Number Three[8].
What a trash
To annihilate each decade.

What a million filaments.
The peanut-crunching crowd[9]
Shoves in to see

Them unwrap me hand and foot—
The big strip tease.
Gentlemen, ladies

These are my hands
My knees.
I may be skin and bone,

Nevertheless, I am the same, identical woman.
The first time it happened I was ten.
It was an accident.

The second time I meant
To last it out and not come back at all[10].
I rocked shut

As a seashell.
They had to call and call
And pick the worms off me like sticky pearls.

Dying
Is an art, like everything else.
I do it exceptionally well.

I do it so it feels like hell.
I do it so it feels real.
I guess you could say I've a call.

It's easy enough to do it in a cell.
It's easy enough to do it and stay put.

It's the theatrical

Comeback in broad day
To the same place, the same face, the same brute
Amused shout:

"A miracle!"
That knocks me out.
There is a charge[11]

For the eyeing of my scars, there is a charge
For the hearing of my heart—
It really goes.

And there is a charge, a very large charge
For a word or a touch
Or a bit of blood

Or a piece of my hair or my clothes.
So, so, Herr Doktor[12].
So, Herr Enemy.

I am your opus,
I am your valuable,
The pure gold baby

That melts to a shriek.
I turn and burn.
Do not think I underestimate your great concern.

Ash, ash—
You poke and stir.[13]
Flesh, bone, there is nothing there—

A cake of soap,
A wedding ring,
A gold filling.

Herr God, Herr Lucifer
Beware
Beware[14].

Out of the ash[15]
I rise with my red hair
And I eat men like air.

1. "Lady Lazarus" 写于1962年，后被收录在普拉斯去世后出版的诗集《爱丽儿》（*Ariel*, 1965）中。拉撒路是圣经人物，他是一个麻风乞丐，经历了种种磨难，在死亡中得到复生。根据《新约·约翰福音》第十一章第四十四节，耶稣行神迹，使病死已四天的拉撒路复活。普拉斯在该诗中自比死而复活的拉撒路，只不过性别不同而已。该诗题中的 lady 一词为名词作形容词用，其作用相当于 female。
2. 联系下文，该处 it 指的是拉撒路死而复生这件事，即下文中所谓的"活的神迹"(walking miracle)。第三行的 it 同样指的是这个。
3. Nazi lampshade 意象涉及纳粹迫害犹太人的史实，据说纳粹德军曾用犹太人的皮肤做成薄如蝉翼，极其精致的人皮灯罩。
4. 普拉斯在此同样指涉了纳粹迫害犹太人的一些典故。paperweight 意指为了防止纸张被吹走而压在其上的镇纸。据说纳粹德军曾用犹太人的头骨做成镇纸。在该行中，普拉斯意指拉撒路的右脚曾被做成镇纸。
5. Jew linen：犹太亚麻布。在此与 Nazi lampshade 和 paperweight 一样都指涉了犹太人曾经受到的迫害和摧残。
6. napkin 在此可被理解为盖在死人脸上的遮脸布。基督教中有著名的维罗尼卡之帕（Veronica's Napkin），一位名叫维罗尼卡的犹太女人递上自己的头帕给耶稣擦脸。
7. 在死亡之后，被墓穴吃掉的肉很快将会回到"我"的身体，"我"复活了。如下文所提到的，"我"这时三十岁，这也正是当时写作该诗的普拉斯的年龄。
8. Number Three：指的是"我"的第三次复活，这与诗歌开头的"One year in every ten"，以及下文的"To annihilate each decade, The first time it happened""I was ten"及"The second time I meant"呼应。
9. The peanut-crunching crowd：嚼着花生的那群人。这些人指的是不敬神，喜欢凑热闹的俗人看客。
10. 该处指涉的可能是普拉斯个人的遭遇。1953年，普拉斯第一次有了自杀行为，她在精神崩溃后试图吞安眠药，她也将这一经历写在了她的半自传式小说《钟形罩》（*The Bell Jar*）中。
11. There is a charge：人们争相付钱来参观所谓的神迹或想得到与"我"有关的神迹纪念物："the eyeing of my scars", "the hearing of my heart", "a word or a touch / Or a bit of blood / Or a piece of my hair or my clothes"。

Notes

12. Herr Doktor：此处使用的是德语，Herr 在德语中类似英文的 Mr. 或 Sir。
13. "I turn and burn"，"You poke and stir" 影射的是二战中纳粹德军用焚尸炉焚烧犹太人的尸体，然后从骨灰中寻找金牙、金饰品的史实。
14. 柯勒律治的诗歌《忽必烈汗》曾写道："And all who heard should see them there, / And all should cry, Beware! Beware! / His flashing eyes, his floating hair!"
15. 该处暗含了凤凰涅槃的典故。传说中凤凰是不死之鸟，它会在火中化为灰烬，然后在灰烬中重生。

Text Analysis

"Lady Lazarus", written in Plath's last period of life, is the monologue of a woman speaking out of pain and psychic disintegration. It is considered as the best example of Sylvia Plath's writing style. Commonly known as Plath's "Holocaust poems", this poem describes lady Lazarus's oppression and suffering in its applying allusions of the sad fate of the Jewish people during World War Ⅱ in Nazi Germany and images of severe integration and dislocation.

The lady of the poem is a quasi-mythological figure, reminding the readers of the biblical Lazarus who is brought to life by Jesus Christ. The poem begins by informing the readers that the speaker has "done it again", in which "it" is quite puzzling. The speaker Lazarus, who is only thirty years old and has nine lives like a cat, is able to return to life after death. She compares herself to a Holocaust victim and talks about the first two times that she returned to life after death. For her, dying is an art. Now, it is Lazarus's third time facing death. She imagines herself again as a Holocaust victim to be burned to death in a concentration camp crematorium. At the end of this poem, she resurrects again, rising with red hair "out of the ash" like a phoenix and "eat[ing] men like air".

Lazarus in this poem shares many similarities with Plath herself. In this poem, there are many references to Plath's life experience, especially to her own suicide attempts. If we have to sum up this poem in just one word, "death" will be the most appropriate one.

Questions

1. What is the effect of all the Holocaust references in the poem?
2. What are the similarities and differences between the real life of Plath and lady Lazarus?
3. Who's the speaker's enemy? Why do you think so?

4. What is your understanding of the ambiguous word “men” in the last line?

Chinese Translation

女拉撒路

我又玩了一回。
每十年我就设法
玩一回——

一种活生生的神迹：我的皮肤
透亮得似纳粹的灯罩；
我的右脚

是一块镇纸；
我的脸是没有五官的、细腻的
犹太亚麻布。

揭掉这块头帕吧，
啊，我的敌人。
我吓人吗？——

鼻子、眼窝、全副牙齿？
酸腐的气息
一天后就会消散。

很快，很快，墓穴
吃掉的肉就会
回到我身上，

我就又是个微笑的女人。
我只有三十岁。
像猫一样，我可以死九回。

这是第三回。
每十年都要清除
多少垃圾呀。

多少亿万根纤维呀。
嚼着花生的人群
拥挤进来看

他们解开我手脚的裹缠——
盛大的脱衣舞表演。
先生们、女士们，

这是我的双手，
我的双膝。
我也许瘦得皮包骨头，

然而，我还是原先那同一个女人。
第一回发生是我十岁。
那是一次事故。

第二回我本想
一去就不复返了。
我像一只海蚌

摇摇晃晃闭合了。
他们只好叫啊唤啊，
从我身上摘掉像黏糊糊的珍珠似的蛆虫。

死
是一门艺术，就像别的一切。
我玩得特别好。

我玩起来让人觉得过瘾。
我玩起来让人觉得真实。
我猜你会说我有一种需求。

在小屋子里玩容易得很。

玩完了呆在原处容易得很。
令我晕倒的却正是

大白天
又戏剧性地回到
同一个地方、同一张脸孔、同一阵野蛮

而兴奋地呼喊——
“神迹啊！”
看看我的伤疤

得付钱。听听我的心跳
也得付钱
还真有销路。

要问一句话或摸一下
或讨一滴血
或我的一绺头发或一片衣裳，

就得付钱，很大一笔钱。
那么，那么，医生先生
就这样，敌人先生。

我成了你的作品
我成了你的宝贝——
融化成一声厉叫的
纯金娃娃。
我辗转燃烧。
别以为我低估了你的极大关心。

灰烬、灰烬——
你又戳又拨。
肉、骨，那里什么也没有——

一块肥皂，
一枚结婚戒指，

一颗金假牙。

上帝先生、魔鬼先生，
小心，
小心！

从灰烬中
我披着红发升起
我吃人就像吃空气。

（傅浩　译）